# Shamans and Analysts

*Shamans and Analysts* provides a model by which to understand the wounded healer phenomenon. It provides evidence as to how this dynamic arises and gives a theoretical model by which to understand it, as well as practical implications for the way analysts' wounds can be transformed and used in their clinical work.

By examining shamanism through the lens of contemporary approaches to archetype theory, this book breaks new ground through specifying the developmental foreground to the shaman archetype, which not only underpins the wounded healer but constitutes those regarded as 'true Jungians'.

Further areas of discussion include:

- Siberian shamanism
- contemporary archetype theory
- countertransference phenomena in psychotherapy
- sociocultural applications of psychoanalytic theory.

These original and thought-provoking ideas offer a revolutionary way to understand wounded healers, how they operate and how they should be trained, ultimately challenging traditional analyst/analysand stereotypes. As such this book will be of great interest to all Jungians, both in training and practice, as well as psychoanalysts, psychotherapists and counsellors with an interest in the concept of the wounded healer.

**John Merchant** is a Consultant Psychologist and Jungian Analyst in private practice in Sydney, Australia. He is a member of the Australian Psychological Society and the International Association for Analytical Psychology, and is a Training Analyst and previous Vice-President of the Australian and New Zealand Society of Jungian Analysts.

# Shamans and Analysts

## New Insights on the Wounded Healer

John Merchant

Routledge
Taylor & Francis Group

LONDON AND NEW YORK

First published 2012
by Routledge
27 Church Road, Hove, East Sussex BN3 2FA

Simultaneously published in the USA and Canada
by Routledge
711 Third Avenue, New York NY 10017

*Routledge is an imprint of the Taylor & Francis Group, an Informa business*

*British Library Cataloguing in Publication Data*
A catalogue record for this book is available from the British Library

*Library of Congress Cataloging-in-Publication Data*
Merchant, John, 1949-
    Shamans and analysts : new insights on the wounded healer / John
Merchant.
        p. cm.
    ISBN 978-0-415-55826-6 (hardback)
    1. Jungian psychology. 2. Shamanism. I. Title.
    BF173.J85M47 2011
    150.19'54—dc22

                                                              2011005285

ISBN: 978-0-415-55826-6 (hbk)
ISBN: 978-0-415-55827-3 (pbk)
ISBN: 978-0-203-61065-7 (ebk)

Typeset in Times by Garfield Morgan, Swansea, West Glamorgan
Printed and bound in Great Britain by TJ International Limited, Padstow,
Cornwall
Paperback cover design by Andrew Ward
**Cover image:** *Mask depicting a dying shaman.* Tsimshian, Northwest Coast,
c. 1850. © National Museums Northern Ireland 2011. Collection Ulster
Museum.

To E and all those who prefer the broken-hearted.


ἀνάγκῃ δ' οὐδὲ θεοὶ μάχονται·

(Plato, *Protagoras 345d*, quoting Simonides)

# Contents

*List of tables*                                                          viii
*Acknowledgements*                                                          ix

1  The 'good analyst' and the 'true Jungians'                               1

2  The wounded healer                                                       5

3  What is shamanism?                                                      23

4  Shamanism and the wounded healer as an archetype                       40

5  Contemporary archetype theory                                          59

6  A re-evaluation of Jung's classic theory of archetype                  71

7  The developmental side to the shamanic wounded healer                  89

8  Case study: The Siberian Sakha (Yakut) tribe                           99

9  The Siberian shaman's wound: A 'borderline type of case'              118

10  Evidence that the Siberian shaman is proto-borderline                 130

11  Conclusions                                                           151

   Appendix A: The implications of Knox's
      emergent/developmental model of archetype                           165
   Appendix B: Borderline personality disorder                            173

   *Notes*                                                                174
   *References*                                                           181
   *Index*                                                                197

# Tables

8.1 The treatment of infants across the first twelve months:
The Sakha (Yakut) tribe compared with other world
cultures                                                    109
8.2 The treatment of children: The Sakha (Yakut) tribe compared
with other world cultures                                   110
N.1 A crude nosology of personality 'disease'               179

# Acknowledgements

The impetus for this book came out of my training with the Australian and New Zealand Society of Jungian Analysts and I would like to acknowledge my appreciation for the commitment of all those involved in that program.

I would also like to express my gratitude to the University of Western Sydney for funding which enabled this project to see completion and for the help and encouragement received from Dr Brendon Stewart and Associate Professor David Russell when they were at the University.

Prior to completion of the book I submitted sections of it for publication in the *Journal of Analytical Psychology* and these appeared as follows: 'The developmental/emergent model of archetype, its implications and its application to shamanism', *Journal of Analytical Psychology*, *51*: 125–44 (2006); 'A reappraisal of classical archetype theory and its implications for theory and practice', *Journal of Analytical Psychology*, *54*: 339–58 (2009); and 'Response to Erik Goodwyn's "Approaching archetypes: reconsidering innateness"', *Journal of Analytical Psychology*, *55*: 534–42 (2010). I am thankful to the editors not only for their comments and editing of these papers but also for their permission to re-use sections of them in this book. Special thanks are due to Jean Knox for her encouragement and critique when she was an editor of the journal.

I would also like to acknowledge my gratitude to the organizers of the conferences listed as follows, who have shown interest in aspects of the book's theme, and to the colleagues who subsequently gave their generous feedback: 'The shaman archetype: Certain uses and abuses' – paper presented at the First International Academic Conference of Analytical Psychology, University of Essex, UK (2002); 'The new biology of Developmental Systems Theory and archetypes: Theoretical and clinical implications' – paper presented at the 50th Anniversary Conference of the *Journal of Analytical Psychology*, Oxford University, UK (2005); 'Shamanic processes as the heart of a contemporary analytic training program – an Australian perspective' – paper presented at the VII International Conference of the *Journal of Analytical Psychology*, McGill University, Montreal, Canada (2006); 'Siberian shamanism, borderline states and analytic training' – paper presented at XVII Congress of the International Association for Analytical Psychology, Cape Town, South Africa (2007); 'A contemporary reappraisal of traditional archetype theory and its implications for clinical practice and training' – paper presented at the VIII International Conference of the *Journal of Analytical Psychology*, Orta, Italy (2008); 'The shaman archetype: Template for individuation or the wounded healer?' – paper presented at XVIII Congress of the International Association for Analytical Psychology, Montreal, Canada (2010).

Further thanks are due to the University of Western Sydney for funding to attend the aforementioned First International Academic Conference of Analytical Psychology, University of Essex, UK (2002) and also to the NSW Psychologists Registration Board for funding to attend the afore-mentioned VII International Conference of the *Journal of Analytical Psychology*, McGill University, Montreal, Canada (2006).

Acknowledgements are due to Princeton University Press for permission to quote from the *Collected Works of C. G. Jung* (Jung, C. G.; *Collected Works of C. G. Jung*, 1977. Princeton University Press. Reprinted by permission of Princeton University Press). Similarly, thanks are due to Routledge & Kegan Paul for permission to quote from the English translations of the *Collected Works of C. G. Jung*, edited by H. Read, M. Fordham and G. Adler, trans. by R. Hull.

Extracts from Bogoras' 'The Chukchee' (1904) and Jochelson's 'The Yukaghir and the Yukaghirized Tungus' (1926) are courtesy of the American Museum of Natural History.

# Chapter 1

# The 'good analyst' and the 'true Jungians'

At the Fourteenth International Congress for Analytical Psychology's symposium on training, for which the theme was 'What makes a good analyst?', Guggenbuhl-Craig (1999) alluded to a 'shaman archetype' as one which is likely to be present in an analyst regarded as 'good'. In so doing he placed shamanism as conceptually central to analytic work. He began by saying, 'To be a good Jungian analyst, I have concluded, is a talent with which, if you are lucky, you are born' (ibid., p. 408). He saw training as being about refining that talent, which he later described as an 'inner drive'. In his view, the talent arises from the activation of certain archetypes, three of which are dominant within analysts and which would need to be present for an analyst to be regarded as 'good'. These are the 'healer archetype' (which he sees as essential although some reject it), the 'shaman archetype' and the 'alchemist archetype' (exhibited in the ability to symbolize).

Guggenbuhl-Craig defined shamans as those who can leave their bodies and make contact with 'demons, with gods, with other dimensions of human existence' (ibid., p. 409) which could be broadly conceived as the transpersonal realm. He went on to draw a parallel between this and analysis by saying that 'We analysts show the patients these other dimensions. For instance we put them in touch with the unconscious' (ibid., p. 411) and this is especially seen through work with dreams which, in his view, is specifically based on the shaman archetype. Guggenbuhl-Craig concluded that 'the selection of future analysts is more important than the precise compulsory organization of the training. We must receive with open arms the ones who have talent and refuse the ones who have no talent' (ibid., p. 411).

Given the overall significance suggested by Guggenbuhl-Craig's comments and the connection to being a 'good analyst', his assertions are highly significant because they not only place shamanism as conceptually central to analytic work but also have implications for the selection and training of analysts.

Shamanism has always occupied a place of considerable importance in Jungian discourse. Jung (1918/1991, 1930/1991, 1931/1991b) seemed to see it in two main ways – first, as an archaic archetype important in earlier human prehistory but which has emerged in recent times to compensate for the West's over development of rationalistic consciousness; and second, as reflective of the individuation process and especially the place of suffering entailed therein. Whilst the views of post-Jungians on shamanism span a broad range from its connection with the countertransference (Stein 1984) to its deliberate evocation in psychotherapeutic work (C. M. Smith 1997), all writers seem to hold a classical view of it, namely, that it is one archetype of the collective unconscious which will be in existence prior to any experience an individual may have of the world. Given the presence of shamanic practices within native American culture, a significant position within the USA has emerged which not only sees the shaman archetype as part of humankind's 'sacred heritage' but also as one which it would be in our best interests to access (see Sandner and Wong 1997). This perspective reflects a fundamental belief within the classical Jungian position that archetypes of the collective unconscious are unaffected by personal experience and if activated can be potential wellsprings of healing and meaning.

It was Jung (1954/1990c) who also saw a connection between shamanism and the concept of the wounded healer for he says in 'On the psychology of the trickster figure' that

> the shamanistic techniques in themselves often cause the medicine-man a good deal of discomfort, if not actual pain. At all events, the 'making of a medicine-man' involves, in many parts of the world, so much agony of body and soul that permanent psychic injuries may result. His 'approximation to the saviour' is an obvious consequence of this, in confirmation of the mythological truth that the wounded is the agent of healing, and that the sufferer takes away suffering.
>
> (p. 256)

Jung is alluding here to one of the common cross-cultural features of shamanic initiation, what Eliade (1964) called a 'pre-initiatory illness' in which candidates experience unsolicited states of derangement entailing dismemberment imagery and extreme distress. But it is not until the initiates can demonstrate mastery over these derangements that they are recognized by their sociocultural others as functioning shamans. The eventual mastery underpins the shaman's capacity to act as healer within their tribe and it is in this way that Groesbeck (1989, p. 267) understands the shaman to be 'the wounded healer, *par excellence.*' It is quite plausible then to view both shamanism and the wounded healer as aspects of one and the same archetype although Groesbeck (1975) and Guggenbuhl-Craig (1989) speak of a wounded healer archetype in its own right.

Whilst the general concept of the wounded healer has become quite popular across a range of other psychotherapeutic schools of thought, the central Jungian perspective in seeing both shamanism and its wounded healer component as reflective of underlying archetypal configurations is an important theoretical position because of its relevance to the selection, training and actual work of analysts. As Guggenbuhl-Craig (1999) suggests, the detection of those who have the shaman archetype is crucial at the time of trainee selection. Analyst training would then need to involve activation of the archetype and a progressive refinement of its application in ongoing work. Consequently, von Franz sees a 'shamanic initiation' (as cited in Kirsch 1982) as central to the vocation of being an analyst and Kirsch (1982), when considering the place of personal analysis in the training of analysts, summarizes her position as follows:

> Von Franz has discussed the vocation of the analyst in the context of shamanic initiation. In primitive tribes, the shamanic initiate is the one who experiences a breakthrough of the collective unconscious and is able to master the experience, a feat many sick persons cannot achieve. Von Franz emphasizes that such an experience must occur in the analysis of a candidate as part of the training of an effective analyst.
>
> (p. 391)

In relation to actual analytic work, Groesbeck (1989, p. 274) goes so far as to say that it is only those who 'function as shamans in the therapeutic process dealing directly with the patient's illness in order to produce a transformational healing experience' who can be considered the 'true Jungians'. Given that the functioning of these 'true Jungians' is understood in the classical view to be dependent on the activation of an actual shaman archetype, it becomes crucial to have a clear understanding of ethnographic shamanism and its pre-initiatory illness component on the one hand and Jung's classic theory of archetype on the other. This is especially so given the more recent contemporary views of archetype based on neuroscience research unavailable to Jung when he wrote. These approaches to archetypes suggest they are not innate *a priori* psychic structures but are better understood as emergent and developmentally produced mind/brain structures forged out of the intense affective experiences of infancy and which once in existence, have the capacity to directly influence psychological life.

Consequently, this book addresses a significant gap in the literature by assessing shamanism and its wounded healer component in light of these new developments in archetype theory. Indeed, there have been very few systematic attempts to evidence both shamanism and the wounded healer as archetypes, it so often being assumed since Jung's time that they simply are so.

Furthermore, Sedgwick's (1994) previous overview of countertransference from a Jungian perspective aligned it with the wounded healer concept but the connection to shamanism was not really developed. For those others who also speak to the wounded healer tradition, no particular wounds or zone of wounding ever seem specified apart from the self-evident aspect of general human vulnerability and suffering. The new emergent/developmental models of archetype when applied to shamanism and its wounded healer component have the capacity not only to specify the zone of wounding relevant to analytic work but also to identify the particular psychological construction emerging from the wounding. This provides the means for explaining the somatic and embodied countertransferential experiences of the 'psychic infection' kind which Samuels (1985a) has specified.

'Psychic infection' was a term Jung coined in 1937, for from his clinical experience he was aware that there can develop between analyst and patient a zone of 'mutual unconsciousness' leading to 'inductive' effects on the analyst which are usually felt in the analyst's body (see Jung 1937/1993). He came to see these unconscious influences as highly important pieces of communication and further argued that 'their nature can best be conveyed by the old idea of the demon of sickness. According to this, a sufferer can transmit his disease to a healthy person whose powers then subdue the demon – but not without impairing the well-being of the subduer' (Jung 1946/1993, p. 72). The connection between the 'psychic infection' way of working and shamanism could not be more succinctly stated.

Since the psychotherapeutic use of such countertransferential 'psychic infections' many see as the quintessential Jungian way of working which, when mastered, leads to the 'good analyst', what is also highlighted is that this style of working reflects the 'true Jungians'. Alarming to some will be the evidence presented in the following chapters to do with the relevant psychological construction of the 'good analyst' for it is suggestive of something 'proto-borderline'. But I believe that it is this psychological construction, derived from woundings in the earliest stages of infancy, together with their sufficient self-cure, which underpins the wounded healer of the 'true Jungian' kind and which ultimately makes for the 'good analyst'.

And so to the wounded healer.

# Chapter 2

# The wounded healer

## Introduction

Within the helping professions the concept of the 'wounded healer' has become a particularly popular notion so that its use occurs across a range of strikingly diverse modalities including nursing (Conti-O'Hare 2002, C. Jackson 2004), psychodynamic psychotherapy (Holmes 1991, 1998), transcultural psychiatry (Kirmayer 2003), humanist psychology (Stone 2008), palliative care (Laskowski and Pellicore 2002), psychotherapy training selection (Barnett 2007, Mander 2004), the clinical use of the countertransference (Sedgwick 1994) and the history of medicine (S. W. Jackson 2000).

Such use would indicate the concept is understood to be of some central importance. This is probably because it acknowledges that all persons working in the helping professions are vulnerable human beings who carry their own individual wounds and that these can be brought to bear on their healing work in a positive way. Jung (1951/1993) puts it this way:

> We could say, without too much exaggeration, that a good half of every treatment that probes at all deeply consists in the doctor's examining himself, for only what he can put right in himself can he hope to put right in the patient. It is no loss, either, if he feels that the patient is hitting him, or even scoffing at him: it is his own hurt that gives the measure of his power to heal. This, and nothing else, is the meaning of the Greek myth of the wounded physician.
>
> (p. 116)

Later, in his autobiography, *Memories, Dreams, Reflections*, Jung (1963/1990) amplifies these points on two occasions:

> Only if the doctor knows how to cope with himself and his own problems will he be able to teach the patient to do the same.
>
> (p. 154)

And later:

> What does he mean to me? If he [the patient] means nothing, I have no
> point of attack. The doctor is effective only when he himself is affected.
> 'Only the wounded physician heals'.
>
> (p. 155)

According then to Jung, analysts cannot facilitate their patients' growth
to a point where they themselves have not been. Nor should they be fearful
of their own wounds for they can be the measure of one's healing power.
Later research has confirmed this view by consistently showing that the
character of the therapist and the therapeutic relationship are directly
related to therapeutic effectiveness (see Wolgien and Coady 1997).

In *The Nurse as Wounded Healer: From Trauma to Transcendence*, Conti-
O'Hare (2002) stresses that central to the notion of the wounded healer
is the need to accept the mutual vulnerability of both practitioner and
patient, and further, that the concept entails the idea of the potential
transformation of suffering. As such, wounds are seen as an avenue to
transcendence and a conduit to healing knowledge because they derive
from some crisis that precipitates transformation and spiritual awakening.
It is with acknowledgement by practitioners of their vulnerability that
wounded healer dynamics can be turned into practical therapeutic action
because awareness of one's own wounds hones empathy. In this perspective,
the idea of the wounded healer underlies the use of empathy, which is one of
the key ingredients discovered by Carl Rogers (1961) and others at the
Center for the Study of the Human Person that leads to positive change
for clients.

On this issue, Hayes (2002) coins the term 'empathic duplication', that is,
making therapeutic use of one's own experiences which in some way
parallel those of the client. He maintains this can lead to 'deep empathic
understanding' and that the therapist achieves this through 'intentionally
calling to mind – or at least intentionally being open to – a personal
experience' (p. 96). Similarly Miller and Baldwin (1987) see the therapist's
conscious attention to their own wounds as leading to healing. They
conclude that 'the therapist's acceptance of his own wounds through conscious awareness of his vulnerability contributes to a sense of wholeness,
which in turn enables the patient to do the same and, thus, empower his
own healer' (p. 150).

As can be seen it is a consistent emphasis among many of these writers
that the health professional's own vulnerabilities and/or wounds can hone
their clinical use of empathy as well as their therapeutic insight. As such,
they provide strong recommendation that therapists actively and consciously engage with their own wounds and vulnerabilities. Remen *et al.*
(1985) put it this way:

There is no essential difference between the two people engaged in a healing relationship. Indeed, both are wounded and both are healers. It is the woundedness of the healer which enables him or her to understand the patient and which informs the wise and healing action.

(p. 85)

Michael Whan (1987), on the other hand, in his 'Chiron's wound: Some reflections on the wounded-healer', somewhat reverses things. He certainly sees empathy as the capacity to 'feel into' the patient's inner life but notes it is this which can *lead to* woundedness (what he calls 'empathic wounding'). He says, 'To be open empathically is to be open to the other's shadow and disturbance' (p. 202) and it is this which raises an important question for him – do therapists respond this way because of their own wounds or are they just taking upon themselves the wounds of the patient?

From a Jungian perspective it is quite understandable for Whan to conclude that this 'empathic wounding' is an experience taking place 'in the context of the unconscious'. What he is really highlighting, however, is Jung's concepts of 'psychic infection' and the 'inductive effect' of the patient's unconscious on the unconscious of the analyst. This is a notable shift in perspective, for whilst the conscious use of one's own wounds in psychotherapeutic work as advocated by so many commentators is commendable, Whan's view that the patient can in some way 'wound' the analyst, and the questions which this then poses for him, are important.

## The concept of 'psychic infection'

'Psychic infection' was a concept Jung (1937/1993) introduced into his discussion of psychotherapeutic work when he said:

> If . . . he [the analyst] is neurotic, a fateful, unconscious identity with the patient will inevitably supervene – a 'counter-transference' of a positive or negative character. Even if the analyst has no neurosis, but only a rather more extensive area of unconsciousness than usual, this is sufficient to produce a sphere of mutual unconsciousness, i.e. a counter-transference. This phenomenon is one of the chief occupational hazards of psychotherapy. It causes psychic infections in both analyst and patient and brings the therapeutic process to a standstill.
>
> (pp. 329–30)

Jung is describing here in a particular way, the emotional responses activated in the analyst as a result of their engagement with the patient. The early psychoanalysts formulated their discussion of such emotional responses through the term 'countertransference'. The problems Jung particularly highlights here in relation to the countertransference are unconscious identification; the analyst's possible neurosis and an occupational hazard with the main problem being a 'sphere of mutual unconsciousness' leading to psychic infections. A noteworthy list. When considering erotic countertransferential reactions, the 'occupational hazard' issue is certainly very real given the occurrence of sexual actings out by therapists, which makes this an issue of critical importance to psychotherapy.[1]

At the time, Jung's statement above accorded with Freud's (1910/2001, 1912/2001) view that countertransferential responses were an interference to psychoanalytic technique because they introduced the analyst's personal material into the process which interfered with the 'evenly suspended attention' he recommended.

## A case example of 'psychic infection'

In his paper 'Symbolic dimensions of eros in transference-countertransference: Some clinical uses of Jung's alchemical metaphor' Samuels (1985b) describes an arresting consulting room occurrence four years into the work with a patient from a difficult family background which succinctly illustrates the unconscious psychic infection kind of experience:

> I had the very strong impression of being in an enormous desert, at the bottom of a wadi. Looking over my shoulder I could see my footsteps stretching into the distance. I felt a thirst so intense I thought I should have to excuse myself and leave the room to get a drink. Instead, something made me tell the patient of my fantasy. Quite unruffled, she replied by saying that this was the desert where, during the war, her father had met the man who probably became his lover and certainly became her mother's lover.
>
> (pp. 210–11)

This kind of countertransferential reaction felt in bodily sensations and apparently induced in the analyst by the patient's material is not that uncommon in psychotherapy – therapists describe on occasion feeling emotionally swamped by patients, attacked by them, left with feelings of repulsion and disgust or being erotically moved. Hayes (2002), however, makes the point that in the general psychotherapy world, far more attention has been given to the deleterious aspects of the countertransference and this can prompt certain responses to either manage such reactions or avoid them. Unfortunately, clinical experience would reveal that the latter alternative is impossible.

The kind of bodily countertransference Samuels experienced above he elsewhere gives the term 'embodied countertransference' (Samuels 1985a).[2]

Critically, Jung's position on such countertransferential reactions substantially changed from that which he held in 1937. By 1946, in 'The psychology of the transference' (1946/1993), he was saying:

> In any effective psychological treatment the doctor is bound to influence the patient; but this influence can only take place if the patient has a reciprocal influence on the doctor. You can exert no influence if you are not susceptible to influence. It is futile for the doctor to shield himself from the influence of the patient . . . By so doing he only denies himself the use of a highly important organ of information. The patient influences him unconsciously . . . One of the best known symptoms of this kind is the counter-transference evoked by the transference. But the effects are often much more subtle, and their nature can best be conveyed by the old idea of the demon of sickness. According to this, a sufferer can transmit his disease to a healthy person whose powers then subdue the demon.
>
> (pp. 71–2)

What is initially noteworthy here is Jung's connection between countertransferential experiences and 'the old idea of the demon of sickness', that is, more primitive modes of healing as in shamanism. Critically, Jung has also changed his attitude toward psychic infections. He adds to this later when he says, 'the unconscious infection brings with it the therapeutic possibility – which should not be underestimated – of the illness being transferred to the doctor' (ibid., p. 176). In other words, psychic infection is now seen as a potentially positive occurrence rather than bringing the 'therapeutic process to a standstill' (Jung 1937/1993, pp. 329–30).

By the time of these statements in 1946, Jung's thinking had gone far beyond that of others in the psychoanalytic movement. Not only was he aware of the unconscious influence of one psyche on another but had also come to the critical realization that these unconscious influences can be important means of communication about the patient's internal dynamics. One important clinical question then becomes: how and why is it that the patient is evoking these effects in the analyst and what use can be made of them?

In the clinical vignette above, Samuels (1985b) does go on to describe the positive incorporation of this incident into the ongoing psychotherapeutic work. So what did the countertransference tell him? He says:

> A mosaic of relationships from which she was excluded and to which she felt inferior came into focus in a way they had not done before: father and lover, mother and lover, father and mother. It was, from the relationship angle, a desert and, moreover, one in which she was still lost. We went on, in that session and subsequently, to talk much more

deeply about the lack of erotic feedback from her father, how this made it difficult to relate to men on anything other than seductress/anima/inspiratrice terms. In fact, in her childhood this reached a climax when the lover of both her parents made a sexual move towards her. As far as the analysis was concerned . . . I had not known consciously where the area of her emotional deprivation lay.

(p. 211)

Jung's 1946 position on the countertransference implies that any positive use of it as an organ of communication similar to this description by Samuels is predicated on the analyst being 'susceptible to influence'. Samuels alludes to this point when he says further:

Certain areas of the analyst's experience are also highlighted: for instance, the need to be aware of bodily erotic feelings as a foundation for understanding. The analyst's being 'in' the treatment just as much as the patient was shown both by my unconsciousness and what I gained from the eventual awareness.

(ibid.)

Apparently, Samuels had been denying his own erotic feelings for the patient which only enhanced the mutual unconsciousness between them. Presumably, though, it was these denied erotic feelings which evoked the zone whereby Samuels became susceptible to his patient's unconscious needs.

Samuels' case is not only a good example of the positive psychotherapeutic use of the embodied countertransference but also highlights Whan's (1987) question asked above, which could be re-cast: do analysts have these kinds of countertransferential responses because of their own wounds or are they just taking upon themselves the wounds of the patient? In other words, what makes the analyst 'susceptible to influence' in the first place? This question is crucial in determining how wounded healers are formed and how they operate.

## The 'susceptibility to influence'

When it comes to the 'susceptibility to influence' issue, it can be noted from Jung's statements in 1937 above, when he says, 'even if the analyst has no neurosis, but only a rather more extensive area of unconsciousness than usual' (1937/1993, p. 329), that responses can be evoked in the analyst which are unconnected to their personal wounds (although the possibility of the analyst's neurosis is also contained in the statement).

In his later comments, Jung (1946/1993) amplifies this point:

When two chemical substances combine, both are altered. This is precisely what happens in the transference. Freud rightly recognized that
this bond is of the greatest therapeutic importance in that it gives rise
to a *mixtum compositum* of the doctor's own mental health and the
patient's maladjustment. . . . It is inevitable that the doctor should be
influenced to a certain extent and even that his nervous health should
suffer. He quite literally 'takes over' the sufferings of his patient and
shares them with him.

(p. 171)

Jung's point here seems to be that the transfer of the patient's illness
material arises out of the unconscious projections underpinning the transference and that the analyst is in the position of having 'mental health'.
However, in a subsequent note in the same paragraph he goes on to say:

The effects of this on the doctor or nurse can be far-reaching. I know of
cases where, in dealing with borderline schizophrenics, short psychotic
intervals were actually 'taken over', and during these periods it happened that the patients were feeling more than ordinarily well. . . . This
is not so astonishing since certain psychic disturbances can be extremely
infectious if the doctor himself has a latent predisposition in that
direction.

(ibid., p. 172n)

This note in Jung's text is quite noticeable because it typifies what I see as a
tension in his perspective that continues to run through 'The psychology of
the transference' – the 'susceptibility' of the analyst either being a result
of unconscious transference dynamics on the part of the patient toward
the analyst or conditional upon the analyst's own 'latent predispositions',
that is, their own mental ill health and/or wounds. This is not Jung's main
point, however, for he continues to address the 'transfer' issue through his
ideas about the inductive effect on the analyst of constellated unconscious
material:

The doctor, by voluntarily and consciously taking over the psychic
sufferings of the patient, exposes himself to the overpowering contents
of the unconscious and hence also to their inductive action. The case
begins to 'fascinate' him. . . . The patient, by bringing an activated
unconscious content to bear upon the doctor, constellates the corresponding unconscious material in him, owing to the inductive effect
which always emanates from projections in greater or lesser degree.
Doctor and patient thus find themselves in a relationship founded on
mutual unconsciousness.

(ibid., p. 176)

The implication here is that the inductive effect on analysts of unconscious contents has to do with material that is not theirs so that the sequence of events runs something like this:

> *Step One*: the analyst consciously engages in the psychotherapeutic process with the patient;
> *Step Two*: a transference onto the analyst is activated in the patient;
> *Step Three*: the transference contains unconscious projections which induce an activation of the analyst's unconscious material;
> *Step Four*: both analyst and patient end up in a zone of 'mutual unconsciousness'.

It seems to me that Step Three is critical and needs elucidation, the question being: is the induction due to unconscious material from the level of the collective unconscious that has been evoked by the transference and has nothing to do with the analyst's personal dynamics or has the analyst's similar zone of wounding (at the unconscious level) been activated by the psychotherapeutic exchange? Or are both occurring together?

Further thought also needs to be given to Jung's phrase about 'the doctor . . . taking over the psychic sufferings of the patient' (ibid.) because embodied countertransference phenomena are not chosen, they just happen in one's body and as an experience whose meaning is initially beyond conscious understanding. Consequently, the implications of the term 'taking over' are not just a moot point about terminology.

A little further on Jung (1946/1993) notably returns to the issue of the analyst's susceptibility and in doing so he introduces other statements of doubt that things are quite so straightforward.

> The unconscious infection brings with it the therapeutic possibility . . . of the illness being transferred to the doctor. . . . The greatest difficulty here is that contents are often activated in the doctor which might normally remain latent. He might perhaps be so normal as not to need any such unconscious standpoints to compensate his conscious situation. At least this is often how it looks, though whether it is so in a deeper sense is an open question. Presumably he had good reasons for choosing the profession of psychiatrist and for being particularly interested in the treatment of the psychoneuroses . . . Nor can his concern with the unconscious be explained entirely by a free choice of interests, but rather by a fateful disposition which originally inclined him to the medical profession. The more one sees of human fate and the more one examines its secret springs of action, the more one is impressed by the strength of unconscious motives and by the limitations of free choice. The doctor knows . . . that he did not choose this career by chance; and the psychotherapist in particular should clearly understand that psychic infections, however superfluous they seem to

him, are in fact the predestined concomitants of his work, and thus fully in accord with the instinctive disposition of his own life.

(pp. 176–7)

The idea of the wounded healer is only alluded to here tangentially through the suggestion that there is something of significance in the analyst's 'instinctive disposition' in relation to the experience of 'psychic infection'. This is probably because of Jung's particular theoretical position on the collective unconscious and its constituent archetypes. Transference is then seen to bring into the foreground the projection of archetypal figures from the deep collective unconscious (specifically those of 'anima' and 'animus') which are not connected to the personal history of the individuals and it is these which can be experienced as infective.

Nonetheless, Jung does pose that something like fate has drawn the analyst to the psychotherapy profession in the first place, that is, there is already something in the analyst's personal constitution. There are a number of options here. The 'fate' aspect could indicate something trans-generational as Jung (1963/1990) elsewhere suggests in relation to himself:

I feel very strongly that I am under the influence of things or questions which were left incomplete and unanswered by my parents and grand-parents and more distant ancestors. It often seems as if there were an impersonal karma within a family which is passed on from parents to children. It has always seemed to me that I had to answer questions which fate had posed to my forefathers, and which had not yet been answered, or as if I had to complete, or perhaps continue, things which previous ages had left unfinished.

(p. 260)

Alternatively it could be that the analyst has inherited in his collective unconscious archetypal contents which become activated under the influence of the transference projections from the patient, and Jungians like Guggenbuhl-Craig (1989) and Groesbeck (1975) have taken this idea further by specifying an actual wounded healer archetype.

A third alternative is that the experience of psychic infection has something to do with the analyst's own wounds, operating at an unconscious level, which have become activated in the psychotherapeutic exchange.

These alternative positions do raise the issue as to what is the nature of the 'fateful disposition' and why it is that people choose to be psycho-therapists in the first place.

## Why do people choose to be psychotherapists?

Contemporary research continues to indicate a connection between the choice of psychotherapy as a profession and one's own woundedness.

Mander (2004) researched it by looking at candidates who wanted to train as either counsellors or psychotherapists and she found one main theme – they felt 'summoned by an internal voice, a call from the super-ego which forms the basis of any vocation' (p. 161). Mander concluded that the wish to help was indeed rooted in an experience of suffering.[3]

Similarly Barnett (2007) was interested in the unconscious motives which drew people to the profession of psychotherapy. Through interviewing a number of experienced psychoanalytic and psychodynamic psychotherapists about their professional and personal histories she found two major themes: one of early loss and narcissistic needs. Little wonder she concluded personal therapy to be desirable for safe and effective practice.

It would appear that one's own wounds are intimately connected with the choice of psychotherapy as a profession. Given this, a clear understanding of the wounded healer dynamic then emerges if we align this with Searles' (1975) idea that all persons have an inbuilt healthy tendency to heal and help the other, an issue he explores in his paper 'The patient as therapist to his analyst'. Presumably for the wounded healer, the natural tendency to heal and help the other is facilitated by one's own wounds, which drive an empathic resonance with the sufferings of others.

Consequently, whilst Samuels (1994, p. 187) can say, 'That analysts are in some sense wounded is scarcely to be doubted', his more recent statement that the 'idea of the wounded healer implies that the therapist must be wounded' (Samuels 2006, p. 188) captures the dynamic more fully – it is actually necessary. However, as Steinberg (1989, p. 11) says, 'little appears in print or public discussion about the specific wounds the healer has to contend with and how they affect treatment.' Specifically, what seems to be missing in Jungian discourse is an articulation of the kind of wounds in the analyst which would relate to the psychic infection experience in embodied countertransferences and this is critical because I would understand use of the latter to be the particular and distinct way of working analytically.[4]

Sedgwick (1994) suggests that the fascination which can occur in the analyst as a result of the inductive action of projected unconscious content occurs because it is 'about the self' (as an archetype) and that some analysts who work in the countertransference may just be born that way (as opposed to being made that way). It is in this way that the classical Jungian approach has been to see the wounded healer as reflective of an inbuilt archetypal pattern which will inevitably get played out in the analyst-patient interchange.

## The archetypal approach to the wounded healer

As we have seen, Jung was one of the first to articulate the concept of the wounded healer in relation to psychotherapy. Classical Jungians have continued this tradition and addressed the wounded healer in terms of an underlying archetype, Guggenbuhl-Craig (1989) and Groesbeck (1975) being the most prominent commentators.

Groesbeck (1975) understands the archetype as being constellated in the analyst but stresses that for cure, it needs also to become constellated in the patient. This position is predicated on two beliefs: first, that the wounded healer archetype is present within the collective unconscious of all persons and can thereby be accessed by the patient; and second, that all archetypes are made up of two opposite poles held in union, in this case 'wounded' at one end and 'healer' at the other. For therapeutic change/cure to come about, the patient needs to access and integrate the healer pole of the archetype which can then operate as their own internal therapist.

Both Guggenbuhl-Craig (1989) and Groesbeck (1975) make the point that at the start of the therapeutic enterprise, the analyst and the patient will consciously identify with their roles, that is, professional healer on the one hand and sick patient on the other. This bifurcation intensifies as the therapeutic interchange progresses due to projections arising from the wounded healer archetype which has become constellated in the interaction. As a consequence, the patient will project the healer pole of their own internal archetype onto the analyst. Conversely, the analyst is likely to project the wounded pole of their own internal archetype onto the patient, especially if their own wounds have not been sufficiently integrated, are operating unconsciously and have become activated in the therapeutic interaction because of similar life experiences and/or woundings.

A therapeutic standstill will result if this situation continues because no improvement can occur for the patient until their own inner healer is activated and until the therapist withdraws any projections of their own wounds. Hence Groesbeck (1975, p. 132) says, 'the analytic physician himself must "have knowledge of, and participate, in his own incurable wounds", similarly as in the primordial mystery of healing that has come down to us from the myth of Asclepius.' For Groesbeck, this is because such participation activates the archetype, thereby allowing the patient's inner healer to be activated. And there is an additional reason for this, for as Guggenbuhl-Craig (1989) notes, if analysts are not related to their own wounds they can project them onto the patient leading to domination and a counterproductive use of power in the therapeutic relationship. The analyst's wounds are then excluded from use in the therapy and this locks the patient into the 'wounded' pole. As a consequence, Holmes (1998) sees in this certain practicalities of psychotherapy concerning the necessary capabilities inherent in the patient which they must access for their healing and this set against the psychotherapist's own emotional damage which has the capacity to derail the therapy.

Because of the assumed archetypal level operating, there is an additional component which Groesbeck (1975) emphasizes in similar fashion to Jung's ideas about the analyst 'taking over' the sufferings of the patient: 'The analyst "takes on" the patient's illness or wounds, and also begins to experience more fully the wounded aspect of the archetypal image. This in turn activates his own wounds or vulnerability to illness on a personal level and/or in its connection with the wounded-healer archetypal image' (p. 132).

Groesbeck is alluding to two things here. Since in the psychotherapeutic exchange we are dealing with the activation of an archetype, deep material from the collective unconscious can get constellated and this can affect the analyst. Consequently Groesbeck goes on to say that the analyst must have courage 'to experience these powerful archetypal contents' (ibid.). However, he is also saying that personal material in the analyst will get activated, with three possibilities – either the analyst's actual personal wounds are activated or the analyst's vulnerability to illness is activated or the analyst can personally experience something from a more collective archetypal level.

There is a similar tension in these statements to that we saw previously with Jung (1946/1993) in 'The psychology of the transference'. It is not clear what exactly is going on, especially the place of the analyst's own wounds in the exchange. The question would be: does the constellation of a wounded healer archetype promote or activate personal (wound) material in the analyst or does personal (wound) material mutually shared between the participants constellate the archetype? A much broader tension in Jungian discourse, to do with the general constellation of archetypes, is contained in this question and this is addressed specifically in Chapter 6. This question does highlight another issue of some importance, for in emphasizing an archetypal level to the wounded healer, reflection to do with the personal material of the analyst, especially that of their own wounds, can get sidelined. This leads to the possibility of a depersonalized perspective creating a 'blindness' in the analyst as to that which has been activated in them on the level of personal wound. If this remains unconscious it could get projected onto the patient – as Guggenbuhl-Craig (1989) suggests – as well as foreclosing on the possibility of using the associated countertransferential responses to get a 'readout' of the patient's complexes.

Overall, the archetypal approach to the wounded healer has led some to reflect on the Chiron myth from ancient Greece to which both Groesbeck and Jung allude. This myth is seen to encapsulate the whole wounded healer dynamic thereby adding further understanding to it.

## The ancient greek myth of Chiron

The classical Jungian perspective on mythic stories is to see them as speaking a 'truth' to people and hence lasting the test of time because they have emerged from the collective unconscious, that is, they represent psychological elements common to the human condition and with which all persons can identify. It is the myth of Chiron which is seen to amplify the wounded healer archetype, that is, the strange conundrum that to be an effective healer means being wounded oneself.

According to Graves (1960), Chiron was the result of the sexual union between Cronos and Philyra but with a particular beginning, for Cronos was surprised by his wife Rhea during the sexual act. To escape detection, Cronos changed himself into a horse, galloped away and left Philyra to bear Chiron. This explains why Chiron was born a centaur, that is, half man and half horse. Philyra found Chiron loathsome and begged to become anything else other than his mother. She was metamorphosed into a linden tree. Chiron grew to become a wise ruler and king of centaurs as well as a teacher of medicine and healing. Consequently Apollo gave his son Asclepius to Chiron to be educated, Asclepius subsequently becoming the father of medicine.

The wounded healer aspect to Chiron is initially seen to come from the incident where he was accidentally wounded in the knee by one of Heracles' poisoned arrows. Heracles was Chiron's friend but the wound remained incurable despite the best efforts of them both. This incident occurred during Heracles' fourth labour where he was to capture the Erymanthian boar and when in being entertained by the centaur Pholus, a skirmish arose. During the ensuing fracas, Graves (1960) tells us, 'Nephele, the Centaurs' cloudy grandmother . . . poured down a smart shower of rain' (p. 113) so that Heracles' aim was affected. One of his arrows accidentally struck his friend Chiron in the knee and as such, Chiron partook of the incurable wound – 'incurable' because being an immortal, he could not die. In this way the one who is connected with teaching the healing arts is himself a sufferer with an incurable wound suggesting the strange interconnection between knowing about healing but being ongoingly unhealed and wounded oneself. There is, as Kerényi (1959, p. 99) puts it, 'the knowledge of a wound in which the healer forever partakes.'

## The psychology of the Chiron myth

Since centaurs are half man and half horse they are often understood to symbolize the division between Apollonian consciousness and the unconscious life of the body with its instincts but in a particular way, for the two aspects are not well integrated or blended together. Rather they are joined but with a noticeable dividing line which emphasizes a split aspect to their being, or, as Kerényi (1959) puts it, Chiron is 'contradictory'. This 'contradictory' nature of the 'half-human, half-theriomorphic god' is further emphasized by the fact that 'despite his horse's body, mark of the fecund and destructive creatures of nature that centaurs are otherwise known to be, he instructs heroes in medicine and music' (p. 98). Furthermore, he participates in this life whilst living in a cave as entrance to the underworld and, paradoxically, as a 'dark god, was able even to restore eyesight' (p. 100).

What is particularly noteworthy is that Chiron's 'contradictory' condition has come about through particular traumatic events associated with his conception and birth – a father who abandons him out of fear of his infidelity being exposed and a mother who abhors his body with its animal instincts, who then abandons him as well. It is not unreasonable to conclude that the later wounding Chiron experiences from Heracles' arrow has come about due to weaknesses emanating from these first woundings he experienced in infancy. Given his early life experience it is little wonder Chiron is not on good terms with his own instinctual life.

Such a perspective on the myth comes from approaching the story as if it is similar to a dream narrative where a later event or scene (in this case getting in the way of Heracles' wounding arrow) is given as the 'effect' of a previous 'cause' (in this case Chiron's traumas in infancy which have led to his 'contradictory' make-up). As such, the 'accidental' wounding from Heracles' arrow is an outworking of issues arising from the earlier infant trauma. Further, approaching the mythic story as if it is a dream narrative would mean that each of the characters in the story represents something to do with Chiron himself. Noticeably, Chiron and Heracles are not on bad terms or at war with each other – quite the reverse, they are friends. So whilst symbolically representing parts of Chiron himself, the actions of each are not well integrated.

From a psychological perspective, the early infant abandonment and rejection trauma has led to a 'contradictory' personality construction (represented by Chiron as centaur) which gets caught in a tension between primitive heroic aggressive tendencies (represented by Heracles' impulsive anger) and the zone of deep protective feeling (represented by Nephele's protection of her grandchildren). This leads to the hero's footing becoming unstable resulting in poor aim that ends in a further wounding to that part of instinctive being which should enable a stand to be taken in the world (represented by the wound to Chiron's knee) but which ends in a constant stumbling, the pains from which are ongoing and incurable.

In this way the Chiron myth highlights the underpinning psychology of the wounded healer. First, it indicates that the dynamic arises in early infant traumas and that these lead to a 'contradictory' kind of split/joined psychological constitution, that is, developed cerebralization on the one hand which is connected to, but not well integrated with, the instinctive life of the body. Second, the infant traumas will have flow-on effects later in life seen in impulsive and unintegrated uses of aggression which are poorly aimed and which cause further stumblings. A critical point is that from the experiential point of view, it is these later difficulties that will be the more obvious to consciousness but the early infant material lies in the background. Arising as the latter does from conception and the earliest months of life, it will reside in a zone of deep unconsciousness despite being of a highly traumatic nature.[5]

Translating this into the modern era, the psychology of the Chiron myth gives us a clear idea of the constitution that makes for the best kind of wounded healer. More than likely it is the conscious difficulties to do with life's stumblings that prompt the contemporary wounded healer into their own therapy but it is the depth of the early infant material in their psychological background which resonates with the deep unconscious of their patients thus explaining the 'psychic infection' kind of countertransferential experiences. In other words, the most significant wounded healers are those whose difficulties arise out of early infant trauma. And it should be noted that the underlying psychological constitution of this wounded healer is 'contradictory' in nature, being of a split/joined kind and suggesting something more 'borderline'.

I believe it is in this way that the Chiron myth not only elucidates the psychological dynamics of the wounded healer phenomenon but also provides us with clues as to the sorts of wounds which are relevant to the modern analyst and to which we may need to pay attention.

It was noted at the beginning of this chapter that Jung, by alluding to the Chiron myth, was one of the first to articulate the concept of the wounded healer in relation to psychotherapy. He extends this view in 'On the psychology of the trickster figure' (Jung 1954/1990c) by saying that

> the shamanistic techniques in themselves often cause the medicine-man a good deal of discomfort, if not actual pain. At all events, the 'making of a medicine-man' involves, in many parts of the world, so much agony of body and soul that permanent psychic injuries may result. His 'approximation to the saviour' is an obvious consequence of this, in confirmation of the mythological truth that the wounded is the agent of healing, and that the sufferer takes away suffering.
>
> (p. 256)

Amongst other things Jung is here connecting the wounded healer concept with shamanism, a connection followed by many other commentators.

## Shamanism and the wounded healer

Jung's (1954/1990c) connection of shamanism to the wounded healer idea occurs because he is aware that 'the shamanic vocation is manifested by a crisis, a temporary derangement' as Eliade (1964, p. xii) puts it. As we will explore in the next chapter, it is this 'pre-initiatory illness' experience of personal derangement followed by its self-cure which indicates to their sociocultural others that a person has been chosen by the spirits to be a shaman. Noticeably though, their capacity to heal is underpinned by their own experience of suffering. In other words, they are wounded healers.[6]

Jung (1946/1993) also sees a connection between shamanism and the countertransference. Whilst he does not mention shamanism directly in 'The psychology of the transference', his view of the countertransference as the analyst 'taking over' the sufferings of the patient, of the 'illness being transferred to the doctor' (p. 176) and of the 'old idea of the demon of sickness' according to which 'a sufferer can transmit his disease to a healthy person whose powers then subdue the demon' (p. 72) are all reminiscent of a shamanic way of working.[7]

As noted above, to be effective amongst their sociocultural group the shaman must be able to self-cure. Basilov (1984, p. 29), in commenting on Siberian and Central Asian shamanism, puts it this way: 'As soon as the shaman lost control over his visions, he would become a neuropath. But having lost control over himself, he would no longer be a shaman.' And Shirokogoroff (1935) goes so far as to say the shaman is 'the madman who has healed himself.' It is not uncommon therefore for the shaman to be seen as a wounded healer 'in the fullest sense' (Miller and Baldwin 1987) and this aspect has been explored by C. M. Smith (1997) in his *Jung and Shamanism in Dialogue: Retrieving the Soul/Retrieving the Sacred*, where he says: 'It is through the tended wound that the shaman is able to see, to empathize, and heal' (p. 97).

Some commentators have extended this view to Jung's own life, drawing parallels between it, wounded healer dynamics and even shamanism (see Dunne 2000, Groesbeck 1989, C. M. Smith 1997 and R. C. Smith 1997).

Jung's connecting of shamanism with the wounded healer concept does draw shamanism into the foreground and this is significant because Jung also saw shamanism as reflecting archaic aspects of the individuation archetype. If that is the case, the most pristine forms of shamanism may be closer to the core of the archetype and may reflect archaic aspects of the wounded healer dynamic as well.

## Jung's views on shamanism

Bearing in mind that it is not part of Jung's purpose to give a full treatment to the phenomenon of shamanism, he does make reference to it throughout his writings and this is generally for the purpose of illustrating aspects to do with his emerging analytical psychology, especially in relation to the individuation process.

Individuation is a central concept in Jung's psychology and it was an area of interest which occupied him for much of his professional career. Most of his writings on alchemy are devoted to explicating the process in one form or another. Jung (1928/1990) defines the term thus:

Individuation means becoming an 'in-dividual', and, in so far as 'in-dividuality' embraces our innermost, last, and incomparable uniqueness, it also implies becoming one's own self. We could therefore translate individuation as 'coming to selfhood' or 'self-realization.'

(p. 173)

And elsewhere:

> I use the term 'individuation' to denote the process by which a person becomes a psychological 'in-dividual', that is, a separate, indivisible unity or whole.
>
> (Jung 1939/1990, p. 275)[8]

It has to be noted that whilst Jung primarily sees shamanism as reflective of an individuation archetype he does also connect it with the wounded healer concept as we saw above from 'On the psychology of the trickster figure' where shamanism is connected to 'the mythological truth that the wounded is the agent of healing, and that the sufferer takes away suffering' (1954/1990c, p. 256). Similarly he notes elsewhere that shamanic initiation has 'the aspect of a healing' (1954/1991b).

In 'The philosophical tree', Jung (1954/1981) argues that it is precisely because of an archetypal foundation that images such as the tree can appear in both shamanism and alchemy, and in modern persons who know nothing of either shamanism or alchemy. He believes that such a trans-cultural and transhistorical phenomenon is due to the fact that each archetype has an unalterable core (what he calls its 'psychoid form') so that the expression of any archetype can undergo cultural modification and development without losing its basic patterns and features.[9]

If this is the case, and taking Jung's classical line on archetypes, it is not unreasonable to conclude that if shamanism with its wounded healer component is an historically early phenomenon it could represent something from an earlier stage in the cultural development of the archetype and as such would be closer to that archetype's unalterable core. Jung alludes to this when he sees shamanism as something archaic. In 'Transformation symbolism in the Mass', Jung (1954/1991b, p. 294) says that shamanism's 'widespread phenomenology anticipates the alchemist's individuation symbolism on an archaic level' and further that the 'numinous experience of the individuation process is, on an archaic level, the prerogative of shamans and medicine men.' Similarly in a private letter to G. A. van den Bergh von Eysinga, Jung (1954, p. 152) relates shamanism to a 'primordial psychic pattern.'

Clearly these statements indicate that for Jung, shamanism represents something from an earlier stage in the cultural development of the individuation archetype and which may be closer to its unalterable core, hence 'archaic' and 'primordial'.

The important point is that for Jung, shamanism, with its wounded healer component, not only represents something archetypal (and hence in the collective unconscious of all persons and presumably then accessible to modern persons) but could also be close to the unalterable core of an archetype to do with individuation and the wounded healer dynamics contained therein. Consequently, a study of shamanism's phenomenology could elucidate that core and help us determine the archetypal components in any contemporary expression of the archetype, especially the wounded healer aspects. Indeed, because of the 'primitive' nature of the cultures within which shamanism appears, the phenomenology of shamanism is likely to be the closest thing we have to such an archetype's unalterable core.

Furthermore, if shamanism is reflective of an archaic archetypal pattern it may very well be the foundational template for all wounded healer dynamics. It is important, therefore, to have a clear idea as to exactly what shamanism is.

# Chapter 3

# What is shamanism?

## Introduction

If shamanism and its wounded healer component are a sociocultural expression of an underlying archetypal pattern, it is important to have a clear understanding as to exactly what shamanism is. This is even further the case if shamanism represents an archaic expression of the archetype as Jung asserted, for the phenomenon would thereby exhibit a more central and pristine core expression of the archetype's essential features which would enlarge our understanding of the whole wounded healer dynamic.

Scholars have noted, however, a number of problems with this field of study. Siikala (1978) has raised concern about an over-reliance on reconstructions from secondary sources and Noll (1990) highlights a Western tendency to romanticize shamanism so that the anthropological accounts become interpreted as 'ideal metaphoric abstraction[s] of what many Westerners believe the experiences of shamans *ought* to be' (p. 213). Grim (1983) thereby cautions against a tendency to 'cultish emotionalism'. Ränk (1967), on the other hand, sees a 'mistake with the existent major comparative research consist[ing] mainly in the attempt of scholars to seek a short cut straight to the meaning and origin of shamanism' (p. 21), hence he believes many have lost their way. Nonetheless, shamanism remains a broad and diverse field of study with many significant researchers contributing to its understanding.

## The work of Anna-Leena Siikala and Mircea Eliade

Anna-Leena Siikala (1978, 1980, 1984, 1987a, 1987b, 1989) from the University of Helsinki has been one of the most significant anthropologists investigating shamanism (primarily the Siberian and Inner Asian expressions) not only through her own work but also in collaboration with the eminent Hungarian scholar of Siberian shamanism, Mihály Hoppál (Siikala and Hoppál 1998).

In her paper 'The interpretation of Siberian and Central Asian shamanism', Siikala (1989) devotes a section to the research of Mircea Eliade and the important place which he occupies. Her opinion is that Eliade 'represents the main stream of studies in shamanism' (p. 22) for whilst he dealt with many of the classic issues, he is noteworthy because of the method he used. Despite the fact that there is diversity at every level across the Siberian and Inner Asian groups, it has been through the comparative approach Eliade used that he has been able to set the phenomenon in a broader transhistorical context by balancing the interpretation of culture-specific facts whilst crystallizing transcultural elements. In so doing, he has combined these two levels of interpretation whilst avoiding any tendency toward homogenization. The overall debt we owe to Eliade is that through his work, much on shamanism has become general knowledge and Siikala believes the fundamental contribution of his research has been the opening up of 'new vistas on the understanding of basic religious experiences common to all mankind' (ibid., pp. 24–5). Eliade is also the only writer on shamanism whom Jung quotes.

Eliade's (1964) classic text, *Shamanism: Archaic Techniques of Ecstasy*, was written from a history of religions perspective and is regarded as one of the most comprehensive treatments of shamanism as it reviewed the vast majority of extant ethnographic literature on the subject up until that time. Its importance lies not only in its comprehensive overview of the definitive characteristics of the shamanic phenomenon but also because it deals with much material from a time before contemporary cultural incursions into shamanic cultures. This is important because, as Guggenbuhl-Craig (1999, p. 409) points out, 'there are hardly any real shamans left.' A succinct summary of Eliade's findings can be found in his 1987 introduction to the 'Shamanism' entry in Macmillan's *Encyclopedia of Religion*.

Eliade (1987, p. 202) begins by stating that 'Shamanism in the strict sense is pre-eminently a religious phenomenon of Siberia and Inner Asia' but goes on to note that similarities occur in other parts of the world. As a phenomenon, Eliade sees shamanism as centred on the mastery of the technique of ecstasy; shamans are particular amongst other magicians and ecstatics for their speciality of the trance state – their soul is believed to leave their body and to ascend to the sky or descend to the underworld. Critically, this occurs without shamans being possessed by their helping spirits but rather through their control of them.

Recruitment of shamans occurs in one of three ways. It is either a hereditary vocation, the result of a spontaneous 'call/election' by the spirits or a neophyte's choice to become a shaman (although these shamans are considered to be less powerful). Despite the method of recruitment, a shaman is not recognized by their sociocultural group until they have undergone two types of teaching – ecstatic (that is through the actual experience of dreams and trance states) and traditional or 'didactic' (through the learning of techniques, the names and functions of the spirits, the mythology and genealogy of the clan, and often a secret language). This twofold instruction given by both the spirits and older master shamans is seen as an initiation. Sometimes there are public initiation ceremonies but this is not always the case.

The recognition of election to the shamanic vocation is similar amongst most groups. Eliade (1987) says:

> Among many Siberian and Inner Asian tribes, the youth who is called to be a shaman attracts attention by his strange behavior; for example, he seeks solitude, becomes absent-minded, loves to roam in the woods or unfrequented places, has visions, and sings in his sleep.
>
> (p. 202)

It was Eliade who coined the phrase, 'pre-initiatory illness' to describe such characteristics. In some groups the symptoms of the pre-initiatory illness indicating election can be of a deranging nature and quite serious. Even hereditary shamans undergo similar changes in behaviour due to their election by shaman ancestors. It is believed that during these states, a shamanic initiation is proceeding. Additionally, there are times when people can become shamans following accidents or highly unusual events of a bizarre or life-threatening nature, though such instances are less common.

Eliade notes that the symptoms of the pre-initiatory illness have led some scholars to conclude that shamans suffer from a mental disorder. He is of the opinion that shamans have generally healed themselves so that their 'initiation is equivalent to a cure' (ibid., p. 203) and that the pre-initiatory illness is part of a mystical initiation which follows a traditional pattern. In Siberian and Inner Asian shamanism the sequence is as follows: in an imaginal state, the shaman is 'killed' by the spirits, then dismembered (generally to the state of a skeleton) and put back together again, followed by an ascent along the world tree where instruction is received in the art of healing and how to orient oneself in the spirit realm, given its inherent dangers etc. The shaman emerges from this ordeal with a strong constitution, powerful intelligence and enhanced energy.

Overall, Eliade sees shamans as functioning by way of mystical trance for four purposes: to take offerings to deities and spirits on behalf of the community; to seek a lost soul which has either wandered off from its body or been stolen by a spirit; to guide the soul of a dead person to its new location; or to gain knowledge from the spirit realm (as in divination). Shamans often act as guardians of their tribe's rich oral traditions but their principal sociocultural function is that of healing. Amongst most groups, sickness is seen as the result of a loss of soul, so a diagnostic séance can be the first phase of the healing process to determine if the soul has just wandered off or has been stolen. All séances involve trance and can be quite structured. They feature drumming, singing, calling on the spirits, a describing of the shaman's soul journey (which can be celestial ascent or descent) and directives received from the spirits. The séance ends when the shaman collapses motionless. A shaman's capacity for soul journey means they can act in the manner of a spirit and this is emphasized in the undertaking of various *faqir*-like tricks. These often have to do with fire.

This overview accords with those of other reputable commentators on shamanism such as Harvey (2003), Ränk (1967), Stutley (2003) and Vitebsky (1995). However, Siikala (1978) notes that although 'the describing and explaining of the phenomenal complex going under the name of shamanism has been one of the central themes of research into ethnology, comparative religion and anthropology, ethnomedicine and folklore, no consistent answer has been found to the question "What is shamanism?"' (p. 12).

## The definitional debate about shamanism

Despite the work of Eliade, there has been over the decades substantial divergence of opinion amongst scholars as to what can accurately define shamanism and this still occurs today. Geertz (1997, p. 39) believes things like 'shamanism', 'animism' and 'totemism' to be examples of 'desiccated' and 'insipid' categories 'by means of which ethnographers of religion devitalize their data', whilst Spencer (1968), in his review of Edsman's (1967) *Studies in Shamanism*, called the whole concept of shamanism into question. Following more contemporary trends in anthropology which deconstruct general theories of cultural evolution and history, Taussig (1989, p. 59) goes so far as to say that 'shamanism is . . . a made-up, modern, Western category, an artful reification of disparate practises, snatches of folklore and overarching folklorizations, residues of long-established myths intermingled with the politics of academic departments, curricula, conferences, journal articles, [and] funding agencies.' Despite these opinions, the research literature on shamanism is vast and it has not been uncommon for scholars to address the etymology of the word 'shaman' in an attempt to bring some clarity to the issue of definition.

## The meaning of the word 'shaman'

All scholars seem to agree that 'shaman' is a Siberian word from the Evenk (Tungus) group, having come into English through Russian sources.[1] The other Siberian tribes use different words for similar functionaries. Czaplicka (1914) says the word functions both as a noun, meaning 'one who is excited, moved, raised' and as a verb, meaning 'to know in an ecstatic manner'. These meanings give some understanding to the phenomenon which goes by the name. It is generally accepted that the most comprehensive etymological account is that of Laufer (1917) who tells us that seventeenth-century Dutch diplomats, after a visit to the Evenks (Tungus), made one of the first uses of the word. By 1875, it had become included in the *Encyclopaedia Brittanica*. However, speculation amongst scholars as to the actual origin of the word is substantial. For those who trace an historical development of shamanism from Chinese and Indian Buddhism into Siberia, there is a suggestion that the word *šaman* could have been incorporated from the Chinese (*sha men*) via the Pali word *samaṇa* (which means an ascetic and religious person). Laufer and other scholars, such as Németh (1913–14, as cited in Siikala 1978), refute this. By tracing linguistic changes, Laufer formed the view that shamanism developed in Central Asia and was not Indic-Buddhist and this conformed to similar ideas put forward by early etymologists such as Banzaroff (1891, as cited in Czaplicka 1914). Shirokogoroff (1935), after his extensive fieldwork among the Evenk (Tungus), concluded that while shamanism was indigenous to them, it was a 'shamanism stimulated by Buddhism', a view with which Siikala (1987b) agrees. Nonetheless, the Indic-Buddhist view still makes its way into later introductions on shamanism, such as that of Peters (1989).

This divergence of opinion around the etymology of the word does make it difficult to be definite about the cultural-historical origins of shamanism. As an Evenk (Tungus) word, the phenomenon is located in a particular cultural and geographical area but it is of significance that it shares common elements with other Siberian groups who use a different word. As Siikala (1978) notes,

> for although the magico-religious rite complexes and their associated concept systems in Siberia and Central Asia are not completely uniform in their phenomenology, due to natural reasons of culture, geography, history and social economy, these phenomenal complexes do still contain a considerable number of common elements of a fundamental nature.
>
> (p. 14)

As such, Siikala is prepared to accept the Evenk (Tungus) word 'shaman' as a *terminus technicus* whilst noting that etymology has not really thrown any specific light on the inherent nature of the shamanic complex. This seems a reasonable conclusion.

Beyond the etymology, the broad issue to do with the cultural-historical origins of shamanism has occupied a number of scholars in relation to the definitional debate.

## The cultural-historical origins of shamanism

As already noted, Shirokogoroff (1935) believes of the Evenk (Tungus) that theirs is a 'shamanism stimulated by Buddhism'. Eliade (1964) concurs with this view of southern influence noting that 'the ancient Near East influenced all the cultures of Central Asia and Siberia' (p. 500). However, he goes further to state that shamanism

> in its structure and as a whole cannot be considered a creation of these southern contributions [for] the ideology and the characteristic techniques of shamanism are attested in archaic cultures, where it would be difficult to admit the presence of paleo-Oriental influences. It is enough to remember, on the one hand, that Central Asian shamanism is part and parcel of the prehistoric culture of the Siberian hunters, and, on the other, that shamanic ideologies and techniques are documented among the primitive peoples of Australia, the Malay Archipelago, South America, North America, and other regions,
>
> (ibid., pp. 502–3)

Eliade is highlighting two important points here. First, that much of shamanism can be considered a universal phenomenon. Indeed, later scholars such as Peters and Price-Williams (1980) include Africa in their treatment of shamanism which Eliade does not. Second, there is a suggestion that shamanism is part of the palaeolithic hunting cultures of ancient Eurasia.

This view as to the palaeolithic origins of shamanism is supported by the growing number of researchers who interpret certain palaeolithic cave paintings as representing shamans. Makkay (1953) was one of the first to interpret the horned figure in *Les Trois Frères* cave at Ariège, France, as a shaman. Such an approach has gained considerable support from the contemporary research of Lewis-Williams (1991) on cave art in both Africa and Europe as well as that of the French scholar Clottes (2003a) and his co-workers. The African and European parallels alongside similarities in the Sahara and Siberia all support the view of a universal palaeolothic origin to shamanism (see Glob 1969, Lajoux 1977 and Okladnikov 1966).

Overall, Siikala (1987b) concludes:

> The wide distribution of the phenomenon of shamanism and the endemicity of certain of its basic ideas . . . in Arctic and sub-Arctic cultures do, however, support the view that the roots of shamanism lie in the Paleolithic hunting cultures.
>
> (p. 2)

A palaeolithic trajectory for shamanism may not be that much of an unexpected situation. Hultkrantz (1973) notes:

> Considering the ubiquity of shamans wherever (or nearly so) there are hunting cultures, and their decreasing importance in more advanced

societies, it is safe to say that shamans are a product of the basically individualistic, predominantly bilateral hunting societies. Since this type of society apparently was represented in the oldest known cultures of prehistoric man there is a strong probability for the high age of the office of the shaman.

(p. 35)

It has not been uncommon for scholars to use the palaeolithic material as evidence at hand to indicate shamanism is a primordial religious phenomenon which underpins all religious experience. Shamanism's connection to religion has thus been used definitionally.

## Shamanism and religion

On the issue of religion, La Barre (1970, p. 352) believed that: 'Essential shamanism is thus at once the oldest and newest of religions, because it is the *de facto* source of all religion.' In other words it is seen as an archaic underpinning to all later religious developments and this would accord with its palaeolithic origins. In this way both Hultkrantz (1973) and Eliade (1964) saw shamanism not as a religion in itself but as an autonomous complex which operates as a segment in different religions – 'a religious configuration within . . . religion' (p. 36). This is a similar position to that held by the members of the 1900–2 Jesup North Pacific Expedition from the American Museum of Natural History into Siberia. They tended to see shamanism as an archaic religious experience operating something like a North-Asian cult and whilst undergoing its own cultural modifications, was kept in various tribes alongside later religious developments.[2]

There are alternative views which see shamanism as a religion in its own right (Klementz 1910), including those of modern scholars such as Diószegi (1968) and Basilov (1984). As Hultkrantz (1988, p. 39) puts it, 'the shaman lives intermittently . . . in the world of trance, which is the supernatural world. . . . Since the supernatural world is the world of religion, shamanism plays a religious role.'

As a consequence, Siikala (1978, p. 12) concludes that 'Most researchers . . . agree that although the practice of shamanism does demand special mental and nervous properties it is nevertheless first and foremost a phenomenon in the realm of religion and magic.' Of more relevance, however, to the archetypal aspects of shamanism is her observation that 'the ideological basis [that is, the belief systems] of shamanism throughout North Asia and Siberia contains similar basic structures and forms of tradition' (ibid., p. 17). She would include in these the cornerstone beliefs about the helping-spirit system, the possibility of the mutual union of human and spirit and animistic beliefs about multiple souls and the spirit realm. The indication of 'similar basic structures' within the ideological systems of different groups does suggest something archetypal as one possible explanation.

Overall, however, from the perspective of religion, we see a significant number of writers viewing shamanism as representative of something archaic and primordial as with those who study the palaeolithic material. Further, a similarity of patterns in belief systems can be noted across the Siberian groups. When it comes to the history of religion, Eliade's (1964) is a most comprehensive account and on the question of definition, he seems to emphasize one phenomenological feature – ecstasy. In his foreword he states that 'shamanism is . . . one of the archaic techniques of ecstasy – at once mysticism, magic and "religion" in the broadest sense of the term' (p. xix) and then goes on to offer the following definition: 'A first definition of this complex phenomenon, and perhaps the least hazardous, will be: shamanism = *technique of ecstasy*' (p. 4). Not all would agree with this view and this raises the issue of the place of ecstasy, trance and possession in the understanding of shamanism.

## Ecstasy, trance and spirit possession in shamanism

Ränk (1967) believes that most scholars would accept 'ecstasy' as the defining characteristic separating shamans from witch-doctors, native healers and fortune-tellers, seeing Eliade as being the most influential scholar with this view. He points out, however, that the early Russian ethnographers saw ecstasy and the engagement with spirits as a later cultural development. Hence, Zelenin (1944, as cited in Ränk 1967) linked shamanism with primitive aetiology and the art of healing within animism and saw in it 'a transitory stage of development which from time to time has been known all over the world' (p. 20). Ränk goes on to note that opinions substantially diverge when the form of ecstasy and the original meaning of the term 'shamanism' are raised. Similarly, Siikala (1978) sees ecstatic trance as one way of delineating shamanism. She says, 'the technique of communication . . . in ecstasy . . . is, despite variation, common to all manifestations of shamanism' (p. 17). She is also aware that it is not uncommon for scholars to emphasize one phenomenological feature of shamanism over others as Eliade (1964) does in specifying ecstasy and magical flight as definitional features. The result for Eliade is that he rejects the notion of spirit possession whereas Findeisen (1957, as cited in Siikala 1978) emphasizes possession over ecstasy. Since then, these alternatives have led to a major divide amongst scholars.

During the 1960s, with a growing societal interest in 'consciousness' and psychedelics, researchers began to focus on the Altered State of Consciousness into which shamans entered during their trances. Harner (1973, 1980) eventually coined the term 'Shamanic State of Consciousness' to describe the particular characteristics of this state. This approach led to what Noll (1985) described as a 'renaissance' of interest in shamanism emerging in the 1980s. This was unlike the earlier ethnography because of the type of psychological perspective upon which it focused in relation to the characteristics of the 'Shamanic State of Consciousness'. Noll (1989, p. 49) concluded that the 'proponents of this school are largely devoted to examining and classifying the subjective phenomenology of the shaman's inner, private experiences without reduction to mechanistic causal principles. Self-reports of ecstatic experience by shamans are generally the focus of these investigators.' In parallel with this research focus, Peters (1978, 1981a, 1981b, 1982, 1987) did further fieldwork of a more experiential kind amongst the Tamang of Nepal and this substantially extended our understanding of the phenomenology of shamanism beyond that known to the early ethnographers.[3]

Eventually this research area fomented a debate as to whether it was 'embodiment' or 'flight' which is aboriginal to shamanism. Peters (1989, p. 118) defined embodiment as 'a controlled and voluntary trance condition [as] distinct from the term *possession* which definitionally may imply that the trancer is a victim of the spirits.' 'Flight' was understood to mean the soul journey that shamans undertook in their trance states. Peters went on to suggest that both embodiment and flight are culturally primordial and he emphasizes the fact that both involve controlled visualizations, which are lucid and non-amnesiac. By extending his definition of a shaman to an ecstatic who employs soul journey and/or embodiment techniques, Peters was able to include in his schema 'controlled ceremonial embodiment' (which may be contiguous with 'possession') and controlled visualization/imaging (usually interpreted as 'spirits' and/or 'soul journeys'). The critical feature is that both are controlled, lucid (meaning a dual conscious awareness of being 'embodied' and 'disembodied' at the same time) and non-amnesiac.

A critical feature of shamanism has emerged from these psychologically oriented investigations. Whilst there has been investigation of the particular kinds of visualizing and imaging which shamans seem to experience in their trance states, what is noticeable is that these can occur without the shamans losing touch with events in the ongoing Ordinary State of Consciousness. Noll (1985, 1990) has thereby stressed alongside Eliade (1964) that a central feature of shamanism is *control* over trance and its subsequent use in cere-monial situations. In other words, shamans attain the capacity to re-enter trance states similar to those experienced in their pre-initiatory illness but without being possessed and overcome. They then use the spirit encounters experienced in their trances to gain the healing information required. Noll sees this capability as the most significant result of the training which they undertake.

Therefore, despite the on-going debate as to whether it is 'embodiment' or 'flight' which is aboriginal to shamanism and the extent to which both are believed to be culturally primordial, they do both involve controlled visualizations. Thus Peters (1989) notes that overall, the ethnographic literature seems to privilege 'controlled possession' as the central feature and concludes that '[m]emory and mastery of visionary trance seem to be crucial definitional elements' (p. 121).

In relation to the 'ecstasy' versus 'possession' debate, Siikala (1978) attempts to resolve it by seeing both of them simply as 'functional alternatives describing the communication between the shaman and the other world' (p. 13). She sees the tendency to emphasize one feature over another as driven by the theory the scholars are developing. An example would be Hultkrantz (1967) who extended Eliade's (1964) definitional emphasis on 'ecstasy' and defined a shaman as 'a practitioner who, with the help of spirits, cures the sick or reveals hidden things etc. while being in an ecstasy. During the trance he may leave his own body, or he may simply summon the spirits to him and ask them to help him' (op. cit., pp. 32–3). This extended definition later allowed Hultkrantz (1973) to consider much North American material where he specifically addressed the question of definition. Aware of the confusion in the literature surrounding the issue, he believed one common agreement to be that shamanism 'refers to religio-magic techniques and the operator of these techniques, the shaman.' (p. 25). From this point on, he noted that agreement amongst scholars ceased.

To overcome such ongoing disagreements, certain writers have been led to take what they consider a phenomenological approach in the way advocated by Wach (1958). For him, the researcher is 'concerned to let manifestations of the religious experience speak for themselves rather than to force them into any preconceived scheme' (p. 24). One of the main commentators who takes such a phenomenological approach to shamanism has been Kraus (1972).

## The transcultural phenomenological approach

Kraus (1972) notes that despite the vast literature on shamanism, there is substantial divergence of opinion as to the concept of the shaman and a precise definition remains elusive. He sees a diverse range of loosely related phenomena included in the study of shamanism with these widespread across many different world cultures. He states that

> one of the problems that has made the definition of shamanism such an elusive matter is that its basic content is of a very primitive, highly personal, primary process nature. In this sense it is part and parcel of the human condition and may correctly be termed ahistorical.

(p. 31)

This is an extremely interesting comment when viewed from an archetypal perspective for things that are 'part and parcel of the human condition' are *ipso facto* archetypal, an issue which will be addressed in the next chapter.

To develop a working model of shamanism, Kraus examined three autobiographical accounts of shamans from different parts of the world and deduced common characteristics, which he used to establish what he described as a 'skeletal' definition of shamanism. He then applied this definition cross-culturally. This is essentially a phenomenological approach to definition and it is not uncommon for such cross-cultural phenomenological approaches to be used as a way of getting around the definitional difficulties. There seems substantial agreement amongst scholars as to what shamanism is, if the issue is approached phenomenologically.

Five main characteristics emerged from Kraus' research. First, the shaman is a chosen person. Second, shamans are involved with powerful spirit familiars whose aim is tutelary and helping. Third, the shaman's initiation is characterized by a period of psychological crisis in which the shaman-to-be withdraws, subsequently experiencing both psychic torment and tutelage. Fourth, the shaman's knowledge is attained through this process and (often) the instruction of master shamans; and fifth, the end result of these experiences leads shamans into a communal focus around aspects of healing for their sociocultural group. These features are not at all dissimilar to those we have already seen Eliade (1964, 1987) deduce.

By applying his 'skeletal' definition of shamanism transculturally, Kraus (1972) placed himself within that tradition which understands shamanism to be a universal phenomenon. Whilst other comparative and phenomenological studies of shamanism, such as those of Peters and Price-Williams (1980, 1983), also tend to regard it this way, we have already seen from Eliade and Siikala that it is more preserved amongst the Siberian and Inner Asian groups, despite occurring in many world cultures, even prehistoric ones. The vast majority of scholars accord with this view, Hoppál calling the region of Siberia and Inner Asia the *locus classicus* of shamanism (see Siikala and Hoppál 1998). This is no doubt due to the fact that these societies have remained over an historically long period of time (until quite recently) 'loosely structured, technologically simple, homogeneous and animistic hunter/gatherer societies' (Saliba 1998, p. 1) which seem to be the kind of society within which shamanism flourishes.

Furthermore, the geographic isolation of these groups would have contributed to the continuity of this kind of culture. Specifically in the Arctic regions, the religious life of the community tends to be centred on shamanism, which is not necessarily the case in other places in the world. Because of its centrality in the discourse on shamanism, the *locus classicus* requires particular attention and it is not unreasonable to expect that this region is able to shed significant light on the whole wounded healer phenomenon within shamanism.

## Siberia as the *locus classicus* of shamanism

In relation to the *locus classicus*, Hultkrantz in 1973 restated his previous conviction from 1967 that there are two types of shamanism: a general type common across many cultures which exhibits substantial variation and is expressed in a form of 'low intensity' and Arctic shamanism (the Arctic including the Inuit peoples, parts of the north-west coast of USA and areas west of the Bering Strait) which is more concentrated in its geographic distribution and intensity, and which overall displays a greater degree of uniformity within its geographic boundaries. In this conception, Arctic shamanism is seen as a cultural modification arising out of general shamanism, which has been its foundation, a common circumpolar historical tradition having in all probability contributed to this development. This is a critical assertion for if this is so, then we are getting a particularly concentrated and intense version of shamanism in the Arctic regions which, whilst dependent to some extent on these particular cultural groups for its characteristics, nonetheless may be encapsulating in this bounded and concentrated locality a distilled form of shamanism which is preserving in a very focused way the essential characteristics of this magico-religious phenomenon. In other words, it is not inappropriate at this stage to speculate that the characteristics of the shamanism in these Arctic regions may be closer to the essential centre and core of the phenomenon.

Hultkrantz's designation of two forms of shamanism does have support from many other scholars and Kraus (1972, pp. 20–1) concludes that the distinction 'is a valuable one because it systematizes the general impression that shamanism, although widespread, is considered by many to be found in its most highly developed form in the circumpolar area, whose historical tradition has contributed to its growth'.

Fortuitously for our purpose, the kinds of society in which shamanism has been noted to flourish have been preserved in the Arctic regions until relatively recently, enabling us to observe a shamanism which has been lost in many other cultures. Additionally, there is an extensive ethnographic literature on Siberian shamanism much of which has been obtained through direct fieldwork and is accessible to most western readers. Most of these accounts go back into the second half of the nineteenth century and the beginning of the twentieth century, reflecting a time before the onslaught of Sovietization and later Western influences. Compared with other places in the world, this material can be considered quite pristine.[4]

An important conclusion to be drawn from Hultkrantz's (1973) assertion that there are two forms of shamanism is that it highlights the role of cultural modification. On this latter point, I believe he rightly concludes that an 'unalterable shamanism cannot . . . exist' (p. 27) because of cultural changes and modifications across space and time. Even North Eurasian shamanism, which has been so popular amongst scholars, Ränk (1967) notes is not a unified phenomenon, for substantial local differences are evident around the shaman's authority, behaviour patterns, paraphernalia and personality construction. Siikala (1978) is of a similar opinion and it needs to be noted at this stage that she understands cultural modification to have occurred within Siberian shamanism despite her observation of its 'similar basic structures' that was previously noted.

Additionally, Hultkrantz's two forms of shamanism explain why we are able to recognize shamanism's different manifestations worldwide as belonging to essentially the same class of things and why when countering Spencer's (1968) criticism that such a thing as shamanism is ill-defined and does not exist, Hultkrantz can assert that shamanism is recognized amongst scholars as a social institution. It may be ill-defined or conceptually flawed to some extent, but this does not invalidate the fact that something of substance is being studied.

On the issue of the two forms of shamanism, Siikala (1978) does make the following important observation:

> The broader the application of the term shamanism and the more varied the systems of rites concerned, the more blurred the conceptual content becomes. I therefore consider it useful to use the term *shamanism* for the real, 'classical' shamanism of Central Asia, Northern Siberia and other arctic regions, in which the similarities of rite technique and belief system amount to more than a few basic features. Shamanic features, elements and ideas are, on the other hand, found in different parts of the world.
>
> (p. 14)

Siikala is making here the valuable point that there is a 'classical' shamanism across the Central Asian, Northern Siberian and Arctic groups and that a substantial similarity exists amongst them.

For the purposes of explicating the wounded healer dynamics within a shaman archetypal configuration I believe it important to concentrate on this *locus classicus* of shamanism for the similarities to which Siikala alludes are likely to indicate any archetypal patterns. And as previously indicated, there is sound ethnography on this *locus classicus*. Furthermore, given the palaeolithic origins of shamanism and the evidence that native American tribes derive from Siberian migration during that era, Siberia (and its shamanism) tends to be placed more centrally; one cannot ignore it.[5]

## The essential features of Siberian shamanism

In concentrating attention on the *locus classicus*, specific features of Siberian shamanism emerge. A general account of the Siberian shaman's duties can be found in Shimkin's (1939) overview of the Ket tribe. He used

Anuchin's (1914, as cited in Shimkin 1939) study of fifteen 'full' shamans to indicate that they tell stories, cure, prophesy, make birth easier, specify hunting regions and find game, direct the procedures to settle disputes and shamanize for amusement. By comparing this material with other groups, Siikala (1978) concluded that a shaman's general function is to handle crises that threaten the normal life of the tribe. The one common feature of these crises is that they are seen to be caused by spirits, demons or super-natural beings. Shamans handle these crises in a particular way – through immediate contact with their spirit helpers in the supernatural realm. This is attained by way of an Altered State of Consciousness (ecstatic trance) wherein mastery is critical, for shamans must, whilst gaining information, get the spirits to do what they want. This is an important feature for at least two reasons. First, as we have seen before, the commonness of ecstatic trance means that it can be one way of defining shamanism; and second, it implies something quite specific to shamanism compared with other manipulators of the transpersonal. It is an activity of direct experiential encounter with the cause of the problem, this being a dissimilar activity to priests who only need to enact a ritual without direct personal involvement.

The other common features of Siberian shamanism which Siikala (1978) goes on to note are the shaman's journey; sickness being explained by the flight of the soul from the body; particular beliefs about the structure of the cosmos; a helping spirit system; and the idea of a mutual union of human persons and spirit. However, she emphasizes four main aspects: the com-munity within which shamans operate; their emphasis on the supranormal world; the shaman as medium of communication between this world and the supranormal one; and the ecstatic nature of the communication. Overall, these features tend to align with those concluded by Hultkrantz (1973, p. 34), who said: 'We may now define the shaman as a social functionary who, with the help of guardian spirits, attains ecstasy in order to create a rapport with the supernatural world on behalf of his group members.' These features also accord with Kraus' (1972) 'skeletal' definition of shamanism and Eliade's work, and they are not contradicted by the conclusions of 1980s fieldworkers such as Peters (1981a, 1981b, 1987, 1989) or Peters and Price-Williams (1980, 1983).

There is, however, one aspect of shamanism which Siikala (1978) seems to underemphasize but which Eliade (1964) and Kraus (1972) note – the psychological crisis which causes the shaman-to-be to withdraw and in which psychic torment is experienced. Apart from the trance states into which shamans enter as part of their healing cures, the involuntary nature of this pre-initiatory illness with its hallucinations, visions and torment alongside bizarre and deranged behaviour has led to the view that Siberian shamans are psychopathological. This issue of psychopathology has a direct connection to views about the Siberian shaman's underlying psychology and the related wounded healer dynamics.

## Siberian shamanism as psychopathology

The early accounts of Siberian shamanism in English by Czaplicka (1914), Bogoras (1904) and Jochelson (1908, 1926, 1933) tended to regard the pre-initiatory illness of shamans as a specific form of neurosis, called 'Arctic hysteria'. Ohlmarks (1939, as cited in Eliade 1964) believed this to be caused by the extremities of the Arctic environment in terms of temperature, the long nights, the solitude and a lack of vitamins. Devereux (1961) similarly believed shamans to suffer from a neurosis.

However, as Siikala (1978, p. 27) succinctly points out: 'How can the visions of the North American Indians, for example, which to a great extent parallel the initiatory visions of the Siberian shaman, be explained by this view stressing Arctic hysteria?' It should be noted, though, that this observation may only call into question Ohlmarks' explanation and not necessarily the possibility that such groups so widely separated could experience a similar psychological state because its cause arises out of experiences common to the human condition.

In another early account Loeb (1929) specified epilepsy as the shaman's problem whilst later researchers including Silverman (1967), Kraus (1972) and Kroeber (1940) tended to see the condition of shamans as something truly psychotic and pathological. Ackerknecht (1943) saw the shaman as more like a recovered psychotic but believed that using Western psychiatric labels could be based in sociocultural bias.

The fact that the pre-initiatory illness can only be cured by shamanizing and that shamans eventually are able to control their trance states has caused some, such as Eliade (1964), to see the shaman as superior in some way, while others, such as Shirokogoroff (1935), view the shaman as 'the madman who has healed himself.' Eliade coined the term 'supernormal' because of the apparent capacity shamans have to transcend their psychological and emotional difficulties. And Basilov (1984) certainly understood the connection between mastery of trance and derangement when he said: 'As soon as the shaman lost control over his visions, he would become a neuropath. But having lost control over himself, he would no longer be a shaman' (p. 29).

The Shamanic State of Consciousness research emerging from the renaissance of study on shamanism in the 1980s had such an influence on the psychopathology question that Atkinson (1992) eventually concluded that 'the argument that shamanism is not a function of mental illness appears to have prevailed' (p. 309). Nonetheless, the literature on shamanism reveals quite polarized opinions as to the mental state of shamans and these generally reflect the areas of academic interest of the researchers. Psychological tests used in the Native American context have proved similarly divergent (see Ackerknecht 1971, J. M. Murphy 1964 and Opler 1936).

There does seem to be general agreement, however, that shamans experience a degree of mental disturbance with which they have done something personally transformative and culturally relevant. Shirokogoroff (1935), Radin (1937) and Devereux (1956, 1961) all hold this view. It cannot be overlooked that whilst the shaman's own cultural group may speculate as to their power, they often see their own shamans as deviant in certain ways. As Bogoras (1904, p. 426) observed, the shaman has been described as a 'very nervous, highly excitable person, often almost on the verge of insanity.' However, to dismiss shamans as 'just pathological', as Kroeber (1940) seems to do, does not do justice to either their apparent personal transformation or their sociocultural services.

The psychopathology view of shamanism is not generally held today by anthropologists. Znamenski (2003, p. 280), when summarizing Basilov's paper on 'Chto takoe shamanstvo [What is shamanism?]', says: 'The old debate about whether shamans were normal or sick people . . . does not make sense and should be excluded from scholarly discussions.' Znamenski believes Basilov takes this position because the psychopathology stance overlooks the shaman's social role from within a particular sociocultural context.

Hutton (2001) makes a similar point:

> Bogoras indeed extended his opinion of Chukchi shamans into the assertion that shamanism in general was a form of mental illness, a theory which enjoyed some popularity among scholars in the early twentieth century but was abandoned by the 1950s as patently untenable. What seems harder to refute is Sieroszewski's perception that shamans were somehow different in kind from the rest of their society. It was repeated long afterwards by Vilmos Dioszegi, after his work among former practitioners in various ethnic communities of southern Siberia. He stated that they all had some distinctive trait, being introverts, invalids, psychopaths or misanthropes. Such first-hand research must be treated with respect, but how it accords with Shirokogoroff's characterization of shamans as spanning the spectrum of social types, and how much it reflects the experiences of Dioszegi's interviewees under Stalinism, now seems impossible to say.
>
> (p. 77)

An overview of the writings on shamanism indicates that the issue of psychopathology has not really been abandoned since the 1950s for it still appears as a point of discussion with those researchers who approach shamanism from a psychological orientation (see Noll 1983, Peters 1982, 1989 and Peters and Price-Williams 1980, as well as more recent commentary by Krippner 2002). Indeed, Peters (1996) could note parallels between the features of transitional crises and Borderline Personality

Disorder, including fasting, Altered States of Consciousness, body mutilation, use of psychoactive drugs, body fragmentation, dismemberment and mutilation, all features seen in shamanic rites of passage. In 2002, deMause was still describing shamans as 'schizoids'.

In relation to the question 'what is shamanism?', the psychopathology issue is actually highly significant for, as Ränk (1967) indicates, once a psychopathology can be determined, the whole definitional debate around shamanism reduces as the difficulties become collapsed and a psychological universalism is introduced which has the capacity to simplify. However, it has to be noted that there are still quite varied views as to the shaman's psychopathology. More crucially, there would appear to be a connection between the shaman's pre-initiatory illness and their later healing function. It is the latter which underpins the view of them as wounded healers and this issue is explored further in later chapters.

## Summary and conclusions

Shamanism with its wounded healer component is a more complicated area of study than it initially appears for much more is going on than rudimentary spirit possession. The palaeolithic material indicates it is representing something archaic in terms of both religion and society whilst most scholars (even those such as Siikala who exclusively study Siberian shamanism) consider that something universal is indicated. However, the concentrated form of shamanism in the *locus classicus* and the sound ethnography that has been undertaken on these Siberian groups means that phenomenal features are quite clear.

Whilst shamanism operates primarily within the realm of religion and magic, one of its main foci is on healing in one form or another and, significantly, the 'call' to this vocation is precipitated by a crisis involving states of derangement. As Siikala (1978, p. 17) notes, this demands 'a certain nervous and psychic susceptibility in those chosen as . . . representatives' and it is this aspect which is of significance to the wounded healer issue. Critically, the shaman's healing capacity is related to their own self-cure which comes about in a two-stage process: an initial overwhelming experience of dismemberment imagery and psychic derangement followed by tutelage with a master-shaman so that trance states can become controlled. The result is that the healing séances entail direct involvement with the cause of a problem without the shaman re-experiencing any derangement.

However, in seeing shamanism as reflective of an underlying archaic archetypal pattern to do with individuation, Jung would see the wounded healer aspects as contained within that archetypal understanding. It becomes necessary, therefore, to determine whether shamanism and its wounded healer component actually reflect an archetype because of the significant conclusions one could draw in relation to contemporary analysts.

Chapter 4

# Shamanism and the wounded healer as an archetype

## Introduction

In parallel with Jung, it is generally assumed by most post-Jungian commentators that shamanism represents an archetype and its phenomenology is then viewed from that starting point – Groesbeck (1989), Moore and Gillette (1993), Ryan (2002), Sandner and Wong (1997) and C. M. Smith (1997) all do this. Few give consideration to any systematic evidencing for this assumption. It is important to determine, therefore, whether shamanism is representative of an archetypal configuration because of the conclusions we may want to draw, especially to do with its wounded healer dynamics, and how these may relate to contemporary analysts.

Groesbeck (1975) asserts that there is an actual wounded healer archetype and if that is so, then the wounded healer component within shamanism will have a nonpersonal aspect to it derived from the collective unconscious and independent of the personal history of any individual experiencing things shamanic. However, if the wounded healer component within shamanism is not an archetypal configuration then the experiences associated with it must be subjective in nature and developmentally derived from particular kinds of wounds. It would be important to specify just what kind of wounds these are so as to understand why it is that certain individuals receive the 'call' to the shamanic vocation while others who may want to become shamans cannot get initiated. Given Groesbeck's (1989) suggestion of a connection between a shaman archetype and 'the good analyst' there would then be flow-on issues to the selection and training of contemporary analysts. And if a sizeable component of shamanism with its wounded healer dynamic is archetypal in the classical sense, then specific selection and training issues for analysts would emerge.

To further these issues, a clear understanding of Jung's theory of archetypes is required, including the way he evidenced their existence, so that this can be applied to shamanism and its wounded healer component.

## The essential features of Jung's theory of archetype

For Jung (1931/1991a, p. 157) the 'totality of all archetypes' is contained in the collective unconscious and it is this concept of the collective unconscious which is both central and unique to Jung's analytical psychology.[1]

In extending his conception of the unconscious from that which had been gained through his initial collaboration with Freud, Jung (1931/1991a) came to see that a 'rationally explicable unconscious' is only a top layer, the material of which has been made unconscious artificially (through repression). He goes on to call this the 'personal unconscious', beneath which, he says is an

> absolute unconscious which has nothing to do with our personal experience. This absolute unconscious would then be a psychic activity which goes on independently of the conscious mind and is not dependent even on the upper layers of the unconscious, untouched – and perhaps untouchable – by personal experience. It would be a kind of supra-individual psychic activity, a *collective unconscious*, as I have called it, as distinct from a superficial, relative, or personal unconscious.
>
> (p. 148)

Nine years later Jung (1940/1990) is saying in 'The psychology of the child archetype' that:

> Modern psychology treats the products of unconscious fantasy-activity as self-portraits of what is going on in the unconscious, or as statements of the unconscious psyche about itself. They fall into two categories. First, fantasies (including dreams) of a personal character, which go back unquestionably to personal experiences, things forgotten or repressed, and can thus be completely explained by individual anamnesis. Second, fantasies (including dreams) of an impersonal character, which cannot be reduced to experiences in the individual's past, and thus cannot be explained as something individually acquired. These fantasy-images undoubtedly have their closest analogues in mythological types. We must therefore assume that they correspond to certain *collective* (and not personal) structural elements of the human psyche in general, and, like the morphological elements of the human body, are *inherited*. Although tradition and transmission by migration certainly play a part, there are, as we have said, very many cases that cannot be accounted for in this way and drive us to the hypothesis of 'autochthonous revival'. These cases are so numerous that we are obliged to assume the existence of a collective psychic substratum. I have called this the *collective unconscious*.
>
> (p. 155)

Clearly Jung saw the collective unconscious as a level of the psyche separate from personal experience which can operate with 'autochthonous revival' (that is, arise spontaneously) despite tradition and transmission by migration having a place.

In relation to the concept of the archetype, as early as 1912, in *Symbols of Transformation*, Jung (1912/1986) spoke of 'primordial images' to explain the universality of certain patterns of behaviour and motif evident across human experience in comparative mythology, comparative religion and even the dreams of modern persons. By 1917 he was referring to '"dominants" of the collective unconscious' and 'nodal points' which attract energy and influence a person's functioning (Jung 1917/1990) but he first introduced the term 'archetype' in 1919 (Jung 1919/1991). As a concept it has attained such cultural coinage that it was eventually included in the Fontana *Dictionary of Modern Thought* in 1977 (Bullock and Trombley 2000).[2]

Jung initially used this term 'archetype' in relation to what he called 'motifs' which appeared in experience as images but this was eventually extended to cover all psychic manifestations which were universal and typical in nature. Eventually he drew a distinction between the archetype *an sich* ('as such' or 'in itself'), which is irrepresentable, and the archetypal images, which are psychically experienced:

> The archetypal representations (images and ideas) mediated to us by the unconscious should not be confused with the archetype as such. They are varied structures which all point back to one essentially 'irrepresentable' basic form. . . . The archetype as such . . . belongs, as it were, to the invisible, ultra-violet end of the psychic spectrum. It does not appear, in itself, to be capable of reaching consciousness . . . [but] . . . when represented to the mind, is already conscious and therefore differs to an indeterminable extent from that which caused the representation. . . . We must . . . constantly bear in mind that what we mean by 'archetype' is itself irrepresentable, but has effects which make visualizations of it possible, namely, the archetypal images and ideas.
>
> (Jung 1954/1991a, pp. 213–14)

Archetypes are also understood by Jung (1940/1991) to be biologically inbuilt structural components of the psyche. As he says elsewhere: 'The collective unconscious contains the whole spiritual heritage of mankind's evolution, born anew in the brain structure of every individual' (1931/1991a, p. 158). Consequently, 'archetypal ideas are part of the indestructible foundations of the human mind' (ibid.). He elaborates:

> However long they [the archetypes] are forgotten and buried, always they return, sometimes in the strangest guise, with a personal twist to them or intellectually distorted . . . but continually reproducing

themselves in new forms representing the timeless truths that are innate in man's nature. . . . The special emphasis I lay on archetypal predispositions does not mean that mythologems are of exclusively psychic origin. I am not overlooking the social conditions that are just as necessary for their production.

(Jung 1948/1991b, p. 130)

This is an important statement because it contains essential ideas about Jung's understanding of archetypes. On the one hand they are 'continually reproducing themselves' (that is, they have autonomy, a point which we have noted above) but on the other hand, Jung allows a place for 'social conditions' in relation to the mythological aspect of archetypal expression.

In his later private letter to G. A. van den Bergh von Eysinga, Jung (1954) makes it quite clear that he is thinking of the archetypes' 'reproduction of themselves' as occurring spontaneously and that this characteristic evidences their autonomous nature:

As animals have no need to be taught their instinctive activities, so man also possesses primordial psychic patterns, and repeats them spontaneously, independently of any teaching. Inasmuch as man is conscious and capable of introspection, it is quite possible that he can perceive his instinctual patterns in the form of archetypal representations. As a matter of fact, these possess the expected degrees of universality (cf. the remarkable identity of shamanistic structures). It is also possible to observe their spontaneous reproduction in individuals entirely ignorant of traditions of this sort. Such facts prove the autonomy of the archetypes.

(p. 152)

Overall, the concept of archetypal 'autonomy' is a centrally distinctive feature of Jung's archetype theory. It is because of this capacity to 'continually reproduce themselves' that Jung sees archetypes as manifesting themselves in some form or another across space and time. This ongoing reproduction of themselves in new forms occurs precisely because archetypes are already part of the human psychic constitution. As such, any similarities around cross-cultural expression will not just be seen as the product of a random coincidence of similar social conditions but rather as the outworking of the archetypal predisposition to experience the world in a certain way for 'archetypes are typical modes of apprehension, and whenever we meet with uniform and regularly recurring modes of apprehension we are dealing with an archetype, no matter whether its mythical character is recognised or not' (Jung 1919/1991, pp. 137–8).

Previously we saw Jung referring to the idea of social context in relation to archetypal expressions. He stressed the 'just as necessary' place social context occupies in the mythological expression of anything archetypal. Presumably, sociocultural conditions can activate, arrange and modify archetypal predispositions so that they become expressed in the terms of a particular culture resulting in what he elsewhere refers to as 'variations on a ground theme' (Jung 1954/1991a, p. 213). In 'A psychological approach to the dogma of the Trinity' he adds:

> [the] archetype *an sich* . . . is an 'irrepresentable' factor, a 'disposition' which starts functioning at a given moment in the development of the human mind and arranges the material of consciousness into definite patterns. . . . Archetypes are, by definition, factors and motifs that arrange the psychic elements into certain images, characterized as archetypal, but in such a way that they can be recognised only from the effects they produce. They exist preconsciously, and presumably they form the structural dominants of the psyche in general. They may be compared to the invisible presence of the crystal lattice in a saturated solution. As *a priori* conditioning factors they represent a special, psychological instance of the biological 'pattern of behaviour', which gives all living organisms their specific qualities. Just as the manifestation of this biological ground plan may change in the course of development, so also can those of the archetype.
>
> (1948/1991b, pp. 148–9)

Given this perspective, it stands to reason that an archetype's expression will always be an intersection phenomenon between the inbuilt archetypal core and the sociocultural context. As a consequence, we should see cultural differences in relation to any archetype's expression but the differences should not be so great that any sense of the underlying commonality is lost.

There is one potential criticism of this 'social context' viewpoint which should be noted. Such an interpretation of similarities and differences surrounding a perceived cross-cultural archetypal expression does enable Jung to have things both ways. Once an archetypal position is granted then any cross-cultural similarity can be interpreted as something archetypal and any cross-cultural difference can be interpreted as social modification of the archetypal predisposition. However, to solve this problem in our context we would have to articulate the development and modification of a shaman archetypal pattern across space and time and this is impossible; we are only in a position to investigate it as recorded in reliable documents to do with actual fieldwork and to see from these whether or not our questions can be sufficiently answered.

There are a number of important points which emerge from this overview of Jung's theory of archetype which are relevant in answering the question: 'does shamanism and its wounded healer component represent something archetypal?' First, Jung's assertion that archetypes are 'irrepresentable dispositions' which can only be known by their effects means that there will be something at the same time known and elusive about them. Second, activated archetypes arrange the material of consciousness into recognisable patterns of imagery; and third, the manifestation of an archetype can change in the course of sociocultural development. So what method did Jung himself use to prove the existence of archetypes?

## Jung's method for proving the existence of archetypes

In 'The concept of the collective unconscious', Jung (1936/1990) does address the question of how to prove the existence of archetypes. It needs to be remembered, however, that his focus is on the experience of individuals rather than broad sociocultural phenomena like shamanism. Nonetheless, aspects of his method will become useful in addressing the question to do with shamanism and its wounded healer component representing something archetypal. Jung begins by looking for sources of unconscious content and turns his initial attention to dreams:

> We must now turn to the question of how the existence of archetypes can be proved. . . . The main source . . . is *dreams*, which have the advantage of being involuntary, spontaneous products of the unconscious psyche and are therefore pure products of nature not falsified by any conscious purpose . . . [W]e must look for motifs which could not possibly be known to the dreamer and yet behave functionally in his dream in such a manner as to coincide with the functioning of the archetype known from historical sources.
>
> (ibid., pp. 48–9)

Jung's emphasis here is on the archetypal, objective and nonpersonal, regarding dreams as being 'involuntary' and 'spontaneous' products of the unconscious psyche, 'unfalsified' by conscious activity. As such they produce motifs unknown to the dreamer and yet which function in the dreamscape in the same way as the corresponding archetype has been seen to operate historically. He goes on to state that similar motifs can appear through active imagination, paranoid delusions, trance states and the dreams of early childhood.

There is some difficulty here with Jung's assertion that dreams are involuntary, spontaneous products of the unconscious psyche not falsified by any conscious purpose. This is a debatable position to adopt but it is one which Jung (1950/1990) emphasizes elsewhere:

> There are products of active imagination, and also of dreams, which reproduce the same patterns and arrangements with a spontaneity that cannot be influenced.
>
> (p. 332)

On this point, Hobson (1971, pp. 73–4) notes that 'in suggesting that dreams arise with a spontaneity that cannot be influenced . . . he [Jung] seems to underestimate the extent of secondary elaboration, which certainly occurs in reported dreams and is probably an important factor in active imagination.'

It would have to be agreed that secondary elaboration is a feature relevant in dream reporting, whilst the imagery arising in meditative states like active imagination is highly questionable and susceptible to inductive effects (that is, the unconscious influence on a client by the therapist) as the debate surrounding 'repressed memories' and their 'accessing' would attest (see Sandler and Fonagy 1997). Can the occurrence of dreams really be excised from their subjective context? Many of Jung's own examples would seem to indicate that they cannot. For instance, his example of the woman patient who dreamed of him as a 'corn god' deity occurs within the context of an intense erotic transference and any reasonable commentator would have to conclude that the dream has not occurred 'spontaneously' (that is, without a subjective context) (Jung 1939/1993). Whilst the dream could be explained as a form of primary process thinking finding the only suitable imagery at hand with which to express its purpose, what still needs explaining is why and how it is that this particular imagery has emerged.

It would appear that Jung, whilst believing archetypal experiences could be connected to things like tradition and migration, had a personal preference for conceiving of them as operating autonomously without any reference to personal experience or environment.

Two related and crucial questions are raised by this position: what is the relationship between the collective unconscious and an individual's personal experience and does the collective unconscious actually operate spontaneously and autonomously? In relation to shamanism and its wounded healer component, these important questions will be addressed below and further in Chapter 6.

To return to Jung's method: he does not believe that a similarity between images occurring in dreams and mythology provides sufficient evidence for the presence of an archetype. There must be a correspondence of *functional meaning* within a similar context (that is, serving the same psychic purpose). Jung (1936/1990) goes on to say:

> In order to draw a valid parallel [between a motif and a similar one from mythology], it is necessary to know the functional meaning of the individual symbol, and then to find out whether the apparently parallel mythological symbol has a similar context and therefore the same functional meaning.
>
> (p. 50)

As an illustration of this technique, Jung summarizes the 'solar phallus' case example gained from his days at the Burghölzli Mental Hospital in

Zurich. The case was of a male schizophrenic patient who in 1906 reported an hallucination of the sun's phallus, the moving of which he said caused the wind. Subsequently, in 1910, Jung came across a book by Dieterich describing a liturgy of the ancient Mithraic cult which contained the same concept as the schizophrenic's hallucination. Jung (1931/1991a, p. 151) concluded that: 'The vision of my patient in 1906, and the Greek text first edited in 1910, should be sufficiently far apart to rule out the possibility of cryptomnesia on his side and of thought-transference on mine.' He saw this as an example of the spontaneous occurrence of an archetype, the image of the sun's phallus producing the wind having arisen autonomously in the patient from a deep layer of the collective unconscious.[3]

Overall, then, Jung (1936/1990, p. 53) concludes that 'first of all, certain symbols have to be isolated clearly enough to be recognizable as typical phenomena, not just matters of chance' and this can be achieved through examining dream series and the content of active imagination. The method requires discovery of typical figures and typical situations which not only regularly manifest themselves with a corresponding meaning but display development and variation. The motifs which emerge from this analysis must then be shown to occur in other times and places to rule out chance coincidence: 'We must therefore show that the idea . . . exists independently . . . and that it occurs at other times and places' (ibid., p. 52).

Clearly, the example of the 'solar phallus' patient's hallucination would fall into this category. Generally then in Jung's method, comparative mythology and ethnology are used to substantiate the conclusion that an archetype is in existence and operative. Alternative explanations, as in forms of transmission through language, education, cryptomnesia and culture, must be ruled out so that spontaneous transmission (that is, 'autochthonous revival of mythological motifs') can be established beyond doubt. This is the critical issue to do with the autonomy of archetypes:

> It is not sufficient to point out the often obviously archetypal nature of unconscious products, for these can just as well be derived from acquisitions through language and education. Cryptomnesia should also be ruled out, which it is almost impossible to do in certain cases. In spite of all these difficulties, there remain enough individual instances showing the autochthonous revival of mythological motifs to put the matter beyond any reasonable doubt.
>
> (p. 44)

Jung (1954/1990b) recognizes that he is not the first to promote the idea of psychic *a prioris*, this being a tradition which goes right back to Plato, but he does say that if he has

> any share in these discoveries, it consists in . . . having shown that archetypes are not disseminated only by tradition, language, and

migration, but that they can rearise spontaneously, at any time, at any place, and without any outside influence.

.   (p. 79)

Jung believed this to be his own particular and unique contribution and as we have seen, it is central to his conception of archetypal theory. However, as Hobson (1971) notes, despite spontaneity and autonomy of archetypes being central ideas for Jung, these are his most difficult assertions to substantiate.

In summary, the active presence of an archetype in an individual can be detected when motifs unknown to the person spontaneously appear and cluster around typical phenomena which can be seen elsewhere to occur across other times and places and which display a correspondence of functional meaning in a situation where no other explanations other than 'autochthonous revival' are possible.[4]

## Is shamanism and its wounded healer component an archetype?

In approaching shamanism as a sociocultural phenomenon, certain difficulties are already apparent in terms of 'unknown motifs' and 'spontaneity' in relation to the experience of specific individuals. Within shamanic cultures, it could not be said that the pre-initiatory illness and its corresponding motifs are unknown for as we have already seen in Chapter 3, it is the actual occurrence of the pre-initiatory illness and its motifs which provides evidence of the 'call' to the shamanic vocation both to the initiate and to their sociocultural group. However, in Jung's view, just because motifs are known to an individual through their culture this does not in itself preclude the operation of an archetype. As he says in 'A psychological approach to the dogma of the Trinity':

> The special emphasis I lay on archetypal predispositions does not mean that mythologems are of exclusively psychic origin. I am not over-looking the social conditions that are just as necessary for their production.
>
> (Jung 1948/1991b, p. 130n)

Presumably, archetypal content can be activated through cultural means so that a difficulty would only arise if 'unknown motifs' were being used alone to deduce the existence of an archetype. What is of more significance is the occurrence of equivalent motifs across space and time where cultural transmission can be ruled out, and this issue will be discussed below.

Furthermore, similar difficulties arise in relation to the issue of the 'spontaneity' and 'autochthonous revival' of archetypes when shamanism is considered as a sociocultural phenomenon. From the perspective of individuals, Hobson (1971) has already noted that it is an immense task to fulfil all of Jung's criteria for demonstrating the existence of archetypes and suggests it is probably impossible actually to substantiate the one of 'autochthonous revival'. We have already seen in Chapter 3 that the spontaneous 'election' of individuals to become shamans does occur but the influence of language, education and culture on them could not possibly be ruled out. Indeed, how could one rule out cultural transmission once mythological stories are incorporated into a culture? Nonetheless, from the sociocultural perspective, there are examples from the ethnographic literature in relation to shamanism where similar motifs appear and cultural transmission can be ruled out. In relation to initiation phenomena in shamanism, Eliade (1964) discusses the parallels between Siberian initiations and those within Australia and states that such 'a parallelism between two groups of mystical techniques belonging to archaic peoples so far removed in space is not without bearing on the place to be accorded to shamanism in the general history of religions' (p. 51). Eliade is here referring to the dismemberment of the initiate's body by spirit beings so that the internal organs can be renewed and replaced but the parallels he describes would accord with an archetypal explanation. Eliade goes on to say that 'this likeness between Australia and Siberia markedly confirms the authenticity and antiquity of shamanic initiation rites' (p. 51). Campbell (1976) has been able to draw similar conclusions when comparing shamanic practices in Tierra del Fuego with those of Alaska. Although these locations are from the same New World continent, cultural transmission, whilst highly unlikely, cannot be entirely ruled out and so Campbell's deductions must be treated tentatively. Nonetheless, they are corroborative rather than contradictory and this is noteworthy.

Generally, in relation to shamanism as a sociocultural phenomenon, the issue of 'autochthonous revival' becomes somewhat questionable because the motifs and imagery to do with the phenomenon are already present in the cultures making it impossible to deduce any occurrence of something purely autochthonous when looked at transculturally. However, this does not seem to be the case in relation to the subjective experience of those individuals who become the most powerful shamans. These initiates experience an unsolicited 'call' to the vocation through the pre-initiatory illness and it is this aspect which appears to occur with 'autochthonous revival' suggestive of a spontaneous upwelling of archetypal content.

This does, however, raise a further question: whilst the concepts, motifs, imagery and ideologies to do with shamanism are present within these cultures, why is it that certain individuals undergo this 'spontaneous calling' and others do not? This is a crucial question for our understanding of shamanism generally and for the operation of the wounded healer component in it and will be addressed further in Chapter 7.

Nonetheless, if shamanism and its wounded healer component represent an archetypal configuration as conceived by Jung then a number of deductions follow. Being in the nature of things by way of the collective unconscious, such an archetype would be seen to express itself across space and time.

### Shamanism across space and time

If shamanism with its wounded healer component is the result of an archetypal constellation which is itself archaic as Jung conceives, then we should be able to find evidence of its expression within prehistoric cultures as well as across diverse and different cultures historically. This is precisely what we do find. The overview of shamanism in Chapter 3 revealed that most scholars agree that much of shamanism is not only a universal phenomenon but also has its origins in the palaeolithic era and this would accord with an archetypal underpinning.

From the historical perspective there has been speculation for some time concerning palaeolithic cave art and shamanism, Frobenius (1933, as cited in Campbell 1976) having made such deductions from his North African research prior to the discovery in France of the Lascaux caves in 1940. Whilst much comment has focused on these famous French caves, Clottes and Lewis-Williams (1998) point out that the actual French scholars of the cave art have tended to be sceptical of any interpretation (like a shamanic one) and have traditionally stuck to facts and a structural rather than interpretative approach.[5]

One main speculation of those scholars studying the French palaeolithic cave art has been how to interpret Leroi-Gourhan's (1967) 'wounded men' figures, found in a number of the caves. These seem to depict humans wounded by spear-like projectiles but N. Smith (1992) interpreted them shamanically, believing the lines to indicate forces emanating from their bodies. From the discovery of a similar figure in the Cosquer cave, Clottes and Courtin (1996) concluded that the speculation could be ended. For them it was clear that the killing of a man was depicted for 'the large sign that overlies him could not in any way be a symbol of forces emanating from within the body: the sign is outside the body and crosses it from one side to the other' (p. 160). It is possible we have here a diagrammatic representation of the shaman's 'wounding' for Clottes and Courtin did not completely discount shamanic possibilities. In particular, they were aware of other human depictions apparently dressed as animals or birds, such as the 'sorcerer' in the Dordogne Gabillou cave. They also noted that most of the other human figures depicted in the caves are drawn completely lacking in detail, despite the artists' capacity to render animal figures with life, beauty and precise characterization. They did wonder then if these figures represented 'extraordinary beings, shamans or spirits in human form who could be depicted only in a somewhat indirect way' (ibid., p. 161), presumably drawn this way to protect the artists against the spiritual power these beings were believed to exercise.

What has been emerging over recent years is a body of contemporary evidence from other parts of the world which is causing the French cave art to be reinterpreted. Most notable is the extensive work of Lewis-Williams (1991) on the caves of the southern African San. He concluded that these painted caves were expressing something shamanic and he then began to look at European cave art in the same way (see also Lewis-Williams and Dowson 1988, 1989).

Clottes subsequently became interested in Lewis-Williams' research and his commentary on the European material. A professional collaboration emerged and they say in their introduction to *The Shamans of Prehistory: Trance and Magic in the Painted Caves* that: 'We have undertaken [this project on European caves] because our initial studies have convinced us that shamanism – both the concept of the universe and the practices it engenders in so many regions of the world – responds better than any other to certain particulars of the art of the deep caves' (Clottes and Lewis-Williams 1998, p. 9).[6]

Their conclusions are based on two premises. First, the view that there is a universal human propensity for the nervous system to enter altered states of consciousness; and second, the ubiquity of shamanism among hunter-gatherer communities. Given these, it is not difficult for them to find evidence of figures from palaeolithic cave art that represent the stages of trance. Also, by taking into account the caves' topography, geographical structure and context, including the positioning of the figures, Clottes and Lewis-Williams (1998) concluded that the caves were sites of ritual. By combining neuropsychology and ethnology in this way, they believe they have demonstrated that a 'shamanic interpretation goes far beyond mere conjecture' (p. 79).

Later, Clottes (2003a, 2003b), with a number of co-workers, returned to reinvestigate the paintings at the Chauvet cave in France and a number of shamanic interpretations followed which are covered in *Return to Chauvet Cave. Excavating the Birthplace of Art: The First Full Report*. In this publication, Le Guillou (2003) argues that the way the so-called 'sorcerer' figure is drawn 'is characteristic of prehistoric depictions of humans such as the "Horned God" that dominates the Sanctuary in the cave of Les Trois-Frères in Ariège' (p. 170n). This figure has often been interpreted in a shamanic way, Campbell (1976) being one of many who does so.

Further evidence follows from the prevalence of bear depictions at Chauvet (up to fifteen recorded in the cave complex at the time of Clottes' publication), which Robert-Lamblin (2003) believes could be interpreted in the same way as bear mythology in Arctic cultures where the bear has a mythical role analogous to that of the shaman. Chichlo (1981) has already seen a link between bear mythology and shamanism in the neolithic rock art of the Siberian Sakha (Yakut) tribe. Robert-Lamblin used his study of Inuit culture, including their shamanic tradition, to interpret what may be the significance and meaning of the cave complex in terms of a site of ritual in a similar way to Clottes and Lewis-Williams above. He concluded:

> Although we cannot assert that Chauvet Cave was the scene of real 'shamanic practices', as we have not so far found any traces of rituals that could have accompanied the production of the depictions, we nevertheless think that it may have been a sanctuary, inside which those who lived essentially from hunting came to celebrate a site that was particularly rich in game or to communicate with the animal kingdom and perhaps the supernatural world.
>
> (2003, p. 207)

In his conclusion to the re-examination of Chauvet cave, Clottes (2003c) reiterates the view he and Lewis-Williams presented earlier that the 'dangerous animal' depictions in the cave are related to mythology within the framework of shamanic practices and beliefs. It is not without significance that he and these other reputable researchers are coming to such conclusions. There would appear to be a growing body of irrefutable evidence to support the view that shamanism was practised by our palaeolithic ancestors. And this is corroborated by other examples of shamanic activity in the art of prehistory which can be found elsewhere. Kent Reilly's (1996) research in Mexico on Olmec art (1500–300 BC) at the Oxtotitlan cave near Chilpancingo in the Guerrero region and at La Venta have been interpreted as depicting shamanic activities such as cosmic flight. Further similarities can be found in the Sahara (Lajoux 1977), Siberia (Okladnikov 1966) and Scandinavia (Glob 1969).

In relation to shamanism's distribution across space, we have already seen Eliade (1964) in Chapter 3 show that it can be found in cultures as diverse as Indonesia, North America, India, Central and North Asia, Australia, ancient China and Persia. Peters and Price-Williams (1980) even include Africa, which Eliade does not. The view that shamanism is a universal phenomenon is also supported by those such as Siikala (1978, 1987b, 1989) who restrict their attention to the Siberian *locus classicus.*

Most of the major researchers on shamanism agree that it has been part of the human experience for a long period of time and that it has been reproduced in the vast majority of the world's cultures as would be expected if it had an archetypal underpinning in the way Jung conceives. As Stein (1987, p. 58) puts it: 'One basis for claiming archetypicality for any human activity is its ubiquity.' Examples would be Siikala's (1978) observation to do with the ideological belief systems of shamanism throughout North Asia and Siberia which contain 'similar basic structures and forms of tradition' (p. 17) and Eliade's (1964) conclusions to do with the universality of the pre-initiatory illness. Such common elements across different groups are in accord with an archetypal underpinning.

### Shamanism as 'irrepresentable disposition'

If archetypes are 'irrepresentable dispositions' which can only be known by their effects as Jung (1948/1991b) maintains, then there will be something that is at the same time both elusive and known about them. If shamanism with its wounded healer component is the result then of an archetypal expression, such an 'elusive but known' aspect would be seen within the conscious articulation or attempts at conscious articulation amongst people but with a difficulty surrounding precise definition, which is exactly what we do see with shamanism. The vast literature on shamanism indicates an agreed sense of something similar being investigated by scholars, despite their difficulties in formulating a precise definition. This is exactly the kind of situation which archetype theory would predict. Furthermore, as Kraus (1972, p. 31) notes on the issue of definition, 'one of the problems that has made the definition of shamanism such an elusive matter is that its basic content is of a very primitive, highly personal, primary process nature. In this sense it is part and parcel of the human condition and may correctly be termed ahistorical.' In terms of classical archetypal theory, things which are part and parcel of the human condition are *ipso facto* archetypal (see Whitmont 1991).

### Shamanism as a cluster of typical phenomena with functional meaning

If the function of archetypes is to arrange psychic material into certain patterns with functional meaning and if shamanism is the result of an archetypal constellation, then a particular pattern to do with this phenomenological expression ought to be able to be deduced from the ethnographic studies and this is what we do find both in Eliade's (1964) comparative morphology and with others including those who have undertaken their own fieldwork, such as Peters and Price-Williams (1980). From Chapter 3 we can see that shamanism has a definitional core and that it expresses itself with functional meaning in those cultures where it occurs. The critical examples would be the mastery aspect emerging from the self-cure of the pre-initiatory illness (which no doubt aids reconstitution of individual initiates) and the subsequent healing séances which shamans are then able to undertake on behalf of their sociocultural others.[7]

### Shamanism and imagery

A further deduction from Jung's theory of archetype is that there will be a connection between an archetype and imagery. The arrangement of psychic material into a pattern which becomes recognizable to consciousness as a particular archetype occurs as a certain set of images. As Jung (1926/1991, p. 322) explains: 'A psychic entity can be a conscious content, that is, it can be represented, only if it has the quality of an image and is thus *representable*.' This is not to say that the concept of the archetype is equivalent to an actual concrete image, rather the archetype orders and directs psychic material into visible images. It is behind the images as a latent invisibility but can become known to consciousness through the set of images it produces. Consequently, within archetypal theory, the presence of a pattern of certain images will indicate the presence of a constellated archetype and conversely, if an archetype is being constellated, strong imagery organized into perceivable patterns will be seen. The presence of both strong and definable imagery within shamanism and around particular themes, such as dismemberment, is further evidence that the phenomenon is archetypally driven.[8]

Overall there seems sufficient indication that shamanism with its wounded healer component conforms to an archetypal configuration in the classical Jungian sense and this can be confirmed by the ethnographers of shamanism, especially those who are not specifically approaching it from an archetypal or Jungian perspective.

## The views of the ethnographers of shamanism

### Mircea Eliade

Having provided the most extensive study of the phenomenon of shamanism, it is not without significance that Eliade (1964) himself concludes that, as a religious experience, it is archetypally based.

In discussing comparative religion (which is the discipline through which Eliade approaches shamanism), his view is that 'the very dialectic of the sacred tends indefinitely to repeat a series of archetypes, so that a hierophany realized at a certain "historical moment" is structurally equivalent to a hierophany a thousand years earlier or later' (p. xvii). Whilst it is this repeating which allows the history of the phenomenon to be written, the mere fact that such a repeating can be observed to organize itself into definable patterns is actual evidence of an archetypal process. An example would be Eliade's explication of the Altaic shaman's ritual of climbing the birch tree. Eliade is positioning his research by arguing that the (religious) history of a phenomenon cannot reveal *all about* the phenomenon. In Altaic cosmology, the birch tree symbolizes the World Tree and 'the steps up it represent the various heavens through which the shaman must pass on his ecstatic journey to the highest heaven' (ibid., p. xiv). Eliade believes there is strong evidence to assert that this type of cosmological view is Oriental in origin and would be one example (amongst a number of others) of the religious ideas of the ancient Near East penetrating far into Central and North Asia and influencing the shamanisms there. But as he points out, there is no reason to believe that these Oriental ideas created the cosmology and rituals of the Altaics because similar ideologies and rituals around themes of ascent and descent appear all over the world and in places where Oriental influence has not occurred (see Grimal 1965 and O'Connor 1993 for examples). Eliade goes on to say:

> More probably, the Oriental ideas merely *modified* the ritual formula and cosmological implications of the celestial ascent; the latter appears to be a primordial phenomenon, that is, it belongs to man as such, not to man as an historical being; witness the dreams, hallucinations, and images of ascent found everywhere in the world, apart from any historical or other 'conditions'. All these dreams, myths, and nostalgias with a central theme of ascent or flight cannot be exhausted by a psychological explanation; there is always a kernel that remains refractory to explanation, and this indefinable, irreducible element perhaps reveals the real situation of man in the cosmos, a situation that, we shall never tire of repeating, is not solely 'historical'.
>
> (1964, p. xiv)

Such primordial phenomena which belong to humankind as such are, from a Jungian perspective, archetypal. Indeed, the myths they spawn last the test of time because, being archetypally based, they have universal significance.

Overall, Eliade's research on shamanism reveals a phenomenon with a cross-cultural distribution of something deemed to be essentially similar but with noted cultural differences, which is exactly what we would expect from an archetypal configuration as conceived by Jung. Since the archetypes are not viewed as static forms which predetermine all behaviour and experience but rather as organizing principles into which specific individual experience can be poured (so that they act more like moulds), the particular culture into which individuals are born will have an influence on the way an archetypal configuration expresses itself. The result will then be an observable similarity of pattern around an archetype's expression across cultures but with specific cultural modification being observable at the same time. Thus Ränk (1967) and Siikala's (1978) observation that even North Eurasian shamanism, which has been so popular amongst scholars, is not a unified phenomenon because substantial local differences are evident around the shaman's authority, behaviour patterns, paraphernalia and personality construction, is not an unexpected outcome if an archetype was in operation.

A range of scholars has been able to demonstrate the underlying characteristics of shamanism with its wounded healer component which appear cross-culturally and it seems justifiable to assume that these are reflective of an underlying archaic archetypal pattern. This conclusion is further supported through Eliade's (1964) methodology. Working as he did as a historian of religion, his method is comparative. He puts it thus:

> The historian of religion does not reach a comprehension of a phenomenon until after he has compared it with thousands of similar or dissimilar phenomena, until he has situated it among them; and these thousands of phenomena are separated not only in time but also in space.
>
> (p. xv)

Applying this methodology to shamanism, Eliade has been able to draw together the cross-cultural characteristics of the phenomenon and describe the various ways an underlying shamanic pattern manifests itself within different cultures. Whilst he interprets this material within a history of religions framework, an archetypalist could just as easily use it to describe the phenomenological characteristics of an archetypal pattern.

Whilst Eliade's position is actually quite archetypal, it is interesting to note that 'Jung' appears nowhere in his references. Given the cultural coinage which Jung's concept has gained, Eliade's use of the word 'archetype' may not be that unexpected but an archetypal perspective actually has the capacity to explain the phenomena he enunciates. Despite this, Eliade is a significant researcher on shamanism and his material does provide evidence of an archetypal configuration for shamanism and its wounded healer component.

### Other ethnographers

In addition to Eliade, other ethnographers have noticed the similar worldwide characteristics of the shaman phenomenon within those cultures in which it appears, Kraus (1972) and Peters and Price-Williams (1980) being notable examples (see Chapter 3). As Kraus puts it, '[shamanism] is part and parcel of the human condition and may correctly be termed ahistorical' (1972, p. 31). The implications this has concerning the underlying psychic structures of humankind has not been lost on other scholars for, as Ducey (1976, p. 174) states, 'the patterns intrinsic to the shamanistic experience . . . are encountered repeatedly the world over.' Similarly Campbell (1976, p. 264) concluded that 'psychology lurks beneath and within the entire historical composition, as an individual controller.' It is difficult to doubt that the phenomenon represents something of general human experience and can thus be interpreted as archetypal.

### Peters on shamanic spirituality

Larry Peters (1978, 1981a, 1981b, 1982, 1987, 1989, 1997) is an important ethnographer to consider because of the extensive first-hand fieldwork he did among the Tamang (a Nepalese ethnic group), which underpins his conclusions. When he compared shamanic practices and techniques with other spiritual traditions, Peters (1989, p. 115) concluded that shamanism is humankind's 'first spiritual discipline . . . the root from which other spiritual disciplines have issued.' As evidence for this, Peters noted that shamans' descriptions of their transpersonal states of mind, despite the cultural relativity of the explanations for such experiences, are similar to those from other mystical and meditative traditions in that they share 'deep underlying experiential features' which he attributed to an 'endogenous transformation process' which underlies all the separate traditions. This process is seen to have an identifiable structure not the least of which is the experience of a psychic death and rebirth, so central to shamanism but common also to many other diverse forms of mysticism. Peters concludes that 'there is a demonstrably similar underlying psycho-transformational process which is precipitated by traditional spiritual practices that utilize ASC [Altered States of Consciousness]' (ibid., p. 116).

There are further features of this 'endogenous transformation process' which Peters again identifies as common across traditions. First, the wedding of such transpersonal and transformative experiences to a career and vocation of compassionate action oriented toward others, this being a primary goal of most major spiritual traditions. Second, in shamanic initiations, a luminous figure is often encountered similar not only to Jung's (1963/1990) account of his Philemon experience in *Memories, Dreams, Reflections* but also to reports of other experiences, such as drug-induced states (Grof 1976) and those of near-death and UFO abduction – which Ring (1988) interestingly calls 'archetypes of the cosmic shaman.'

Overall, Peters (1989, p. 127) concludes that the 'endogenous transforma-tion process' is 'psychologically prototypal, paradigmatic, and archetypal' which accords with the previous conclusion that the shamanic phenomenon is reflective of an underlying archetype.

## Conclusions

It would seem a reasonable conclusion that shamanism with its wounded healer component can be viewed as an archetype in the classical sense of the concept. As indicated previously, this would highlight the non-personal aspect to the phenomenon because it would derive from the collective unconscious and be independent of the personal history of any individual experiencing things shamanic. This would have to be taken into account when assessing the wounds of the wounded healer, the ways in which they become healed and the ways they are then used for the therapeutic benefit of others.

The situation in relation to this archetypal perspective, however, may not be that straightforward. Given the discoveries from contemporary neuro-science to do with the way mind/brain structures develop and emerge, classical archetype theory is undergoing certain revisions. It is becoming increasingly difficult to assert the innate *a priori* aspect to archetypes on which Jung's theory stands. The alternative position is to see archetypes as developmentally derived structures forged out of the intense affective experiences of early infancy which once in place have the capacity to direct psychological life. Imagery which is later experienced as 'archetypal' is then understood to be an emergent phenomenon derived from these develop-mentally produced mind/brain structures. It is to these contemporary revi-sions of archetype theory that the next chapter is addressed so as to determine the actual underpinnings to shamanism and its wounded healer component.

# Chapter 5

# Contemporary archetype theory

## Introduction

Whilst it is possible to show at one level that shamanism and its wounded healer component represent a classical archetypal configuration there is currently emerging substantial debate about archetype theory and this bears directly on our understanding and interpretation of them. The critical issue is the extent to which archetypes can be evidenced as innate *a priori* psychic structures which have the capacity to operate autonomously and spontaneously divorced from the subjective and personal experience of individuals. If shamanism and its wounded healer component represent an archetype in this classical sense, its manifestation would be understood to emerge from a pristine level of psychic life untouched by personal experience making it a 'sacred heritage' into which modern persons can tap for their healing as Sandner and Wong (1997) propose. The 'wounds' of the wounded healer would then have to be understood from that perspective. However, there is growing evidence to suggest that the psychic structures which underpin archetypal experience are developmentally produced. If the shaman's wounded healer constitution is developmentally produced, an entirely different perspective is opened from which we can not only gain insight into the kinds of wounds which predispose to the vocation in the first place, but also explain why it is that certain individuals (rather than others) are drawn to the vocation. Furthermore, if the wounded healer component of modern analysts is of a shamanic kind then this vocational understanding would aid in the selection and training process of these analysts. It is important, therefore, to evaluate the developmental and emergent approaches to archetype theory.

## The new approaches to archetype theory

Samuels (1994) in his classic text *Jung and the Post-Jungians* gave a comprehensive overview of both Jung's theory of archetype and the major critiques of it up until that time. By the mid 1990s, however, contemporary concepts such as emergentism, supervenience and complexity theory were being used to describe archetypes thus heralding in a new way in which they were being discussed. Other views arguing for archetypes as 'symbolic forms' without any biological underpinning generated substantial debate in Jungian circles. One main area of comment has had to do with the *a priori* and innate status of archetypes and opinion has polarized on the one hand toward those who argue for a biological base to archetypes (and hence an assumed innate aspect) and on the other toward those who hold the counter view which argues against innatism and instead uses aspects of Dynamic Systems Theory, self-organization and emergentism in its articulation. As Hogenson succinctly puts it, 'the archetype itself and the archetypal image are emergent properties of a complex dynamic system' (Stevens *et al.* 2003, p. 376).[1]

There would appear to be two quite provocative lines of thought which have developed out of these new approaches to archetype theory and which need to be considered in relation to a shaman archetype and its wounded healer component. The first comes from the work of Saunders and Skar (2001) who have taken the position that it is the complexes, not the archetypes, which arise out of self-organization. Instead, the archetype can be seen as a property of the developmental dynamic that forms the complexes, and can be defined as a class of complexes that fall into the same general category. As such, archetypes cannot in any way be considered *a priori* entities. Skar (2004) further clarifies that

> [Jung] postulated an archetype at the core of each complex which somehow affected the formation of the complex. Our modern understanding of the processes of self-organization allows us to see how complexes can form without some pre-existing entity at the core, but it is still convenient to use the term archetype to separate the developmental aspect from the individual manifestation of the complex. . . . The words 'archetype' and 'archetypal' remain effective in describing these key human processes, if we remember that the archetype is not the *cause,* but rather the *essence* of the experience.
>
> (pp. 247–8)

Whilst Saunders and Skar (2001) assert that their position is in line with the original development of Jung's ideas in that he derived the concept of the archetype from his earlier discovery of the feeling-toned complex, Hogenson (2004a) has pointed out that this is a radical reversal of classical archetype theory which most commentators have failed to appreciate. I believe that the most radical assertion is in not seeing archetypes as pre-existing entities at the core of complexes, driving their formation. If this is the case then shamanism with its wounded healer component is not an innate psychic structure which organizes aspects of psychological life.

Rather, the use of the word 'archetype' in this context would simply be a categorizing word describing clusters of similar complexes. More specifically, shamanic and wounded healer phenomena would be due to the outworking of personal complexes which only appear to represent something archetypal in the classical understanding of the concept.[2]

The second provocative line of thought emerging from the new approaches to archetype theory has to do with the biological base to archetypes. As one critic puts it, 'genetics – or, strictly speaking, any branch of science based on biological premises – has so far not given any evidential support for the much-discussed thesis of the inheritance of archetypal structures' (Pietikainen 1998a, p. 342). This issue is critical because if archetypes are genetically inherited mind/brain structures then shamanism and its wounded healer component would have innate *a priori* status once it can be demonstrated they reflect an underlying archetypal configuration, as was done in Chapter 4.

One prominent defender of the classical approach to archetype theory has been Anthony Stevens who stresses the genetic and biological underpinning to Jung's theory. In his view, 'the biological implications of archetypal theory are enormous in their ramifications and help to place the whole Jungian edifice on firm epistemological foundations' (Stevens 1998, p. 351).[3]

## The biological base to archetypes

It is certainly clear that Jung (1912/1986) held to a biological perspective in relation to the theory of archetypes, as he states in one presentation of his 'solar phallus' case:

> This observation is not an isolated case: it was manifestly not a question of inherited ideas, but of an inborn disposition to produce parallel images, or rather of identical psychic structures common to all men, which I later called the archetypes of the collective unconscious. They correspond to the concept of the 'pattern of behaviour' in biology.
>
> (p. 158)

And elsewhere he says, 'The collective unconscious contains the whole spiritual heritage of mankind's evolution, born anew in the brain structure of every individual' (Jung 1931/1991a, p. 158).

As Stevens (1982, p. 16) concludes, 'Jung asserted that all the essential psychic characteristics that distinguish us as human beings are determined by genetics and are with us from birth. These typically human attributes Jung called archetypes.' As such, Stevens understands archetypes to be biologically based innate capacities of mind, the biological base itself having arisen out of selection pressures during the course of human evolution. Thus, archetypal predispositions are not only understood to have an adaptive function but also to be dispositions that are inherited in the genome.[4]

Hogenson (1998) points out that Stevens has been relatively alone in addressing the importance of the biological underpinning to archetypal theory and he hits the mark when he realizes that the issue is not an incidental or minor epistemological one. Hogenson is also aware that the argument for the innateness of archetypes can no longer occur in a context which does not take into account biological research. It is 'rather . . . the extent to which it [biology] plays a role and the precise nature of the role played' which is critical (p. 363).

For many, Stevens' biological approach to archetypes has substantial face validity but the appeal to biology has also led to questions about the innate, *a priori* aspects of archetype theory. This is because the findings of current neuroscience are calling into question the very thing to which Stevens is appealing – innatism and what Developmental Systems Theory in biology calls 'preformationism' (see Oyama *et al.* 2001). Preformationism in biology is the view that the information for producing an organism is contained in the genetic constitution of the zygote and becomes 'read-out' in an environment. This concept does relate to analytical psychology when archetypes, conceived as biologically based and pre-existent in the psyche, are understood to be 'read-out' into experience in some predetermined way, an approach I have critiqued previously (Merchant 2006, 2009, 2010).

## Gene–environment coaction

The issue of 'preformationism' is one of considerable importance in contemporary research on the biological base to psychological experience. The neuroscientists Nelson *et al.* (2006) advocate a position in opposition to what they call 'biological determinism' which I see as their way of referring to the concept of 'preformationism'. They critique the unidirectional assumption imbedded within 'biological determinism', that is, the view that genetic activity leads to structure which leads to function. What seems to be emerging from the sciences of genetics, embryology and the neuroscience of neonates and infants is irrefutable research evidence to indicate bidirectionality, that is, genetic activity also leads to function which leads to structure. Gottlieb (2007) puts it this way:

> Neural (and other) structures begin to function before they are fully mature and this activity, whether intrinsically derived ('spontaneous') or extrinsically stimulated ('evoked') plays a significant role in the developmental process.
>
> (p. 2)

Gottlieb believes that development plays a fundamental role in the generation of phenotypes and has coined the term 'gene-environment coaction' as the best way to describe the reciprocal influence of genes, neural activity, behaviour and the physical, social and cultural influences of the external environment on each other. In this approach, it is acknowledged that genetic start points do exist but, critically, final outcomes are not predetermined. This is because the final mind/brain structures we do see are honed out of functional experience in the environment during the earliest stages of human development.

Such a perspective is not lost on those who approach things from a psychological perspective and who argue a place for the mind as something not reducible to brain states. In his introduction to the Colloquium of Neuroscience and Psychoanalysis, held at the Anna Freud Centre, Fonagy (2002) puts things this way:

> The psychosocial environment . . . profoundly influences the development of neural structures. For example, the complex transition from genotype to phenotype will be conditioned by the child's experience of the environment. There are behaviour genetics data on both schizophrenia and criminality to support this. . . . Mental experience is orchestrated by neural structures, but that very psychological experience has the capacity to filter and modulate environmental effects upon neural structures that in their turn will have the power to determine a subsequent psychological response.
>
> (pp. 4–5)

It is the research area of epigenetics which provides evidence for the 'gene-environment coaction' approach that Gottlieb advocates. And a psychological example can be found in the research on intelligence.

### A research example: Intelligence

One of many possible epigenetic examples of the above fact from the psychological domain comes from a study of IQs in seven-year-old twins (Turkheimer *et al.* 2003). The twin pairs were selected from a range of socioeconomic backgrounds. For those twins living in impoverished environments, most of their intelligence could be accounted for by their shared environment whilst the genetic contribution was virtually zero. However, in affluent families the result was almost exactly the reverse. Epigenetic findings like these have prompted Gottlieb (2007, pp. 3–4) to conclude that 'individuals of the same genotype can have different neural and behavioural outcomes according to the *dissimilarity* of their relevant life experiences.' It would appear that the environment plays a very potent role in mediating genetic input and this calls into question our whole understanding of what it means for something to be 'innate'. It clearly cannot mean 'predetermined' as if things unfold in some kind of unidirectional way. Contemporary neuroscience progressively confirms this perspective.

## Contemporary neuroscience

Modern imaging techniques are vastly expanding our capacity to study the neuroscience of newborns and young infants and Nelson *et al.* (2006) give an accessible overview. When this research is examined, one of the leading researchers, Barbara Karmiloff-Smith (2009), draws similar conclusions to those of Gottlieb. She concludes that

> cortical networks are not genetically predetermined or built in to be preserved or impaired in genetic disorders. Rather, they are the emergent outcome of progressively changing processes, which dynamically interact with one another and with environmental input over developmental time, ultimately to give rise to the structured adult brain. But this is not to imply that the neonate brain is a blank slate with no structure. . . . On the contrary, neuroconstructivism maintains that the neonate cortex has some regional differentiation in terms of types of neuron, density of neurons, firing thresholds, and so forth. These differences are not domain specific . . . [or] . . . domain-general constraints. Rather, they are domain relevant (i.e. different parts of the brain have small structural differences, which turn out to be more appropriate/relevant to certain kinds of processing over others). But initially, brain activity is widespread for processing all kinds of input and competition between regions gradually settles which domain-relevant circuits become domain specific over time.
>
> (p. 59)

There would certainly appear to be growing evidence from 'cognitive damage' studies in particular which supports the view that the neonate brain is not initially organized around innate domain-specific modules. One example from the research of Paterson *et al.* (1999) succinctly illustrates this point, for the cognitive functioning of Williams syndrome patients actually changes over developmental time (Williams syndrome is a rare genetic disorder which causes both medical problems and developmental impairment). For numerosity judgements, these patients do well in infancy but poorly in adulthood, whereas for language, they perform poorly in infancy but well in adulthood. It is findings like these which militate against the idea of intact innate modules because in this case, the later cognitive functioning of these patients in adulthood is not determined by their initial functioning in infancy.

Such neuroscience research is indicating that the neonate brain is not initially organized around innate domain-specific modules and this informs the way we now understand mind/brain structures to emerge.

## The emergence of mind/brain structures

Nelson *et al.* (2006) point out that at the outset, there would appear to be very little neural specialization in humans and this allows for maximum flexibility in interaction with the environment. Rather, there is extensive prenatal neural proliferation in neonates as well as subsequent synapto-genesis (that is, the establishment of connection points between different neurons). This means that broad neural networks appear first and these are then honed by later experience into functional structures. Whilst the neural overproduction is genetically controlled, it would appear that the later pruning and circuit connections are experience dependent. As Nelson *et al.* say, 'the newborn brain has countless more neurons and synapses than an adult brain, and many of these are not yet committed to particular circuits or functions' (ibid., p. 41). Overall, the 'basic architecture [of the brain] occurs during the first two trimesters of fetal life, with the last trimester and the first few postnatal years reserved for changes in connectivity and function' (ibid., p. 29).

Language acquisition is an excellent example of the developmental emergence of mind/brain structures. This is significant, for since Chomsky's (1968) positing of 'deep structure' in relation to the acquisition of language, it has not been uncommon for nativists to use the brain's left hemisphere dominance for language as evidence for an innate human capacity and for this to be used as an analogy for inherited archetypes (see Stevens 1982).

## An example: Language acquisition

Research is revealing that it is the actual experience of language which leads to the development of the specialized mind/brain structures responsible for it. Nelson *et al.* (2006) state that

> the brain is constructed with certain anatomical biases toward acquir-ing language [with] regions seemingly poised to subserve language, most of which reside in the left hemisphere . . . [T]hese regions *become* committed based on experience. In other words, cortical specialization develops and is not prewired (what may be prewired is the potential of the brain to become specialized).
>
> (p. 70)

Nelson *et al.* are aware that left-hemisphere dominance for language processing does look like it supports innatism. They point out, however, that whilst research indicates that the neonate brain is prepared to learn a language, actual speech perception requires developmental experience and is quite plastic. As a consequence, they draw a distinction between a system that is innate and one that is simply biased in a particular direction. They argue that the former would show little plasticity following early brain damage whereas the latter would exhibit more plasticity. They outline research to show that if the left hemisphere does become damaged in infants then the right hemisphere can take over language function and this 'suggests that the neural substrate for language is not fixed, but rather, is biased in a particular direction. Should the normal pathway become impossible (due to early brain damage), other options are available to support language (notably, other brain circuits develop to take over function)' (ibid., p. 70).

The research on face recognition in infants is coming to similar conclusions, that is, that the brain's early developing structures begin with initial biases which are honed by experience in the environment. Casia *et al.* (2004) have shown that infants' face preferences are produced by a domain-general bias toward certain configurations and as such there is no necessity to assume the existence of a pre-wired tendency to orient toward the geometry of the face. In other words, faces do not possess a special status in the newborns' visual world. Similarly Johnson and Morton (1991) have argued against intricate innate perceptual mechanisms underlying face recognition. Rather, they propose minimalist startpoints so that the neural areas finally responsible for face-recognition have become specialized for that function through developmental experience. What appear to be innate face recognition modules are in fact structures which are developmentally acquired. Findings such as these have prompted the influential nativist Baron-Cohen (1998) to reformulate his position.

## Apparent innateness

Of significance, Nelson *et al.* (2006) make the point that the developmental emergence of mind/brain structures can give the impression of innateness because it appears as if 'these events simply unfold of their own accord . . . [and this] vastly under-represents the powerful role of experience in sculpting the final architecture of the brain' (p. 30). The critical point here is that the appearance and functioning of mind/brain structures can make it appear as if these outcomes are somehow predetermined and innate when in fact they are developmentally derived from minimal startpoints. This assumed innateness can then be compounded by the capacity of these developmentally produced mind/brain structures once they are in place 'to determine a subsequent psychological response', as Fonagy (2002, p. 5) puts it.

Clearly, neuroscience research is revealing a different kind of biology to that advanced by Jung or Stevens. The sorts of mind/brain structures which underpin archetypal experience are not produced by some kind of genetic preformationism but emerge as a result of developmental experience. What we now know about neural plasticity (especially in neonates and newborns) and the bidirection between biological structure and function forces the conclusion that genetic determinism is an outdated concept. Such findings are already being successfully applied to archetype theory as in Knox's (2003) model which sees archetypes as 'image schemas' onto which archetypal imagery is later scaffolded through experience in the environment. In such a model, shamanic phenomena and the associated wounded healer components would be better understood as developmentally acquired complexes and 'wounds' leading to the establishment of particular mind/brain structures which when in place have the capacity to direct psychological life.

## Knox's model: Archetypes as 'image schemas'

It is Knox (2001, 2003, 2004) who has extensively applied the findings of neuroscience to archetype theory and as such she takes a stand against psychic innateness, especially any attempt to designate archetypal imagery as genetically specified or to see archetypes as operating like preformed innate pieces of imagery and fantasy waiting to be called forth by the 'correct' environmental stimulus. She offers instead a 'developmental model in which mental contents emerge from the interaction of genes, brain and environment' (Knox 2004, p. 1). She goes on to argue her case for

> self-organization of the human brain and the recognition that genes do not encode complex mental imagery and processes, but instead act as initial catalysts for developmental processes out of which early psychic structures reliably emerge . . . [Archetypes are] emergent structures resulting from a developmental interaction between genes and environment that is unique for each person. Archetypes are not 'hard-wired' collections of universal imagery waiting to be released by the right environmental trigger.
>
> (ibid., p. 4)

In this way Knox does not deny the existence of archetypes or their key role in psychic functioning or as a source of symbolic imagery, but she does not see them as innate *a priori* psychic structures; rather, she understands their formation and operation in a particular way.

In advocating the self-organizing emergent properties of the human mind, Knox refers to Schore's (1994, 2000, 2001) ongoing research as providing evidence of an interaction between early life experience and brain development, that is, the intense emotional experiences in early life directly influence brain development.

Knox understands this process of development to be founded upon certain automatic subcortical innate biological processes which can predetermine behavioural responses and which work effectively in the species-typical environment. She sees these processes as underpinning instinct as we have come to know it – for example, Lorenz's (1952) imprinting is an example she uses to illustrate on the one hand the predetermined tendency to imprint (geese chicks normally follow their mother when she is the first thing they see after hatching) and on the other hand the environmental susceptibility of the response pattern (the geese chicks follow Lorenz and not Mother Goose if he is the first thing they see after hatching).

Specifically in relation to our understanding of archetypes, Knox considers the place of perceptual analysis as an early developmental process for infants, that is, the active comparing between stimuli leading to the emergence of an early structure called the 'image schema'. She believes image schemas constitute the basis of later concept formation: 'The image schema is a mental gestalt, developing out of bodily experience and forming the basis for abstract meanings' (Knox 2004, p. 9). As she says:

> Whilst image schemas are without symbolic content in themselves, they provide a reliable scaffolding on which meaningful imagery and thought is organized and constructed, thus meeting the need for a model that provides for the archetype-as-such and the archetypal image. If we adopt this model for archetypes, we have to discard the view that they are genetically inherited and consider them to be reliably repeated early developmental achievements.
>
> (ibid., p. 9)

Knox goes on to combine this idea of the image schema as core gestalt with that of implicit models which organize the infant's early experience into patterns of expectation. Overall, then, she argues that:

> The archetype, as image schema, provides an initial scaffolding for this process, but the content is provided by real experience . . . Repeated patterns of experience are stored in the form of internal working models in implicit memory. This kind of memory is not accessible to consciousness, but acts outside awareness, structuring our perception of the world by interpreting it in light of the generalized gestalt patterns of implicit knowledge.
>
> (ibid., p. 10)

In summary, it is the intense affectivity of infancy which drives the developmental formation of image schemas. Image schemas are stored in implicit memory as 'internal working models' and would equate with Jung's idea of the archetype-as-such. It is these image schemas which provide the scaffolding for more complex and elaborate symbolization through various processes of emergence and self-organization as the individual interacts with its environment. The ongoing significance of intense affectivity will drive this later scaffolding. Consequently, when similar affective experiences occur in adult life they will resonate with the original scaffolding and constellate imagery. However, it needs to be noted that given the implicit level of organization from which the later imagery arises, the imagery will appear *as if* innate and unknown. As such, the imagery can be interpreted as 'archetypal' in the classical Jungian sense even though it has arisen from mind/brain structures which were themselves developmentally produced.

Knox's model is particularly important for a number of reasons. It is underpinned in biological research and combines a developmental perspective with an emergent one thus enlarging its explanatory power. The developmental component has to do with the formation of the image schemas (archetype-as-such) in the first place and the emergent component has to do with the later scaffolding process (which underpins archetypal imagery). For this reason I have previously referred to this approach as an emergent/ developmental kind of model (Merchant 2006).

## Implications of Knox's model[5]

If image schemas equate with the archetype-as-such and they are developmentally produced then this is a radical reformulation of Jung's conception of archetype. For him, the archetype-as-such whilst understood to be a psychic structure with biological underpinning, was not viewed as being developmentally produced. It was inherited and hence innate.

Knox's model, however, implies there need be no such things as pre-existent, innate archetypal structures which direct psychological life and which are at the core of complex development. Rather, the developmentally produced mind/brain structures (image schemas) underpin a later scaffolding through various processes of emergence and self-organization. It is the latter which has the capacity to generate symbolic imagery. The crucial point is that such imagery would be arising out of mind/brain structures which are themselves derived from early preverbal developmental experience and not from innate archetypes. The ramifications are substantial, for the very existence of archetypes as Jung conceived them is called into question. This raises the possibility that the whole way we have envisaged the collective unconscious needs reformulating, for the conceptual division between it and the personal unconscious would collapse. In other words, there is no collective unconscious, only differential layers of unconsciousness depending on the age of a person when the image schema start points became imbedded through developmental experience. Consideration of this important issue is one to which I have alluded previously (Merchant, 2006).

It does need to be noted at this point that it is still not clear why any one person's 'archetypal' imagery would take the form that it does if it is not arising from innate archetypes. There are, however, a number of possibilities involving the cultural context within which the later scaffolding to image schemas occurs, a position to which Pietikainen's (1998a) work may point. Similarly, Skar (2004) notes in discussing the various cultural expressions of mother/child that these can be instantly recognizable to us not because of innate archetypes but due to the ubiquity of the common (species-typical) human experience of mothering. At our current stage of knowledge, however, it needs to be admitted that providing an extensive explanation about any one individual's archetypal imagery will be difficult if we cannot trace their every environmental experience and encounter.[6]

The critical question which Knox's emergent/developmental model poses is the extent to which Jung's classical theory can be read in that way and the effect this has on our understanding of shamanism and the wounded healer as archetypal configurations. To this issue the next chapter is addressed.

# Chapter 6

# A re-evaluation of Jung's classic theory of archetype

## Introduction

The implications derived from contemporary approaches to archetype theory such as Knox's (2003) emergent/developmental model have direct bearing on how we are to interpret and understand both shamanism and its wounded healer component.

If as Guggenbuhl-Craig (1999) suggests 'the good analyst' has the shaman archetype constellated within them, then it is important to know if the associated wounded healer component is a phenomenon derived from the objective psyche and unconnected to an individual's personal history or whether the experience of something archetypal is actually the outworking of a developmentally produced mind/brain structure. If the latter is the case then the wounded healer component within shamanism would be derived from particular kinds of wounds, the healing and use of which would underpin the 'good analyst'. There would then be significant flow-on issues to do with the selection and training of contemporary analysts.

Consequently, it is important to see if Jung's theory can be read in light of an emergent/developmental model of archetype such as that of Knox and whether Jung is able to provide sufficient evidence for his classical theory.

## The critical features of Jung's theory of archetype

### The place of compensation and affectivity

In classical theory, it is generally agreed that archetypes become activated, as Jung (1953/1993, p. 677) says, 'when a certain lack in the conscious sphere calls for a compensation on the part of the unconscious.' This is not a surprising statement given Jung's medical training because it sees the psyche in homeostasis terms, that is, if the psyche is imbalanced toward certain attitudes held consciously then the unconscious becomes activated so as to bring the psychic system back into balance.

An example would be Jung's (1951/1991, 1952/1991a) patient who experienced a synchronicity to do with a scarab beetle when in the consulting room. Jung describes this female patient as displaying an exceptional rationalism which she used as a defensive manoeuvre so that the psychotherapy had become stagnated in an impasse. She then had a dream of being given a gold scarab. At the precise moment of telling Jung this dream, he hears a tapping at the window and opens it to find a scarabaeid beetle trying to enter the room. These kinds of beetles are rare in Switzerland and on catching the beetle, Jung presented it to the woman saying, 'here is your scarab.' This synchronous event had such a profound effect on the patient that the therapy progressed markedly from that point on. Of this case Jung (1952/1991a, p. 440) says: 'It is this kind of situation that constellates the archetype with the greatest regularity.' In other words, the impasse in the therapy had activated a compensatory archetypal constellation to do with (psychic) rebirth, for Jung knew that the scarab beetle was an ancient symbol of rebirth.

Whilst this explanation by Jung seems quite plausible, I want to highlight the way the archetype gets constellated in the first place. We can safely assume that for the patient, the therapeutic impasse would have been an emotionally distressing occurrence and further, that this situation would have unfolded with Jung before the appearance of the archetypal image of the beetle in her dream. The point is that the personal context is important to note in the sequence of events and that *affectivity* is suggested as being operative in the archetype's constellation. This sequence of events would accord with an emergent/developmental model such as that of Knox (2003). The archetypal imagery has been activated by the intense affectivity of current subjective life experience because current experience is similar to a pre-existing 'internal working model'. The archetypal imagery has not arisen independently even though the unconscious 'choice' of the beetle image needs explaining.

There is every reason to believe that a similar situation is occurring in the shamanic pre-initiatory illness because of its general onset during adolescence (which presumably involves the heightened emotionality of puberty) or less frequently after some experience later in life involving intense affectivity. What requires further explanation is the pre-existing 'internal working model' which has been activated in the shaman initiate and its connection to the 'wound' component of the overall phenomenon.

Jung (1912/1986) did believe that archetypal content can be activated by the heightened affectivity of distressing life experience, for he says: 'The changes that may befall a man are not infinitely variable; they are variations of certain typical occurrences which are limited in number. When therefore a distressing situation arises, the corresponding archetype will be constellated in the unconscious' (p. 294). It is this position which Jung maintains when he goes on to elaborate his theory of synchronicity.

## Synchronicity

In 'Synchronicity: An acausal connecting principle', Jung (1952/1991a) devotes some attention to Rhine's classic experiments on extrasensory perception and psychokinesis undertaken at Duke University's Paranormal Psychology Laboratory. What seems noteworthy is that despite Rhine being able to demonstrate both extrasensory perception and psychokinesis beyond chance occurrence and whilst these were seen to operate over vast distances which precluded fabrication, there was a decline effect over time, that is, the best results were obtained at the beginning of the experiments. Jung suggests that this is because of an initial emotional engagement and expectation on the part of the subjects. Jung's description of the poor results in the experiments from the English medium (Mrs Eileen Garrett) attests to this: 'as she herself admits, she was unable to summon up any feeling for the "soulless" test-cards.' (ibid., p. 434). Emotional engagement seems crucial in the whole process even if Jung's overall explanation relies on his theory of synchronicity about a constellated archetype which separates into a physical occurrence and a psychological one. On summarizing Rhine's experiments he says:

> [Rhine] would never have got the results he did if he had carried out his experiments with a single subject . . . He needed a constant renewal of interest, an emotion with its characteristic abaissement mental, which tips the scales in favour of the unconscious. . . . The mantric procedures owe their effectiveness to this same connection with emotionality.
>
> (ibid., pp. 480–1)

What I believe an emergent/developmental model of archetype such as that of Knox (2003) suggests is that archetypal constellation will always depend on heightened emotionality so that it is not compensation alone which is operative. Rather, affectivity activates archetypal imagery because of its ability to lower the threshold of consciousness (which is Jung's point when developing his theory of synchronicity), which sets up a resonance with a pre-existing image schema template. Affectivity arises in people from their personal life experience and this means in an emergent/developmental model that archetypal imagery is always constellated through personal experience with the operative cause being emotionality. This is because the image schema (archetype) on which the imagery is based has been developmentally produced in the first place out of the intense affectivity of preverbal infant experience and the current affectivity in adult life is activating it.

This would suggest that in relation to shamanism and its wounded healer component the pre-existing 'internal working model' which has been activated in the pre-initiatory illness has arisen from mind/brain structures developed out of the intense affectivity of the initiate's preverbal infant experiences.

However, arguing for such an explanation to the apparent archetypal phenomenon is not to discount the fact that Jung saw connections between the psyche and its environmental conditions.

### The place of the environment

In relation to environmental conditions Jung (1931/1991a) does say:

> We are all agreed that it would be quite impossible to understand the living organism apart from its relation to the environment. There are countless biological facts that can only be explained as reactions to environmental conditions. . . . The same is true of the psyche. Its peculiar organisation must be intimately connected with environmental conditions.
>
> (p. 152)

What needs to be noted is that such a statement is in perfect accord with an emergent/developmental model of archetype such as that of Knox (2003). The peculiar organization of the psyche is most definitely connected with environmental conditions if archetypes (image schemas) become imbedded as mind/brain structures through early infant developmental experience.

In a similar way, Jung's (1954/1991a) following statement to do with phenomenal experience can be understood by an emergent/developmental model of the archetype: '[The archetypes'] essential being is unconscious to us . . . they are experienced as spontaneous agencies' (p. 216). In an emergent/developmental model, archetypes would be experienced 'as spontaneous agencies' because of the process of their emergence. Any particular mind/brain structural template (image schema) underpinning the activation of emergent imagery has originally been laid down developmentally in a state of early infant 'unconsciousness'. We only have to assume that when some resonating 'now' affect occurs, the pre-existing 'internal working model' is activated. But since it resides in the implicit/unconscious layer of the psyche, it will be experienced as if alien, 'spontaneous' and probably 'innate' and as if unconnected to anything which we can consciously understand.

In a similar way the spontaneous aspect of the pre-initiatory illness in shamanism does not necessarily have to indicate some kind of autonomous archetype at work. Knox's (2003) model can just as easily explain the phenomenon.

Consequently, an emergent/developmental model of archetype generally and shamanism with its wounded healer component in particular are not necessarily in disagreement with Jung's position on synchronicity and the significance of environmental conditions. This is not the case, however, with Jung's view of archetypes as innate *a priori* psychic structures which have the capacity to direct psychological life. Here, Jung appears to give emphasis to the autonomous and spontaneous activity of archetypes divorced from personal experience. This aspect diverges substantially from an emergent/developmental model of archetype and requires re-examination because it is important to know if the 'wounds' of the wounded healer are developmentally acquired or constellated out of the objective psyche.

## The 'autonomous' archetype re-evaluated

We have previously seen that Jung eventually came to describe the collective unconscious as an absolute unconscious which is untouched by personal experience and is a psychic activity which goes on independently of consciousness. It is conceived as being so independent that its activity supposedly occurs spontaneously and autonomously with an 'autochthonous revival'. Here the fundamental differences from an emergent/developmental model of archetype could not be more explicitly stated because, in Knox's (2003) view, the archetype-as-such is an image schema which has actually come about *through* outside influence, that is, experience in the environment. The archetype-as-such is not only touched by personal experience, it comes into existence through it and later personal affective experience activates the archetypal imagery. The imagery is not spontaneously produced.

The question is raised: can it really be evidenced that archetypes operate spontaneously and autonomously as if divorced from personal experience and would this then be the only way to understand shamanism and its wounded healer component?

By re-examining the two main examples Jung uses to evidence the existence of autonomous archetypes unconnected to personal experience – that of the army officer and of the 'solar phallus' case – it is evident that archetypes do not operate spontaneously and autonomously as if divorced from personal experience.

### Jung's case of the army officer

The army officer had presented to Jung (1931/1991a) with three hysterical (conversion disorder) symptoms: heart pains, a choking sensation in the throat and a piercing pain in the left heel. Nothing was wrong with the officer organically, his symptoms were psychogenic. Dreams revealed that just prior to the onset of his symptoms he had suffered a relationship breakdown when his girlfriend jilted him and became engaged to another man. During psychotherapy with Jung, the man's real but unconscious affects were able to be expressed; the symptoms of the heart pains (having analogously represented his 'broken heart') and the lump in the throat (having analogously represented his 'swallowed tears') disappeared. But the pain in the heel remained. The man then had a dream about being bitten in the heel by a snake and becoming instantly paralysed. This dream image does give some clue as to why the man feels pain in his heel but as Jung points out, the unconscious is striking in its use of a mythological motif reminiscent of the Genesis story where Jahweh, speaking to the serpent in the Garden of Eden, says: 'I will put enmity between you and the woman, and between your seed and her seed; he shall bruise your head, and you shall bruise his heel' (Genesis 3:15).

Because the dream image did not accord with any obvious rational explanation, Jung concluded that it 'probably derives from some deeper layer [of the unconscious] that cannot be fathomed rationally' (1931/1991a, p. 146). However, Jung also tells us that in discussing the dream with the man, other relevant factors emerged:

> He had been the darling of a somewhat hysterical mother. She had pitied him, admired him, pampered him so much that he never got along properly at school because he was too girlish. Later he suddenly swung over to the masculine side and went into the army, where he was able to hide his inner weakness by a display of 'toughness'. Thus, in a sense, his mother too had lamed him.
>
> (ibid., p. 146)

Jung goes no further and yet this information would appear critical in giving an interpretation to the dream imagery, a point which I will take up below.

To continue with Jung's explication. He acknowledges that the man had probably heard the Genesis story at some stage in his life despite his knowledge of the Bible being at a 'lamentable minimum' and that the snake image is now being remembered from the deep unconscious and used at this suitable opportunity. Given the situation between the officer and his mother, the line 'I will put enmity between you and the woman' is likely to have had significant psychic resonance with his own personal dynamic. However, Jung concludes that this 'part of the unconscious evidently likes to express itself mythologically, because this way of expression is in keeping with its nature', such that

> [the] dream of the snake reveals a fragment of psychic activity that has nothing whatever to do with the dreamer as a modern individual. It functions at a deeper level, so to speak, and only the results of this activity rise up into the upper layer where the repressed affects lie, as foreign to them as a dream is to waking consciousness.
>
> (ibid., pp. 147–8)

Jung goes on to say that the heel symptom is therefore raising all the man's life disappointments to the 'level of a mythological event' and that this corresponds to a kind of 'magic by analogy' known in both ancient and primitive cultures, such that he can identify or participate in the pain of all humanity. 'The healing effect of this needs no proof' (ibid.), Jung concludes.

However, it seems that Jung quickly passes over the possibility of the paralysing snake image being the most apt way for the officer to express the paralysing effect on him of his own hysterical mother. It could be understood as no more than this. Jung does note that such an 'as if' motif accords with the metaphorical way of thinking encountered in primitive cultures. Something similar is probably going on here with the officer. The image is related to early (and thus more primitive) levels of psychic functioning corresponding to the man's early experiences with his mother. Thus the mythic imagery is pointing to the 'earlyness' of the experience for him since early infant experience coincides with a time when the psyche and the affects it experiences are 'primitive'. In fact, mythological motifs derived from the broader culture may be the best way for the unconscious to articulate deep and early trauma (as if it is coming from another world) rather than these motifs saying anything about a hypothesized part of the unconscious expressing itself mythically 'in keeping with its nature', as Jung asserts.

It needs to be noted that there is still a difficulty here in explaining why the specific snake imagery is constellated in the officer but the cultural context to do with the Genesis story would seem relevant. My main point is that the officer's imagery does not have to be seen as arising spontaneously and autonomously from some zone untouched by personal experience. It is possible to understand it as a way of expressing something 'psychically primæval' having to do with the officer's early problems with a hysterical and paralysing mother from which we know he is in later life endeavouring to effect a compensatory solution. So the dream reveals that the officer sees his mother as a Satan/serpent whose affects have had a paralysing effect on his masculinity. Hence it is not necessarily the case that the 'content . . . probably derives from some deeper layer that cannot be fathomed rationally' (1931/1991a, p. 146), as Jung puts it. Lack of clear rationally understood connections is not sufficient reason for us either to give up on the task or to resort to 'autochthonous' explanations. The imagery is perfectly understandable in light of the material about his mother relationship and therefore has everything to do with the dreamer as a modern individual. Indeed, the fact that the dream reworks the mythic image more than likely points to this, for the Genesis story tells of a bruising not a paralysing sting, and there must be some very personal reason why this is changed by the officer's unconscious to produce the paralysis image. There must be some psychic resonance between this and his own personal dynamic.

So it would appear that the unconscious is using a metaphorical mythic image because it is endeavouring to express deep early problems from a time when the psyche operated in such primary process images. Thus it may not be that an 'immemorial pattern' of the human mind 'which we have not acquired but have inherited from the dim ages of the past' (ibid., pp. 149–50) has been stirred but rather that the unconscious has latched onto this image as the most appropriate way to express the problem of the deep unconscious and unresolved affects it contains from actual early life experience. The point to consider is that whilst archetypes in an emergent/developmental model can conceptually exist, they do not operate autonomously in a way disconnected from subjective and developmental experience. Rather, archetypal imagery emerges from particular image schemas which have arisen developmentally from specific affective experiences of childhood. In the case of the army officer, it could be argued that an original image schema to do with an emotionally paralysing mother has been activated by the intense affectivity of the adult relationship breakdown. The biblical snake image has been picked up from the broader culture so as to express the personal complex.

Jung does consider the possibility that the dream image of the paralysing snake may be no more than a 'concretized figure of speech' and concludes that his thesis really needs as proof 'a case where the mythological symbolism is neither a common figure of speech nor an instance of cryptomnesia' (ibid., p. 148) to show that the 'absolute unconscious' has nothing to do with personal experience. It is here he turns to the 'solar phallus' case.

### Jung's case of the 'solar phallus' man

In Jung's early career, around 1906 at the Burghölzli Mental Hospital, Zurich, he came across a male schizophrenic patient who reported an hallucination of the sun's phallus, the moving of which caused the wind. Subsequently, in 1910, Jung came across a book by Dieterich describing a liturgy of the ancient Mithraic cult which contained the same concept as the schizophrenic's hallucination. Jung (1931/1991a, p. 151) concluded that: 'The vision of my patient in 1906, and the Greek text first edited in 1910, should be sufficiently far apart to rule out the possibility of cryptomnesia on his side and of thought-transference on mine.' Jung saw this as another example of the spontaneous occurrence of an archetype, the image of the sun's phallus producing the wind having arisen autonomously in the patient from a deep archetypal layer of the psyche.

In *Symbols of Transformation*, Jung (1912/1986, p. 157) says of this patient that he 'was a small business employee with no more than a secondary school education. He grew up in Zurich, and by no stretch of imagination can I conceive how he could have got hold of the idea of the solar phallus.' However, Dieterich's publication had a first edition in 1903 prior to Jung's contact with this schizophrenic patient in 1906. This fact is noted by the editors of the *Collected Works* (Jung 1931/1991a, p. 150n, 1936/1990, p. 51n) but since the patient had been committed prior to 1903, any concerns were considered inconsequential. Nonetheless, Jung (1931/1991a) discounts both the possibility of this schizophrenic with a 'mixture of intelligence' having esoteric interests (as many schizophrenic people do) and the possibility of him being sufficiently self-educated to have come across the material or some cultural variation of it. After all, there is a suggestion of the theme (that is, the spirit descending through the disc of the sun) in medieval paintings which Jung notes by saying that this 'conception is common to the whole of late classical and medieval philosophy' (ibid., p. 151). And elsewhere he says that '[t]he association of sun and wind frequently occurs in ancient symbolism' (Jung 1936/1990, p. 52). Jung knows that there were no paintings like this in the man's home town of Zurich and that the patient had not travelled. The man did, however, work in a consulate through which many travellers would have passed. I do not believe that the possibility of actual contact with the material or of cultural transmission can be entirely ruled out. As Rivers (1923, p. 178) says on the issue of the cultural transmission of archetypes, 'the possibility cannot be excluded that the common tradition reaches the individual in infancy, childhood and youth through the intermediation of parents, nurses, school-fellows, the overhearing of chance conversations, and many other sources.'

The possibility of the transmission of such a 'common tradition' makes this case too inconclusive to support Jung's hypothesis that the archetypal imagery is divorced from personal experience. Jung (1936/1990) is, of course, aware that the issue of proof is actually more complicated than the single presentation of this case would suggest. As he says:

> If we had only such cases, the task of investigation would be relatively easy, but in reality the proof is much more complicated. First of all, certain symbols have to be isolated clearly enough to be recognizable as typical phenomena, not just matters of chance. This is done by examining a series of dreams, say a few hundred, for typical figures, and by observing their development in the series. . . In this way it is possible to establish certain continuities or modulations of one and the same figure . . . [and] . . . one can discover interesting facts about the variations undergone by a single type. Not only the type itself but its variants too can be substantiated by evidence from comparative mythology and ethnology.
>
> (p. 53)

It is this method which Jung uses in 'Individual dream symbolism in relation to alchemy' (Jung 1952/1992) by tracking an extensive dream series of Wolfgang Pauli. However, whilst Jung was not working directly with Pauli, having sent him to analyse with a colleague, Pauli may be far too familiar with Jung's theories and concepts for the dream material to be considered sufficiently uninfluenced. He was in personal communication with Jung and later co-authored *The Interpretation of Nature and the Psyche* with him (Jung and Pauli 1955). This same critique could be applied to other examples Jung uses to evidence archetypal content as in the woman patient used in 'A study in the process of individuation' (Jung 1950/1990) who had been a student of psychology for nine years (and thus not naive) before working directly with Jung. Jung tracks her emerging artwork to illustrate the individuation process and by picture two (out of 24), he announces that the 'personal relationship to me seems to have ceased: the picture shows an impersonal natural process' (p. 294), which would seem to discount any interpretation to do with transference dynamics. One gets the impression that all too often Jung is interested in removing any personal context, or not focusing on it, or minimizing its influence so as to emphasize the objective nature of the psyche.

Given the specific examination of the case examples of the army officer and the solar phallus man above, I believe Jung's evidence is too inconclusive to prove that archetypes arise autonomously and spontaneously. What is noteworthy is that the case of the army officer is just as easily explained using an emergent/development model of archetype (with the caveat that it is still difficult to provide the linkages that explain why the officer's particular archetypal imagery has arisen).

### The place of Jung's own experience

In relation to his unfolding ideas, it is not unreasonable to assume that Jung was influenced by his own personal experience of archetypal imagery and its apparent 'autochthonous revival'. We know from his own admission that the split with Freud in 1912 affected him deeply. He describes his experience in some detail in his autobiography *Memories, Dreams, Reflections* (Jung 1963/1990) as a 'disorientation' and a 'confrontation with the unconscious', from which particular personifications emerged, such as the Philemon character. Other commentators have described Jung's experience more in terms of a psychotic episode (Winnicott 1964, Atwood and Stolorow 1977).

Of this experience Jung (1963/1990) says:

> Philemon and other figures of my fantasies brought home to me the crucial insight that there are things in the psyche which I do not produce, but which produce themselves and have their own life. Philemon represented a force which was not myself. . . . He confronted me in an objective manner, and I understood that there is something in me which can say things that I do not know and do not intend, things which may even be directed against me.
>
> (pp. 207–8)

In a later section speaking of unconscious contents he says:

> It is not too difficult to personify them, as they always possess a certain degree of autonomy, a separate identity of their own. Their autonomy is a most uncomfortable thing to reconcile oneself to, and yet the very fact that the unconscious presents itself in that way gives us the best means of handling it.
>
> (ibid., p. 211)

Whilst *Memories, Dreams, Reflections* is not included in the *Collected Works* as part of Jung's scientific writing, there is nonetheless something important about the inherent tension in these passages which is likely to give clues as to the subjective underpinning to his academic writing on the theory of archetypes. On the one hand, archetypal imagery is described as 'presenting itself' in a particular way, which may be nothing more than a statement about how it is phenomenally experienced. However, archetypal images are also described as possessing a 'certain degree of autonomy' such that they can 'produce themselves'. Given Jung's (1929/1993, p. 336) assertion that 'every psychology – my own included – has the character of a subjective confession', it is not unreasonable to conclude that his personal experience of the split with Freud was not only significant in terms of the appearance of the archetypal imagery but would have had an influence on the 'autonomy/autochthonous revival' aspect of his theory of archetype. If Philemon had appeared to Jung without the context of the split with Freud there may be more justification for Jung's position on the autonomy of archetypes. However, a similarity between the Philemon image and Freud (despite not being a perfect correspondence) has been noted by Kaufmann (1992, p. 361), who said that Jung 'made a painting of Philemon, and it looks unmistakably like Freud.'

Consequently, Jung's experience could just as easily be read in terms of an emergent/developmental model of archetype such as that of Knox (2003). Again, personal context is important to note in the sequence of events and affectivity is suggested as being operative in the archetype's constellation. The archetypal Philemon image would be understood to be activated by the intense affectivity of Jung's current subjective life experience with Freud. Presumably, the current experience was similar to a pre-existing internal working model around father–son transferences, a theme which R. C. Smith (1997) has explored. The archetypal imagery has not then arisen independently even though the particulars of the Philemon image would need explaining.

Apart from these issues to do with Jung's personal experience, an emergent/developmental model of archetype can help explain other difficulties in Jung's classic theory to do with the separation of personal and collective psychic content and his apparent Lamarckism.

## The separation of personal and collective psychic content

Jung (1916/1990) did see difficulty in separating personal and collective psychic content. In the context of assessing the needs of individuation he says:

> This distinction [between the personal unconscious and the collective psyche] is far from easy, because the personal grows out of the collective psyche and is intimately bound up with it. So it is difficult to say exactly what contents are to be called personal and what collective.
>
> (p. 279)

Subsequent writers, such as Williams (1963), have also commented on the indivisibility of the collective and personal unconscious both conceptually (because experience makes them hard to separate) and in terms of clinical technique. Neumann (1955) makes the point by stating that the connection between archetypal manifestations and an individual's personal life experience ought to be possible theoretically but is difficult to achieve practically. Other Jungians, such as Satinover (1985) and Stein (1987), conclude from their own clinical work that the distinction between the collective and the personal psyche is difficult to maintain in practice. (They also argue that as much as possible this distinction needs to be achieved clinically lest the patient succumb to ego-inflation).

What an emergent/developmental model suggests is that these statements by both Jung and others may be reflecting a true state of affairs and not just practical difficulties. Seeing archetypes (image schemas) as 'reliably repeated early developmental achievements' (Knox 2004, p. 9) and not present in any preformationist sense before experience means that they have arisen from developmental experience and this means there need be no division between a collective psyche and the personal unconscious. As such, Jung's statement above ('the personal grows out of the collective psyche') would need reversing to read: 'the experience of something apparently collective grows out of the personal'.

An emergent/developmental model of archetype has the capacity to make understandable other statements by Jung (1954/1990a), such as the following from 'Concerning the archetypes, with special reference to the anima concept':

> The *représentations collectives* [archetypes] have a dominating power, so it is not surprising that they are repressed with the most intense resistance. When repressed, they do not hide behind any trifling thing but behind ideas and figures that have already become problematical for other reasons, and intensify and complicate their dubious nature.

For instance, everything that we would like, in infantile fashion, to attribute to our parents or blame them for is blown up to fantastic proportions from this secret source.

(p. 63)

An emergent/developmental model of the archetype provides an explanation as to why the interaction between archetypal imagery and personal experience would be noted as occurring this way. The situation will appear like this not because archetypes are preformed in the psyche and operate autonomously but because early infant experience, from which archetypal imagery is derived, is very affectively intense. In other words, archetypes are not hiding behind other difficulties and intensifying them, rather, the intense affects of early experience have led to the development of an 'internal working model' at the structural level of the psyche and the emotions of current life experience activate it leading to the emergence of imagery. Again, this would reverse the direction of Jung's perspective such that we could say that problematical material arising from personal experience actually forms mind/brain structures which leads to both archetypal imagery and numinous affect.

## Jung's apparent Lamarckism

A further difficulty in classic archetype theory which commentators such as Hogenson (2001) have noted has to do with an apparent Lamarckism in the way Jung understood archetypes to become structural components of the psyche. (Lamarkism is the discredited view in Biology that acquired characteristics can be inherited.)

On this issue, Stevens (1982) notes that Jung's early concept of 'primordial images' did suggest Lamarkism, a charge not that surprising given some of Jung's views as to how archetypes arise. Jung's (1931/1991a) most explicit statements are made in 'The Structure of the Psyche' and these seem to arise from his belief that 'the unconscious . . . is the deposit of all human experience right back to its remotest beginnings' (p. 157).

An example would be:

[T]he daily course of the sun and the regular alternation of day and night must have imprinted themselves on the psyche in the form of an image from primordial times. . . . [T]he physical process imprinted itself on the psyche in this fantastic, distorted form and was preserved there, so that the unconscious still reproduces similar images today.

(ibid., p. 153)

And at a later point:

> The psychological conditions of the environment naturally leave similar mythical traces behind them. Dangerous situations, be they dangers to the body or to the soul, arouse affect-laden fantasies, and, in so far as such situations typically repeat themselves, they give rise to *archetypes*.
>
> (ibid., p. 155)

So in relation to an everyday phenomenon like the family, Jung goes on to conclude that these 'ordinary everyday facts, which are eternally repeated, create the mightiest archetypes of all' (ibid., p. 156).

Overall, this would appear to be a Lamarckian explanation as to how archetypes arise – situations of 'danger' evoke 'affects' which lead to 'fantasies', the multiple repetition of which over a long period of time leads to archetypes as structural components of the psyche which somehow become imbedded in the genome.[1]

If on the other hand the emergent/developmental model of archetype is correct, then such statements as: 'Dangerous situations . . . arouse affect-laden fantasies, and, in so far as such situations typically repeat themselves, they give rise to *archetypes*' (op. cit.) become quite understandable at least at the level of the infant's psychic development. An emergent/developmental explanation would be in accord with this statement whilst avoiding anything Lamarckian. Dangerous situations arouse affect, which gets bio-structurally templated as 'internal working model' image schemas leading to archetypal imagery as an emergent phenomenon. Jung is right, then, in that dangerous situations, especially if repeated, can give rise to archetypes. However, this does not imply that these archetypes need get incorporated into the genome, for the process can be based, as Knox (2004, p. 9) says, on 'reliably repeated early developmental achievements'.

## Conclusions

Knox's (2003) emergent/developmental model of the archetype understands archetypes to be developmentally produced mind/brain structures which initially operate as implicit 'internal working models' from which complex 'archetypal' imagery can later emerge. They are initially produced by, and later activated through, intense affectivity. Hence, they are not present in the psyche in any preformationist sense nor do they express themselves with 'autochthonous revival'.

It can be seen that such an emergent/developmental model of the archetype is in accord with Jung's position on affectivity and environmental conditions with respect to the expression of an archetype. Without recourse to innate, preformed psychic structures, the model is also able to explain Jung's case examples, his apparent Lamarckism, his own Philemon experience and the difficulties encountered in separately describing personal and collective psychic content. This highlights the possibility that such a model, derived from neuroscience to which Jung had no access, could be representing the true state of affairs and as a consequence, such a model requires further consideration because of the implications which flow from it.

A significant strength of Knox's model derives from the fact that it is based on the findings of contemporary neuroscience and as such it can take into account all of the research evidence up to this point in time whilst aligning with other emergentist positions and without having to challenge sociocultural approaches to archetypes which emphasize environmental input.

Notably in the model, 'archetypal' experience emerges from actual mind/brain structures so that the observations of those such as Stevens, who detect a correspondence between archetypes and brain locations, are not that unexpected. The main difference is in the explanation as to how such mind/brain structures get there in the first place.

Knox's model of archetype also enables us to explain instinct as we observe it because these response patterns are understood to arise within species-typical environments from the automatic subcortical biological startpoints which she posits. This is important for archetype theory because Jung from his earliest years was drawing a connection between instinct and archetype. In 1919 he said: 'The primordial image [i.e. archetype] might suitably be described as the *instinct's perception of itself*, or as the self-portrait of the instinct' (Jung 1919/1991, p. 136) and in 1931: 'the archetypes are simply the forms which the instincts assume' (Jung 1931/1991a, p. 157).

By 1954, Jung had developed his position in detail in 'Psychological aspects of the mother archetype' where at one point he states:

> The archetype in itself is empty and purely formal, nothing but a *facultas praeformandi*, a possibility of representation which is given *a priori*. The representations themselves are not inherited, only the forms, and in that respect they correspond in every way to the instincts, which are also determined in form only.
>
> (Jung 1954/1990b, p. 79)

It is important to note that Knox's model does contribute an explanation as to the way instinct can function which ties in with Jung's adherence to it in relation to archetype theory.

Furthermore, by positing a biological base to image schemas, which underpin the later emergence of complex archetypal imagery, Knox's model provides a way to explain the psychophysical nature of the psychoid core to archetypes, making Jung's (1954/1991a) concept of the 'psychoid' much more understandable. The physical side would coincide with the bio-structural image schemas and the psychological side with the emergent archetypal imagery. In a similar way the model can retain the distinction between the archetype-as-such (image schemas) and the later emergent imagery which is phenomenally experienced.

The model can also explain why archetypal imagery appears as if it is innate when in fact it has emerged from mind/brain structures which were initially developed out of the preverbal affective experiences of infancy. As a consequence, the model asserts that there will always be a nexus between particular archetypal imagery and specific affective environmental conditions which have led to the development of the mind/brain structures in the first place. Or putting it another way, the emergent imagery will be environmentally specific which is not the same as saying some preformationist archetypal potentiality can express itself once the appropriate environmental fit is supplied. Rather, the model implies that a vector would exist running in the opposite direction so that the emergence of particular archetypal imagery in a person's life will be connected to a similarity in their current affective environment with the original affective environment during the mind/brain structure's original developmental imbedding. It is the interactive resonance between these two states (the 'then' and the 'now') which will constellate the emergence of archetypal imagery in the present, for this interaction between the environment and the mind/brain structure will formulate imagery out of 'then' (early experience) and 'now' (current affect) so long as there is a correspondence between the two which has been initially established in the developmental process. One value of this implication is its capacity to explain clinical phenomena such as 'transference love' and repetition compulsions.

In relation to transference love, Freud (1914/2001, p. 167) notes that 'it exhibits not a single new feature arising from the present situation, but is entirely composed of repetitions and copies of earlier reactions.' It is the very aspect of 'repetition' which Freud saw as revealing the infantile aspect (the 'then') to the phenomenon. Clinicians see such things all the time – the same dynamic played out in the transference and in every other significant relationship into which persons are (projectively) attracted.

An explanation in terms of an emergent/developmental model would run something like this: the 'then' affects of early developmental experience around the unresolved Oedipal situation get bio-structurally embedded in the psyche of the individual as an 'internal working model' or template. The 'now' situation of the later analytic encounter has such similar affective resonance with the infantile experience that the bio-structural 'internal working model' becomes activated. Imagery-affects emerge and are projected onto the therapist so that the earlier unresolved infantile dynamic gets played out in the 'now' of transference love.

The 'repetition compulsion' is a way of describing similar dynamics as seen in those individuals who go through a sequence of abusive relationships which many psychotherapists find difficult to explain – surely people do not like abuse and learn from their experience? Something much more powerful than learning from one's experience is at hand, because we are dealing here with another example of an activated 'internal working model'. Again, the 'then' of early affective developmental experience around abuse has become bio-structurally embedded in the psyche of the individual. Later, in the 'now', a person is encountered who sufficiently resonates with the original abuse situation (with all its excitements, potentialities and connectabilities) so that the mind/brain 'internal working model' becomes activated. Imagery-affects emerge and an emotional vector is established which gets projected onto the object. This can be of such energy that individuals may have very little choice over the (unconscious) compulsive quality to the experience.

The fact that individuals tend to be attracted to the same sorts of people can be explained in a similar way, that is, as the end result of a resonating 'internal working model' template being projected.

The following points from this discussion are noteworthy for archetype theory. First, since there is a bio-structural 'internal working model' template which underpins the emergent imagery-affects in these situations, it is not unreasonable to describe the individual as 'hard-wired' to experience the world in this way. This explains the compulsive nature of the phenomena. Second, the repetition aspect makes the subjective experience of the phenomena appear as if something innate is operative. In some ways, the situation is 'innate' but not because anything is genetically specified before developmental experience but because the mind/brain bio-structure, once there and operative, is experienced *as if* innate. It is by drawing these two aspects together that we have the classical description of an archetype. Knox's emergent/developmental model of the archetype is, however, radically different to classical theory but it should be kept in mind that Jung (1952/1991b) in his foreword to White's *God and the Unconscious* does say that his concept of the archetype is 'an auxiliary idea which can be exchanged at any time for a better formula' and should not be seen as a 'metaphysical postulate' (p. 306). On this theme, Skar (2004) has alluded to the fact that we may no longer need the concept of the archetype-as-such. She says:

> When we employ a dynamical systems view of development, we no longer need the 'archetype-as-such' to explain the formation of complexes. *In fact, we could do without it altogether and still have the same basic psychological system that Jung proposed.*
>
> (p. 247)

If the neuroscience research does ultimately reveal that the archetype-as-such is not innate and preformed as originally conceived, then the question is raised: is the word 'archetype' too suffused with innatism and preformationist meanings to prevent confusion? Most Jungians would not like to lose the term 'archetype' and neither Knox nor Skar argue for it to be dropped. However, Jungians have to face the possibility that this is not just an esoteric theoretical argument, for if they continue to think, act and clinically practise as if archetypes are *a priori*, innate psychic structures which determine psychological life when this is not the case, then they could become irrelevant to the broader psychotherapeutic community.

Applying Knox's emergent/developmental model of the archetype to shamanism and its wounded healer component we can see these apparently 'archetypal' phenomena as expressions of mind/brain structures which have become psychically imbedded through particularly intense affective experiences during preverbal infancy. Presumably, then, early developmental experiences will be different in those who never experience a shamanic 'calling' because the individuals who become shamans have been wounded in a particular way. Despite any appearances to the contrary, the later emergence of shamanic and wounded healer phenomena and imagery are not arising autochthonously; rather, their constellation will depend on the particular affectivity in the 'now' which resonates with the affectivity experienced in the original developmental bio-structural imbedding of the 'internal working model' template.

Overall, the critical point is this: if the mind/brain structures leading to archetypal phenomena are initially developmentally produced then shamanism with its wounded healer component would be no different. It is important to assess, therefore, what developmental experiences underpin the emergence of shamanic phenomena and what kinds of experiential 'wounds' underlie the wounded healer component within it. Fortunately for this purpose, developmentally oriented approaches have been undertaken on Siberian shamanism.

# Chapter 7

# The developmental side to the shamanic wounded healer

## Introduction

If archetypes are developmentally produced mind/brain structures forged through the intense affective experiences in preverbal infancy then an understanding of such experiences in shamanic cultures becomes crucial in explicating the shaman archetype and its wounded healer component. This perspective places us squarely in the realm of psychodynamics, an approach to ethnography which still has contemporary validity as seen in Mimica's (2007) *Explorations in Psychoanalytic Ethnography*. To date, the most comprehensive examination of the specific psychodynamic and early developmental sources of the Siberian shaman's life experience, healing techniques and fantasy life has been undertaken by Charles Ducey (1976). His approach is unquestionably psychoanalytic and he highlights the connection between early infant experience and the emergence of shamanic phenomena within the *locus classicus* of shamanism.

Ducey's (1976) investigation begins by posing the question 'is the shaman sane?' He suggests that the noted polarization of opinion around this issue can be driven by investigators emphasizing one side or another of the shaman's liminality for he sees the shaman as one who 'bridges the gap between the known and the unknown' (p. 175). That the shaman occupies some kind of liminal/borderline zone has indeed raised comment by others, such as Peters (1989). Ducey's opinion is that the liminal/borderline 'bridging' phenomenon in shamanism has prompted investigators to emphasize either a psychopathological perspective or, alternatively, like Eliade (1964), 'supernormality'.

Psychoanalytic approaches to shamanism such as Ducey's have tended to see it psychopathologically as a defensive activity attempting to cure a preexisting mental disturbance which has come about from wounds which have occurred in the earliest stages of infant development – the oral stage in particular. For Ducey (1976), this indicated the paranoid-schizoid position (see Klein 1946[1]) and he proposed a standard psychoanalytic aetiology for this situation, severe emotional trauma in early childhood through either actual death of parents or other causes of substantial oral frustration which have ruptured the 'good-enough' mother–infant bond. His view is that the Siberian environment is harsh and unpredictable, the resulting lack of food leading to a 'commonness of oral frustration of children in these cultures, since mothers cannot nourish themselves and their children adequately' (1976, p. 185). Such experiences would understandably be compounded by any actual loss of parents.

Alongside this view of the Siberian shaman as employing 'neurotic and psychotic defenses to confront the anxiety arising from specific infantile and childhood situations and fantasies for a cathartic, curative purpose' (ibid., p. 178), Ducey acknowledges that the shaman's sociocultural activities and position are indispensable to their culture. He also believes that their 'healthy and pathological patterns are too deeply interwoven to be meaningfully separated' (ibid., p. 177). This is important because it gives us a clue as to the particular psychological construction of Siberian shamans and the wounds which underpin their wounded healer capacities. A kind of borderline dynamic is suggested where substantial functional and dysfunctional components intersect within the one personality. It is noteworthy that one of Schmideberg's (1947) early descriptors for borderline patients was 'stable instability' reflecting their capacity to oscillate between times of considerable emotional distress and degrees of internal consistency.

## Evidence for developmental 'wounds' in the Siberian shaman

Initial evidence for Ducey's (1976) proposition he gains from a psychoanalytic interpretation of the symptoms which shaman-initiates display during the phases of their pre-initiatory illness. We know that Siberian shamans suffer a serious and disturbing psychological experience/illness early in life (often at adolescence) and that this pre-initiatory illness is interpreted as a (mostly unsolicited) calling, which is not only experienced as a destiny/fate but is articulated in their cultures as an election by the spirits. A strenuous and difficult initiation follows involving altered states of consciousness, dismemberment imagery and death/rebirth phenomena, which follows a *rite de passage* structure of departure, initiation and return (as outlined by van Gennep, 1908/1960).

Ducey (1976) divides the pre-initiatory illness into three distinct stages. This follows an outline proposed by Lot-Falck (1970) which although being an obscure French publication, is not a model significantly dissimilar to that of Eliade (1964, 1987).

### The Siberian shaman's pre-initiatory illness: Stage one

Ducey (1976) describes the first phase as a 'spirit possession' which has been historically described as 'Arctic hysteria' (Czaplicka 1914) and in which the initiate experiences a series of recurrent 'attacks' by particular spirits (the unquiet, wandering dead from deceased lunatics or suicides). The ethnographic records describe the symptoms in terms of uncontrolled spasms, trances, wild dancing, howling, epileptoid seizures, frenzied flight, erotomania, fainting, conversion symptoms, fits, singing and chanting often in unknown languages and/or the senseless repeating of overheard words with extended sleep and amnesia following such attacks. Ducey asserts that all these symptoms are schizoidal in nature indicating some kind of conversion and/or dissociation state. By this he means that emotionally distressing states are being split off from the initiate's psyche and converted into symptoms of the body.[2]

From a psychoanalytic perspective, such schizoidal symptoms do indicate a pathological reaction to losses in early childhood and this is further evidenced by other symptoms, such as withdrawal from social relationships and hallucination of torture by ancestral spirits. Indeed, the epileptoid seizures, trances, amnesia and other symptoms are dissociative phenomena that represent a periodical re-emergence of disruptive infantile wishes and anxieties. Similarly, the erotomania could suggest an early frustration of emotional needs arising from a subjectively undifferentiated mother who both withdraws (leading to intense frustration) and uncontrollably approaches. It is the latter which is experienced as a tantalization and hence eroticized.

It is noticeable, however, that there are other symptoms that do not make the condition easily identified as a Western psychiatric illness such as conversion disorder (hysteria). Ducey (1976) notes such symptoms as irregular habits, detachment from others with a need to be alone, cyclic characteristics such as sudden mood swings from irritability to affability and from depression to agitation (which is more suggestive of bipolar disorder) and hallucinatory fantasies of torture by spirits (as in the persecutory delusions of paranoid schizophrenia) which seem both universal and indicative of a more profound disturbance. There is also no *la belle indifférence* as in Western conversion disorder (hysteria), the shaman-initiate expressing real distress. It is these symptoms which cause Ducey to reconsider the 'Arctic hysteria' diagnosis of earlier writers and his analysis of the second phase of the pre-initiatory illness adds further to this reconsideration.[3]

### The Siberian shaman's pre-initiatory illness: Stage two

The second phase of the pre-initiatory illness is characterized by a 'soul loss' and is experienced as a chronic and stable melancholic/depressed condition. Apparently the subjective experience has changed from something having 'come upon/into' the initiate to a situation where something has been 'taken away'. Other characteristics of this stage noted in the ethnographic reports are apathy, helplessness, *taedium vitae*, sexual obsession, delusions of persecution, hallucinations, seizures and fugues. In particular, the experience of dismemberment is intensified and a master shaman is called in to tutor initiates so that their lost soul can be found. This is followed by instruction about the various spirits and how to summon and control them, and teachings around techniques, names and functions of the spirits, mythology, genealogies and a shamanic secret language.

What Ducey (1976) particularly notes about the second stage is that feelings of worthlessness are reportedly absent and that this is unusual in (neurotic) depression. What are reported are apathy and a sense of emptiness (from soul loss). In citing Guntrip (1970), Ducey believes this to be further indication of a schizoid condition. Of note, a subjective sense of emptiness would indicate early deprivations in the infant–mother relationship because something in early experience has not been 'put in' in the first place. The result in adulthood can be a flat, empty and monochromatic version of depression alongside *taedium vitae* and boredom. Clinicians often encounter such cases in the consulting room with individuals who have suffered a deprivation of emotional needs from the earliest stages of infant development.

### The Siberian shaman's pre-initiatory illness: Stage three

The initiate eventually emerges from the second stage into a third which is experienced as a cure. The critical features of this third stage are a resulting mastery of the spirits and the capacity to enter and leave trance states at will, without being possessed. This is the most critical stage because without mastery, the initiate cannot function as a shaman and would not be recognized as a shaman by their sociocultural group. One can see that it is this stage which has direct relevance to the wounded healer component within shamanism.

## Summary

Overall, Ducey's (1976) extensive analysis of the 'Spirit Possession' and 'Soul Loss' phases led him to conclude that shamans display underlying schizoid tendencies despite the conversion (hysterical) and depressive symptoms which are more obvious. As he says, 'the shaman's hysterical tendencies seem to be founded upon an underlying but pervasive schizoid predisposition' (p. 187). Ducey's position is corroborated through the well received position that a splitting of the psyche occurs in all conversion disorder (hysteria) and he cites Federn (1940) and Fairbairn (1952) to that effect. What this situation indicates is that severe difficulties have been encountered in the earliest stages of development 'when the crucial differentiation of self and other is at issue.' (p. 185). From a Kleinian perspective, the 'depressive position' and its concern with whole objects has not been

reached and this is evidenced by the feelings of fragmentation and emptiness that are present rather than the more usual depressive affects.[4]

Ducey concludes that

> hence only representations of part-objects (bad and good spirits,
> sexually and aggressively conceived), splitting of the psyche through
> introjections of and projective identifications with part-object imagoes
> (abduction of soul and torture by spirits), and consequent confusion of
> self/object boundaries (one's own oral-sadistic impulses projected onto
> spirits, gender identity confusion) appear in the future shaman's fan-
> tasies; in other words, he seems caught in the paranoid-schizoid position
> (Klein, 1946), and 'depressive' and 'hysterical' manifestations are mere
> elaborations on this underlying theme.
>
> (ibid., p. 189)

Ducey's final diagnostic conclusion is that shamans suffer from what he
calls 'hysterical psychosis'. 'Hysterical psychosis' is not a current psychiatric
diagnostic category, nonetheless it is an interesting concept as it combines
something to do with both neurosis and psychosis and may have been the
best descriptor Ducey could have coined due to the limited clinical understanding of borderline dynamics at the time he wrote.

We can see that by concentrating on the first two stages of the shamanic
pre-initiatory illness, Ducey has deduced a layered view to the psychopathology and he proposes a standard aetiology for this situation: severe
emotional trauma in early childhood either through actual death of parents
or other causes of substantial oral frustration. It is certainly the case, as
Ducey says, that psychoanalytic research has determined that inadequacy
of emotional satisfaction at the earliest stages of infant development can
result in dissociative splitting, schizoid withdrawal, psychotic denial and
attempts to restore reality through psychotic hallucination. Shaman-
initiates certainly do exhibit the adult behavioural characteristics of these
dynamics as in their withdrawal from relationships, their experience of
hallucination and their dissociative symptoms.

These conclusions of Ducey (1976) reached through his psychoanalytic
interpretation of the symptoms of the pre-initiatory illness are augmented
by his interpretations of shamanic imagery, healing rites and functions.
For example, a developmentally driven identification with the mother is
evidenced in the female nature of the shaman's trappings and insignia
and in the emphasis on a sex change in their initiation. Similarly, cannibalistic imagery and that of the soul being stolen by female figures is
interpreted as indicating oral frustrations with sadistic resolution and/or a
sado-masochistic mother–child relationship indicative of deprivations at
the earliest (oral) stage of development. Further, the fantasy of the soul
being stolen and removed to the upper world is seen by Ducey as a concrete

representation of the early splitting of the psyche in response to the subjectively undifferentiated mother.

From a psychoanalytic perspective such interpretations are quite sound but they are, nonetheless, lines of argument which could be interpreted in other ways. For instance, Jung (1912/1986) could just as easily argue that cannibalistic female imagery is indicative of the negative side of the Great Mother archetype. It is important, therefore, to examine the external evidence in support of Ducey's conclusions.

## Evidence for the developmental components to the shamanic wounded healer

It must initially be noted that none of the ethnographic writers on Siberian shamanism are endeavouring to assert any point about the centrality of emotional trauma in the earliest stages of infant development so it is a case of gleaning relevant comments from their other observations. Nonetheless, the use of direct ethnographic fieldwork is an important issue because, as Siikala (1978) notes, one criticism of shamanism research is that authors will quote upon the quotes of others to the point where we have an iterative discourse so removed from the original data that conclusions become questionable.

It is certainly the case that orphanhood is often mentioned by ethnographers in relation to the emergence of the shamanic vocation. For instance, in discussing shamanic imagery, Campbell (1976), in his *The Masks of God*, refers to Ksenofontov's 1930 account of the legend of the Sakha (Yakut) shaman, Aadja, which begins with two brothers whose parents had died when they were very young.

More significantly, because of the direct fieldwork from which his conclusions were drawn, Bogoras (1904) in his 'The Chukchee' does state that 'a number of Chukchee [Chukchi] tales tell of young orphans, despised and oppressed by all their neighbours, who call to the "spirits", and with their assistance become strong men and powerful shamans' (p. 424).

Furthermore, Castagné (1930, p. 60), when commenting on the Kazak Kirgiz tribe, says: 'Autrefois les *baqças* [shamans] engageaient parfois de tout jeunes Kazak-Kirghizes, le plus souvent des orphelins, afin de les initier à la profession de *baqça*.' Eliade (1964, p. 20) translates this as: 'In former days the *baqças* sometimes enlisted very young Kazak Kirgiz, usually orphans, in order to initiate them into the profession of *baqça*.' Similarly, Novik (1984) notes that it is not uncommon in Siberian legends for the shaman-hero to be an orphan or one who is abandoned (usually by celestial parents). Novik goes on to relate the Nganasan legend of a future hero shaman being summoned to help an old shaman resurrect his dead daughter when 'a very young child ("he only just started to walk")' (p. 208*ff*).[5]

In his *Shamans and Their Religious Practices*, Alekseev (1987) notes that 'exclusive to the Yakuts [Sakha] was the belief that each shaman has an *iie-*

*kyyl* (beast-mother), a supernatural being who is sometimes involved in the upbringing of the shamanic *kut* [that is, soul], but is considered to be the shaman's magical double' (p. 103). The presence of this kind of imagery can be interpreted as a (positive) psychological identification with the mother and this would accord with the view that wounds have occurred for the shaman-to-be in the earliest stages of their infant development.

More significantly, Lopatin (1940–1) gives an interesting first-hand account of a shamanistic performance by the Orochi (Orochee) shaman, Ghindia. This performance was enacted to regain the favour of Ghindia's patron spirit and had become necessitated by the drama and scandal involving the death of her husband who was thirty years her senior and whom she disliked:

> She began singing in a low, almost whispering, voice, now and then striking the drum gently . . . 'I am a poor woman. There is nothing in me that would distinguish me from any other woman in our village. I was a poor orphan. I was a deserted girl. My parents died very early. I do not remember my mother. My youth was hard; my childhood was without joy and my girlhood lonely. My relatives reared me. . . . I have always worked hard. . . . My marriage was unhappy. Oh, I was very, very unhappy. But I must not speak of that at all. . . . If I do not touch memory then memory will not touch me.
>
> (p. 353)

Not only is Ghindia relating here her difficult childhood but this is contextualized in terms of her being an orphan from such an early age that she cannot remember her mother. It would appear this was experienced by Ghindia as traumatizing. This account quite directly supports the view that wounds have occurred for the shaman-to-be in the earliest stages of their infant development.

Additionally, it is easy to establish from ethnographic accounts that the psychological disturbance associated with shamanism often appears in childhood/youth and that many groups in their recruitment of shamans will seek out children who display such characteristics of disturbance. Czaplicka (1914), in quoting the nineteenth-century Russian observers Agapitoff and Khangaloff, says: 'A child chosen to be a shaman is recognized among the Buryat [a Neo-Siberian group like the Sakha (Yakut)] by the following signs: "He is often absorbed in meditation, likes to be alone, has mysterious dreams, and sometimes has fits during which he is unconscious"' (p. 185). What is noteworthy is that Czaplicka in summarizing Agapitoff and Khangaloff goes on to say: ·

> After a period of trial the soul of the child returns to the body, which for a time resumes its normal life. But on his reaching adolescence,

peculiar symptoms show themselves in the person who has undergone these experiences. He becomes moody, is easily excited into a state of ecstasy, leads an irregular life, wandering from *ulus* to *ulus* to watch the shamanistic ceremonies.

(ibid., p. 185)

In other words, early symptoms are evident which re-emerge in adolescence. This could indicate that the shaman's particular wounds have occurred in childhood and/or infancy and that the experience of puberty draws them into the foreground.

In a similar way, appearance in childhood of the characteristics indicating a shamanic 'call' amongst the Alarsk Buryat is confirmed by Sandschejew (1927, 1928, as cited in Eliade 1964) who observed that those children elected by the spirits to become shamans cried in their sleep and became nervous and dreamy. And Mikhailowski (1894, p. 90) says of the Altaians: 'The future *kam* [shaman] begins to realize his destiny at an early age; he is subject to sickness, and often falls into a frenzy. . . . The tendency is hereditary; a *kam* often has children predisposed to attacks of illness.' Mikhailowski also discusses cases where a boy or girl can be subject to fits even in families where there is no shaman. Similarly, Eliade (1964) concludes on the Altaians that: 'While still a child, the future shaman . . . proves to be sickly, withdrawn, contemplative' (p. 20). All these observations are indicative of a connection between childhood experience and the later shamanic 'call'.

We have already noted Castagné's (1930) observation of the Kazak Kirgiz shamans who would sometimes enlist orphans for training. He goes on to say: 'cependant, pour la réussite du métier, une prédisposition aux maladies nerveuses était indispensable. Les sujets se destinant au *baqçylyk* étaient caracterisés par des changements subits d'état, par le passage rapide de l'irritation a l'état normal, de la mélancolie a l'agitation' (p. 60). Eliade (1964, p. 20) translates this as: 'however, to succeed in the profession a predisposition to nervous disorders was essential. The subjects intending to enter the *baqçylyk* were characterized by sudden changes in state, by rapid transitions from irritability to normality, from melancholia to agitation.' It would appear again that the disturbance associated with shamanic election manifests in childhood and it is of note that the *baqças* thought that such a predisposition to nervous disorders would occur amongst orphans, that is, where there is a possibility of early emotional deprivation.

## Conclusions

The ethnographic examples suggest that since the emotional disturbances evidencing the shamanic call occur in childhood/adolescence without any apparent concurrent causative trauma, we are dealing here with an issue of re-emergence, that is, a particular wound is already present from the time of infant development but it emerges at a later age (for some reason).

It is quite possible that in shamanism we are dealing with wounds to do with an overall disrupted emotional atmosphere in the early mother–infant bond rather than the effects of a specific trauma per se. Ducey (1976) does state that

> the reasons for the defectiveness of the mother–child relationship can be inferred only from vague clues. . . . The scarcity of food and the unpredictability and harshness of the environment doubtless contribute indirectly to, but do not in themselves account for, its insecurity and frustrations. But the mother's anxiety over these external difficulties may well be transmitted to the infant.
>
> (pp. 189–90)

In terms of the connection between infant development and psychopathology it is a substantially acknowledged psychoanalytic position that a disrupted emotional atmosphere in the early mother–infant bond can be causative *apart* from any specific trauma. Winnicott (1948, p. 159) particularly argues this point, saying that the 'mental health of the human being is laid down in infancy by the mother, who provides an environment in which complex but essential processes in the infant's self can become completed.'

Such a perspective is substantiated by later clinicians. For example, Gunderson (2001) makes a similar point when discussing the childhood experiences of those with Borderline Personality Disorder (BPD).[6] He states that any childhood trauma experienced by these patients is 'emblematic of sustained developmental problems that formed the patient's disturbed personality' rather than the cause per se of their problems. So whilst he can go on to state that 70 per cent of BPD patients have childhood histories of physical or sexual trauma, he concludes that

> the social conditions needed for BPD to develop require emotional estrangement from parents. This estrangement gives abusive experiences during childhood an impact that is far more traumatic in warping character development than is the impact of similar events on children who have the opportunity to find support, talk about the events, and react with their families.
>
> (pp. 44–5)

Clearly, as with Winnicott, Gunderson sees that it is the early experience of developmental problems in infancy which is critical in Borderline Personality Disorder, even before the impact of later trauma.

A problematic situation for the infant can become even further compounded if it has to incorporate any illness patterns of the mother as in a mother's anxiety being transmitted to the infant in the way Ducey (1976) suggests above. For Winnicott (1956, p. 305), 'the theme of the infant's introjection of the illness patterns of the mother [is a] subject . . . of great importance.'

Overall then there are developmental tasks which can only be completed by the infant when in an emotional environment that is 'good enough' (Winnicott's term) and this is largely connected to the mother's preoccupation with the care of her infant, one that is a sensitive and active adaptation to the infant's needs. As Winnicott (1952b) puts it,

> mental ill-health of psychotic quality arises out of delays and distortions, regressions and muddles, in the early stages of growth of the environment–individual set-up [that is, the mother–infant pair]. Mental ill-health emerges imperceptibly out of the ordinary difficulties that are inherent in human nature and that give colour to the task of child care.
>
> (pp. 227–8)

The conclusion to be drawn is that the environmental conditions under which mothering occurs in Siberian groups are such as to foment affective states in certain mothers (such as depression and/or anxiety) which could constitute a 'failure of the environment' (Winnicott's term) for their infants in the earliest stages of preverbal development. It is the emotional difficulties arising from these early experiences which developmentally produce the shaman archetype and it is this which underpins the later emergence of shamanic phenomena. Furthermore, it is the wounds from this preverbal zone of infant development which shamans have then been able to self-cure, which underpins their status as wounded healers.

It becomes important then to look at the Siberian tribes where shamanism predominates to see if their customs and lifestyle are such as could produce sufficient emotional rupture within mother–infant pairs to explain a later emergence of the shamanic phenomenon. As an entrée, the Siberian Sakha (Yakut) tribe affords a useful case study for not only are they a *locus classicus* tribe on which extensive ethnographic material is available but, as Ducey (1976, p. 190) notes, their shamanism is also 'the "most classical" representative of classical shamanism.'

# Chapter 8

# Case study: The Siberian Sakha (Yakut) tribe

## Introduction

Of all the Siberian groups, the Sakha (Yakut) have been the most extensively studied and ethnographic material resulting from more than one direct observation is available on them. On two occasions, Jochelson (1926, 1933) undertook direct fieldwork amongst them, first, from 1884 to 1894 as a member of the Imperial Russian Geographical Society expedition; and second, from 1900 to 1902 as a member of the famous Jesup North Pacific expedition undertaken through the American Museum of Natural History. Sieroszewski (1902) also had the opportunity for direct observation when he spent twelve years living with the Sakha (Yakut) as a political exile. An abridged overview of Sieroszewski's early findings was subsequently translated by Sumner (1901).

In addition to having such extensive material available on the Sakha (Yakut), we are in an even more fortunate position, for Jochelson (1926) notes that by comparison with the Yukaghir (another Siberian tribe whom he was studying at the time), Sakha (Yakut) shamanism is very well preserved. Previously, Jochelson (1908, p. 48n) had gone even further, asserting that 'among the Yakut, a people with a more developed primitive culture [compared to the Koryak who were another Siberian tribe] . . . [p]rofessional shamans can be found everywhere . . . even at the present time.' This situation adds considerable weight to the conclusions which can be drawn from Jochelson's direct observations of Sakha (Yakut) culture and shamanism.

Furthermore, to the early ethnographers, Sakha (Yakut) culture seemed less well developed compared with other tribes, such as the Buryats (see Krader 1954). As a consequence, Sakha (Yakut) shamanism had not become accommodated to other cultural uses, such as determining sociocultural class and rank. It primarily deals with the spirits in relation to animistic beliefs and is likely, thereby, to be a more 'pristine' expression of shamanism.

For these reasons, as Ducey (1976, p. 190) states, Sakha (Yakut) shamanism is so often regarded as 'the "most classical" representative of classical shamanism.' It is, therefore, a most appropriate tribe to use as a case study to evidence the assertion that shamanism is connected to a developmentally produced archetype which has been forged through intense emotional difficulties in the early mother–infant bond and that the shaman's ultimate self-cure underpins their status as a wounded healer.

It is important at this point to emphasize that I am not necessarily interested in arguing for a pejorative comparison between Sakha (Yakut) and Western childrearing practices or to read Western interpretations into the experience of another culture. Most cultures have quite different and presumably satisfactory ways of organizing and carrying out childbirth and childrearing. However, post-Freudian infant research has shown that particular emotional patterns of the mother in the early weeks and months after childbirth can have long-term effects on the psychological well-being of the infant. It is legitimate to conclude that this psychoanalytic research has made discoveries that are applicable to the general human condition, irrespective of culture. Hence, it is important to ascertain whether the environmental conditions under which mothering occurs in the Sakha (Yakut) (and other Siberian tribes as well) could in any way foment affective states in certain mothers (such as depression and/or anxiety) which could constitute a 'failure of the environment' to such an extent as to be aetiologically implicated in relation to a bio-structural imbedding of a developmentally produced shaman archetype.

## An overview of Sakha (Yakut) culture

### Harsh environment and life

No one would deny that Siberia is a particularly harsh and difficult environment in which to live and the Sakha (Yakut) and the Yukaghir in the Upper-Kolyma region encounter the most severe climate in Siberia. Sumner (1901) says that the hard winters and bad meadows place many Sakha (Yakut) households on the verge of distress, the least accident overthrowing the security of their existence. Since children become labourers who cost nothing, they had high birth rates (on average ten children to one husband). However, this situation was paralleled by high rates of infant mortality (one example Sumner quotes is of a woman who had 22 babies of which 11 died). He goes on to conclude: 'Infant mortality amongst them is frightful . . . This is due to the misery in which they live, on account of which they cannot give care to their children, even when they are rich' (ibid., p. 80). This situation would appear even worse for the girl children. Sieroszewski (1900, as cited in Czaplicka 1914, p. 112), when commenting on the decline of polygamy amongst the Sakha (Yakut), makes an interesting statement: 'Another reason for the decline of the custom [i.e. polygamy] is that girls die in infancy more frequently than boys, as they are not so carefully tended.'

There would seem to have been flow-on effects of this harsh way of life into other mores and attitudes for there appeared to be an overt exploitation of the weak by the strong inside the family groups. According to Sumner (1901), younger members of the family could be forced into marriage or put to work under harsh conditions, children could be given away as labourers to outside persons or simply sold and the beating of wives and young children was not that uncommon. In fact, Jochelson (1933) describes the Sakha (Yakut) as warlike and blood vengeance occurred between clans, which was often resolved through ransom or the giving of a girl in marriage.

Similarly, Sumner states that the old are treated badly and often beaten and intimidated so that, fearing a lonely old age, they make up the greatest number of suicides. This is substantiated by Jochelson (1933), who says that

> according to a Yakut tradition, aged parents and also sick and crippled people, unable to work, were doomed to die and were even buried alive after three days of abundant entertainment.
>
> Trostchansky, who lived as a political exile among the Yakut for about twenty years, characterizes them as egotistical utilitarians. He says that aged people are not in favour; they are beaten by their own children and are often forced to leave their dwellings and to beg from house to house. They are not admitted by the rich and the poor people force them to do hard work, like dressing skins . . . for every bit of food.
>
> (pp. 132–4)

It is not unreasonable to conclude that a conjunction of a number of the factors outlined above could place certain mothers in a position of such stress as to have flow-on effects into the efficacy of the mother–infant bond. It is possible that other customs specifically to do with the status and position of women in Sakha (Yakut) society could further exacerbate these stressors on young mothers.

### The status and position of women in Sakha (Yakut) society

According to Sumner (1901), the women occupy a remarkably low status in Sakha (Yakut) society – they have no rights to land, property or independent existence. Within the family, the girls are treated as subordinate to the boys (who will one day take over sovereignty of the family). Girls are considered as 'outsiders' because they will eventually marry and become the property of their husbands. As Jochelson (1933, p. 132) puts it, '[a] girl, say the Yakut, is really a lot of aliens.' Hence, Sumner describes them as having a sense of being 'worthless' and 'rightless' so that they display 'servile' and 'cringing' behaviours and attitudes. Furthermore, since societal emphasis is on the woman's capacity to breed, polygamy is practised but this is in an environment where multiple wives may not be affordable because the wives have to be housed separately. Sumner concludes: 'Everything is against the women; the conditions of labour . . . and the land tenure which recognises the men only as having a share; and traditions and education' (op. cit. p. 95). Their low status is further amplified by the fact that the Sakha (Yakut) employ chastity girdles, which were worn constantly at night, and through the custom of *chotunnur*, which Sumner reports, whereby brothers do not let their sisters go off in marriage whilst still a virgin. Such customs may not be that unusual in patriarchal/patrilineal societies but what is noteworthy is the position in which the new wives/mothers can be placed and the emotional impact of this on them and their infants.

Furthermore, the wife's labour is exploited and the husband is revered:

> To acquire an extra gain, win food or money, or earn something by outside work is considered more desirable [to the husbands] than to follow heavy daily labour which would maintain the life of the family from day to day.
>
> (Sumner 1901, p. 78)

Hence they pursue interests in external affairs, are lazy, attend village assemblies and leave the women to do the hard work. Sumner (ibid., p. 78) goes on: 'Inside the house he [the husband] is treated with almost slavish respect and consideration. His presence puts an end to cheerfulness, the excuse for which is that he must maintain respect.'

In the Sakha (Yakut) marriage system, most marriages are brought about without the participation or consent of the young people. Apparently the girls have little input into the marriage decisions by their fathers and Sumner says that even repugnant suggestions can be forced upon them through threats and beatings. This situation can be exacerbated through their bride-price system, for although payment is made for a bride, there is a reciprocal system of dowry so that the bride is expected to bring gifts when she takes up residence within her husband's *sib*. Notwithstanding the fact that the bride-price system can help the woman over the emotional threshold of leaving her own blood relatives because she is seen to have and is treated with value, Sumner notes that difficulties can arise if there are price disputes:

> She is very coldly received by his relatives if she brings less than was expected. . . . Often there is a complete rupture. . . . In [this] case, they boycott her and she suffers all kinds of petty household persecutions which poison her existence.
>
> (p. 84)

Moreover, because the wife comes from another *sib*, she can often be undermined by the maiden sisters of the husband. Sieroszewski (1902) knew cases of suicide by young wives under the persecution of the husband and his relatives.

The emotional impact of these situations could be compounded by what Sumner (1901) describes as the strict rules to do with bride interaction with in-laws, especially the father-in-law and other male relatives. These are called 'avoidance customs' and they entail a whole range of rules to do with approach, dressing and verbal address, which could only exacerbate any tense emotional atmosphere, making everyday interactions difficult and placing a strain on domestic relationships.

Again, it is not unreasonable to conclude that these factors to do with the position and status of women in Sakha (Yakut) society could further exacerbate the stresses under which women endeavoured to do their childrearing. However, it is with childbirth practices that Sakha (Yakut) customs seem most extreme. This is an area of particular interest because of the connection between adult psychopathology and disruptions to the emotional well-being of the infant during the early months of life, exactly the kind of situation underpinning the development of the shamanism in Siberian tribes that Ducey (1976) proposed.

### Sakha (Yakut) childbirth

'Women, especially when they are pregnant . . . are considered in some sense unclean' says Sumner (1901, p. 96). Even before the birth of the infant, therefore, a sense of personal inclusion by the mothers-to-be would be difficult. If other factors compounded this atmosphere of emotional estrangement then a more problematic situation could emerge for the future mother–infant dyad.

Jochelson (1926) makes a most interesting statement in relation to childbirth amongst the Sakha (Yakut):

> The view is commonly held that women of primitive and low-cultured peoples have easier childbirths than those of civilized and cultured nations; that with the former this process is much the same as any of the other natural and painless organic functions. I had more than one opportunity, while living among the Yakut and the Yakaghir, to convince myself that this view is erroneous. Of course, the women of these tribes are not as delicate as the women of civilized nations; but the absence of proper obstetric methods, and the necessity of being on their feet soon after childbirth, result in chronic suffering, *nervous diseases*, and premature age. Besides, many cases have come to my knowledge where young women have died as a result of an irregular birth, or of the barbarous practices of native midwives [italics mine].
>
> (p. 96)

It is of significance here that Jochelson is attributing a connection between 'nervous diseases' in the mothers and the 'barbarous practices' they have had to endure during childbirth.

In particular amongst the Sakha (Yakut), the presence of the actual father at the birth is considered advantageous because he can loosen 'what he fastened'. That childbirth is attended by much fear for the women is evidenced by the consequent willingness of the mothers to name the father no matter what the circumstances of the conception.

Sakha (Yakut) birthing is facilitated by the mother leaning across a bar with pressure being applied to the abdomen by the midwife. If this is to no avail, the shaman is called because the Sakha (Yakut) believe difficult childbirth, premature birth and hard labour to be due to evil spirits having entered the mother.

Jochelson elaborates:

> no consideration is shown to either mother or child; for women possessed of evil spirits are regarded by the Yakut as no less perilous to society than those infected with epidemic germs. This accounts for the entire absence of compassion, and for the cruelty, manifested by the Yakut towards women suffering the pains of labor.
>
> (ibid., p. 102)

Jochelson goes on to outline as an example the case of one woman who died from a ruptured perineum and punctured bladder as the result of a shaman's interventions. He gained the following account of the incident from a Russian observer (a man named Gebler):

> The woman was a primipara, and the wife of the clan elder. As soon as the first labor-pains came, which, according to the subsequent assertion of the unfortunate woman, were premature, the husband sent for the shaman to hasten the delivery. The shaman arrived, and at once began his performances, and, having invoked his guardian spirits, set himself to the task of exorcism.
>
> A structure made of birch poles [a structure with a bar across which the woman leans while pressure is applied to the abdomen] . . . was built by the husband with the help of the shaman, and the unhappy woman was dragged to it by force. Her cries and resistance were of no avail. With the aid of the shaman's son and her sister-in-law, the woman was dragged to the structure. Her hands and feet were fastened with skin straps to the side-poles of the structure, and her neck bound to the cross-piece. While the assistants held the woman, that she might not tear herself away from it, the shaman began to squeeze the child out, pronouncing incantations at the same time. The woman's cries were disregarded.

At length the shaman declared that he saw a long-tailed evil spirit holding the child. The husband of the poor woman begged the shaman to expel the spirit. Then the shaman armed himself with iron tongs, such as are used by a blacksmith, and pulled the child out piecemeal. Gebler, who was in the hut at the beginning of the performance, and who did not dare to interfere, had to leave the dwelling, not being able to witness the sufferings of the woman.

When he returned in the evening, the victim, already released, lay in a pool of blood on the bare ground, covered with a fur coat, moaning feebly [the ground is permanently frozen in the region of the Yakut]. The Yakut drank their tea quite unconcerned about the sufferer. Gebler intimated to the Yakut how cruel it was to mutilate a woman in childbirth and then to cast her away on the floor. The master of the house replied that his wife was not ill, but that the evil spirit had possessed her. Then Gebler carried the woman from where she lay and put her upon a reindeer-skin, and covered her over with a coat.

(ibid., pp. 102–3)

Gebler informed an official and the woman was transported to an infirmary where she died. The shaman was arrested and apparently died of fright.

Given the fact that Jochelson indicates such practices and procedures were the norm, it is not stretching the point too far to say that these Sakha (Yakut) cultural practices could set-up the kind of traumatizing conditions required for difficulties to emerge in certain of the early mother–infant dyads. It is exactly these kinds of intense emotional experiences which could be the first wounds in a presumed chain of experiences in the environment leading to a developmentally produced shaman archetype in the infants.

### After childbirth

Information on the subsequent childrearing practices among the Sakha (Yakut) is also informative. Sumner (1901) says

the Yakut mothers have not much milk. Not a child grows up without using a sucking horn. The mothers suckle the children long. The author saw five-year-old boys who demanded the breast when they saw their little brothers enjoying it. Children are often suckled at night to keep them quiet, but in the daytime they lie cold, damp, and neglected, while their uproar fills the house, the mother being employed in her [demanding] household work. Some mothers employ a means of putting their children to sleep, especially if they are fretful boys, which often causes spermatorrhea.

(p. 80)

The last sentence is a rather academic way of saying the boys are masturbated.

This is a description of an emotional atmosphere where the infants could experience the mother as subjectively undifferentiated in that she both withdraws (leading to intense frustration) and uncontrollably approaches (and this in a specifically sexual way with the boys). Such situations can lead to a confused and confusing early frustration of emotional needs providing the kind of experience for some infants which could add to other factors leading to a developmentally produced shaman archetype which has been forged through these kinds of emotional difficulties in the early mother–infant relationship.

And there are further factors indicated in the ethnographic records which could compound an already tense emotional atmosphere in certain mother–infant dyads. First, Jochelson (1926) says there is some evidence that infanticide was not unknown amongst the Sakha (Yakut) and he recounts a probable case when a child was born to a woman who had sexual relations with the Cossack with whom she was travelling. Aggressive impulses towards one's infant are probably not that unusual for any mother but the infant is in an entirely different situation if murderous impulses are concretely entertained as an actual solution to a problem.

Second, the ownership of children could lead to a mother and her infant being permanently separated in a very rupturing way. Sumner (1901) points out that such situations could come about because a general economic value was placed on children due to their subsequent labour. As a consequence, they were owned by the entire *sib* group, so if a widow remarried into another *sib*, the members of her first *sib* group would take away her son(s). It would appear that such situations could be more common than we may first think, for amongst the *locus classicus* tribes, marriage was not necessarily too permanent and divorce was common. This issue is dealt with in further detail later in the chapter.

These factors add to the possibility that certain mothers may be put in a position of such stress as to have flow-on effects into the efficacy of the mother–infant bond. If there is a preponderance of rupture and difficulty in the mother–infant dyads as seems to be suggested from the above, then we ought to be able to find descriptions of anxiety-ridden behaviours amongst young children. And this is what we do find.

### Descriptions of the Sakha (Yakut) children

Sumner (1901) provides an informative description of the behaviour patterns of the Sakha (Yakut) five- to ten-year-olds:

> [They] are by no means sprightly or enterprising, and they are excessively obedient. Even when playing they do not make half the noise and

movement which our children make. When there are several in a family, you may not notice their presence for a long time. They hide themselves away in the corners . . . busy with something or other . . . but all of it only half aloud. They are hardly ever so far carried away as to cry aloud or to sing aloud. At a threatening shout of a grown person, they come to silence and scatter. Only when they are alone do they become lively. This happens in summer, in the woods and groves, and in the fields. They are very fond of assembling to play there.

(pp. 80–1)

We have here a description of behaviour which is excessively self-monitored and riddled with anxiety. Such behaviours in children usually arise from early experience of an environment that is untrustworthy, threatening and unprotective. Notwithstanding the occurrence of infanticide impulses as already noted, early emotional deprivation and a frustration of needs can be experienced by the infant as an attack. The environment is then experienced as potentially punitive. Furthermore, if the mother is excessively emotionally distracted and/or disturbed then she is unable to offer the kind of emotional protection to her infant which the Oedipal stage necessitates. The resulting defensive activity for a child is often of withdrawal from threat. Sumner's description fits perfectly with this whilst the underlying cause of such behaviour resides in a mother–infant relationship that is not 'good enough'.

Furthermore, if conditions can become so difficult for a number of Sakha (Yakut) mothers that they are pushed into psychopathology with flow-on effects to their children, then we would expect to see the prevalence of some kind of anxiety phenomenon in the culture. This is what we do find in terms of the early ethnographers' descriptions of 'Arctic hysteria'.

### Arctic hysteria[1]

According to Jochelson (1926), the Sakha (Yakut) is one of the Siberian tribes for whom 'Arctic hysteria' is more frequent and more serious. The highest degree of the disease seemed to occur amongst those from the Upper-Kolyma region and Jochelson could find a sufferer in each of the families from this region. In addition, one half of the older Sakha (Yakut) women were seen to suffer from a version of the disorder which involves involuntary mimicry symptoms, that is, they would senselessly repeat overheard words. He also noted among the Sakha (Yakut) women in particular that some suffered melancholia (depression), that is, they became apathetic and indifferent to everything, ate little and sat in silence.

Jochelson believed there to be a connection between 'Arctic hysteria' and the psychical effects of the environment, that is, the cold, the dark winters, the light nights in summer and the general monotony of the landscape. The disease also seems linked to certain stressors as it occurred more acutely during times of famine and food shortages. These factors are no doubt implicated but the fact that across the Siberian tribes 'Arctic hysteria' can be observed most frequently and severely amongst the Sakha (Yakut) women is not that unexpected given the evidence so far as to the quality of their lives in their culture. This finding adds weight to the proposition being forwarded here that the emotional atmosphere for certain of the mothers is distressing enough to foment substantial anxiety and/or real psychopathology which will have flow-on effects into their childrearing and their mother–infant relationships. For certain infants, problems could be further compounded beyond their needs not being met because they may end up either absorbing the illness patterns of the mother or reacting in response to those patterns. A simple example of the latter would be the infant of a depressed mother who has to keep the mother happy so as to get its needs met. Such a compounding of difficulties could quite plausibly affect the 'good-enough' mother–infant bond leading to real psychopathology in the infants.

Later ethnographic material on childrearing practices of the Sakha (Yakut) does give further evidence that the emotional atmosphere for certain mothers could be distressing enough to foment real psychopathology which will have flow-on effects into their childrearing and thus onto the quality of the mother–infant relationship.

### Sakha (Yakut) childrearing practices as seen in the Human Relations Area Files (Yale University)

In relation to childrearing practices, Ducey (1976) cites research by Barry *et al.* (1955) who undertook cross-cultural ratings of infant care from 111 cultures worldwide. The data they used came from ethnographic publications and the Human Relations Area Files kept at Yale University. Using this data, two separate researchers averaged their ratings on a scale of one to fourteen for each culture on fourteen items to do with infant and childcare. The results are summarized in *Table 8.1*. The researchers found that the Sakha (Yakut) were overall one of the lowest scoring cultures on each of the childrearing measures. Ducey makes special mention of one particular dimension (Item 9: diffusion of nurturance) which indicates the extent to which infants are cared for exclusively by the mother during the first twelve months. The Sakha (Yakut) received quite a low rating on this dimension (five out of a possible fourteen) and Ducey concludes: 'This combination of a defective but intense relationship with the mother is precisely the pattern identified by our intrapsychic theory' (1976, p. 190).

However, neither Ducey (1976) nor Barry *et al.* (1955) provide any statistical analysis of the data to corroborate their conclusions. When this is done, the Sakha (Yakut) are definitely significantly different to all other

Table 8.1 The treatment of infants across the first twelve months: The Sakha (Yakut) tribe compared with other world cultures

| Item | Description | N | Mean: Other cultures | Mean: Sakha (Yakut) | t (significant at the p<0.05 level) | df |
|---|---|---|---|---|---|---|
| 1 | The display of affection toward the infants, i.e. the extent to which the infants were held, fondled, caressed and played with | 96 | 10.25 | 9 | 4.76 | 95 |
| 2 | Protection of the infants from environmental factors | 93 | 8.9 | 4 | 22.79 | 92 |
| 3 | Degree of drive reduction, i.e. how fully are the infant's needs reduced? | 89 | 11.25 | 7 | 19.32 | 88 |
| 4 | Immediacy of drive reduction, i.e. how quickly are the infant's needs reduced? | 82 | 11.28 | 6 | 18.44 | 81 |
| 5 | Consistency of drive reduction, i.e. how consistently are drives reduced? | 81 | 10.49 | 5 | 19.46 | 80 |
| 6 | Consistency of presence of nurturant agent, i.e. is there a substitute if the mother is not present? | 100 | 11.78 | 9 | 14.6 | 99 |
| 7 | Absence of pain inflicted by the nurturant agent, e.g. cold baths, depilation, rough handling or physical punishment | 92 | 9.03 | 8 | 3.45 | 91 |
| 8 | Overall indulgency during infancy | 100 | 10.33 | 7 | 14.76 | 99 |
| 9 | Diffusion of nurturance, i.e. the extent to which nurturance of the infant is shared | 101 | 7.75 | 5 | 11.94 | 100 |

Source: Adapted from Barry et al. (1955).
Note: Based on a one sample t test of mean scores against Sakha (Yakut) ratings.

*Table 8.2* The treatment of children: The Sakha (Yakut) tribe compared with other world cultures

| Item | Description | N | Mean: Other cultures | Mean: Sakha (Yakut) | t (significant at the p<0.05 level) | df |
|------|-------------|---|------|------|------|------|
| 13 | The degree of anxiety about dependence developed during the transition period from infantile dependence to status of child | 93 | 7.41 | 12 | −14.96 | 92 |
| 14 | Overall childhood indulgence (ages 5–12) | 108 | 8.94 | 5 | 16.41 | 107 |

Source: Adapted from Barry et al. (1955).
Note: Based on a one sample t test of mean scores against Sakha (Yakut) ratings.

cultures on Item 9 and as Ducey realizes, this result is particularly telling because it means the infants in Sakha (Yakut) culture are cared for exclusively by the mother. As he says with regard to schizoidal psychopathology, it is the conjunctions around an intense but defective relationship with the mother which is aetiological. This finding does add weight to his hypothesis.[2]

When the other childcare items specified by Barry et al. (1955) are also subjected to statistical analysis, an interesting pattern emerges in terms of care over the first twelve months of life. The average scores for all the other cultures are significantly above the scores given to the Sakha (Yakut) (see *Table 8.1*). This means that the Sakha (Yakut) are not performing as well on these infant-care dimensions as all the other cultures.[3]

The final two dimensions on which information was available for the Sakha (Yakut) were Item 13 (anxiety about dependence during the transition period from infantile dependence to the status of child) and Item 14 (childhood indulgence), which make up an overall rating of the degree of indulgence shown to older children prior to puberty. Results of the statistical analysis for these two items are summarized in *Table 8.2* and show that the average scores for all the other cultures were significantly below the score given to the Sakha (Yakut) for Item 13 but significantly above for Item 14.[4]

The result for Item 13 indicates that the Sakha (Yakut) display significantly more anxiety about transition-period dependence than the other cultures overall. The result for Item 14 indicates that the Sakha (Yakut) are less indulging of their children than the other cultures overall.

These findings from the Yale data indicate that the Sakha (Yakut) do not perform as well as other cultures in relation to their infant and childcare, which in all possibility could foment conditions whereby the needs of certain infants would not be met in the earliest months of life. This supports the view that the shamanism the tribe exhibits is connected to a developmentally produced archetype which has been forged through emotional ruptures in the early mother–infant bond. The assumption is that the shaman archetype will only be developmentally produced this way in certain individuals thus explaining why some go on to become shamans and others in the tribe do not.

On this theme there is also corroborative material from the childbirth practices of other Siberian groups who have a shamanic tradition.

## Corroborative examples to do with childbirth from other Siberian groups

Jochelson (1926) notes what he calls similar 'barbarous practices' to Sakha (Yakut) childbirth amongst the Yukaghir and he goes on to relate that the many taboos and rules among the Yukaghir require a host of wearisome exercises which aid neither the mother's health nor that of the child. In relation to childbirth in particular, the Yukaghir mother will walk about the room with the onset of labour until she has to be helped by other women. Eventually she sits on her husband's lap and he encircles her body with his arms and squeezes down on her abdomen, aided by two other women and another man to increase the pressure. Sometimes a towel or leather belt is added. 'The harmful effects of these obstetric performances upon the patient and the child are obvious. They frequently kill the former, especially when her pelvis is too narrow, or when the child is in a wrong position,' says Jochelson (ibid., p. 101). It may be little wonder that Jochelson also notes that there are many barren women amongst the Yukaghir for this could be a self-protective manoeuvre, their anxiety inhibiting ovulation.

The Yukaghir mother generally lies down for only two or three hours after the birth and walks outside the next day. Similar taboos as apply with menstruation are observed for up to the next forty days. Jochelson also noted that in the past, infants who had lost their mothers at birth were often killed.

This material shows that certain mothers from another Siberian *locus classicus* tribe with a developed shamanic tradition could be having similar emotionally disturbing experiences as do the Sakha (Yakut), with flow-on effects into the 'good-enough' mother–infant bond. This further supports the view that the shaman archetype has been developmentally forged through such emotional ruptures in that early bond.

In relation to another *locus classicus* tribe with a developed shamanic tradition, the Chukchi (Chukchee), Bogoras (1904) tells us that the mothers here are not allowed to express pain or distress or to receive any help during childbirth, so the birth often occurs when the mother is alone. He says:

> Custom strictly forbids the woman to groan, or to give way to the pain
> by any audible sign. Nor may help be given by other women. The
> woman who has been delivered has to attend to her own needs herself,
> and to those of the new-born infant. . . . The woman who accepts help
> . . . will be mocked her whole life long.
>
> (p. 36)

Conceivably, such a situation would add to the mother's stress and could
compound with other factors leading to pathological responses. Bogoras
also indicates that if the mother dies, the child is smothered but occasion-
ally such a child is reared. For another tribe, the Gilyak, Czaplicka (1914)
indicates that birth occurs in a specially constructed hut outside the home
despite the season or weather. Winter in Siberia can be exceptionally
uncomfortable and the flimsy nature of the huts means the mother and
infant would be exposed to the cold and wind. It has been suggested that
this custom, where the mother and infant remain away from the main home
for eight to twelve days, is in response to the fear of death. Again, the
isolation implied in this custom could place certain mothers under such
stress as to contribute to the kind of psychopathological reactions argued
for here.

## Corroborative evidence from a circumpolar group: The Inuit

Whitney (1910) was a hunter and adventurer who spent a year amongst one
of the northernmost tribes of Inuit and he had occasion to witness a few
incidents of 'problokto' (the Inuit word for 'Arctic hysteria'). He explains
'problokto' in the following way:

> Problokto is a form of temporary insanity to which the Highland
> Eskimos are subject, and which comes upon them very suddenly and
> unexpectedly. They are liable to have these attacks more particularly at
> the beginning or during the period of darkness.
>
> (p. 67)

One occasion Whitney witnessed is described by him as follows:

> At half-past one that night I was awakened from a sound sleep by a
> woman shouting at the top of her voice – shrill and startling, like one
> gone mad. I knew at once what it meant – some one had gone
> problokto. I tumbled into my clothes and rushed out. Far away on the
> driving ice of the Sound a lone figure was running and raving. . . . At
> length I reached her . . . She struggled desperately, and it required the
> combined strength of the three of us to get her back to the shack, where

she was found to be in bad shape – one hand was frozen slightly, and part of one breast. After a half hour of quiet she became rational again, but the attack left her very weak.

In the meantime I went over to her igloo to look after the child. There I found the poor little pickaninny without a stitch of clothes on, crying her eyes out, while five of the wolf dogs, which had broken into the place, were eating everything they could find.

(pp. 83–4)

We can see here the possible negative effects on the infants exposed to this kind of emotional atmosphere, particularly if it is regularly repeated or runs in parallel with other symptoms of disturbance and/or the frustration of emotional needs.

In addition to this material, an overview of the ethnographic literature reveals other general features in the *locus classicus* which could have a detrimental effect on the mothers in these tribes and thus on the 'good-enough' mother–infant bond.

## Other general features in the *locus classicus* which parallel Sakha (Yakut) society

It would seem that across the *locus classicus*, women are regarded quite abjectly. The point in outlining the following is to indicate that as with the Sakha (Yakut), there is a possibility of certain negative factors and stressors compounding so as to disturb the 'good-enough' mother–infant bond, potentially producing psychopathological effects on certain infants.

Amongst a number of tribes, women were treated like property not persons. According to Pallas (1788a, p. 305), the Ostyak (Ket) consider their wives to be like 'necessary domestic animals' and accordingly treat them like 'slaves not consorts'. Similarly, Pallas (1788b, p. 9) describes the Samoyeds as treating their wives like 'slaves . . . scolding and cursing them.' And Montefiore (1894–5), in the following century, says of them:

Girls . . . are more or less valuable property, and the impecunious parent frequently sells his children at a very early age, in order that he may realise their value. . . . It is not uncommon for a Samoyed to sell his wife to another for the consideration of a few teams of deer, and he sometimes barters her for a lady whose husband may be willing to accept the view that exchange is no robbery.

(p. 405)

Pallas (1788b) goes further in his descriptions of the Samoyed, saying they treat their wives as 'impure creatures', subjecting them to many taboos and rules, especially when menstruating. Pain in childbirth apparently indicated the wife had had an illicit affair and this often (as one could imagine) produced a confession.

Bogoras (1904) gives a number of examples which indicate the inferior place of women amongst the Chukchi (Chukchee). He says:

> The position of women, on the whole, is inferior to that of the men. 'Since you are a woman, be silent' . . . these words are repeated every time that a woman severely reproved dares to say a word back in her own defence.
>
> (pp. 546–7)

Bogoras also gives an account of a woman's protest against 'intolerable ill-treatment' by her father-in-law resulting in her leaving her husband and returning to her family home. He notes that this story is 'characteristic of Chukchee family life' and adds: 'The wife is often harshly treated by her husband. I have mentioned the case of a husband killing his wife with a blow of a fire-brand. Blows, though less severe, are not infrequently dealt out to women' (p. 551).

Furthermore, Bogoras notes that the abduction of women had been practised in the past amongst the Chukchi (Chukchee) which could be followed by the exchange of another woman to replace her or by a blood-revenge incident. A similar situation held true for the Gilyak (Czaplicka 1914). Bogoras also reports that amongst the Chukchi (Chukchee), older brothers can carry their sister off from their husbands against their wishes.

In relation to marriage customs, polygamy was practised amongst the Koryak (Jochelson 1908), the Gilyak (Czaplicka 1914), the Ainu (Batchelor 1901), the Samoyed (Montefiore 1894–5), the Chukchi (Chukchee) (Bogoras 1904) and the Ket (Ostyak) (Pallas 1788a). Polygamy is not that unusual outside of Siberia but in the *locus classicus* it can result in particular stress. As Jochelson (1933) indicates, the custom is that wives are housed separately but the Siberian environment is not economically viable enough for this practice to be affordable. Tensions thereby arise between the wives.

There is evidence of a bride-price system among the Yukaghir (Jochelson 1926), the Gilyak (Czaplicka 1914), the Ket (Ostyak) (Pallas 1788a) and the Samoyed (Pallas 1788b) so that tensions can arise if the reciprocal dowry is not regarded as sufficient, a similar situation to that of the Sakha (Yakut).

Bogoras (1904) notes that for the Chukchi (Chukchee), marriage was not necessarily too permanent and wives could be returned easily. In fact, he found that one third of the Chukchi (Chukchee) had been divorced. Divorce is also easy amongst the Koryak (Jochelson 1908), the Kamchadal (Czaplicka 1914), the Ainu (Batchelor 1901) and the Samoyed (Montefiore 1894–5). As indicated with the Sakha (Yakut) previously, this can lead to mothers being separated from their children because the *sib* groups own the children.

Infanticide was also a practice amongst a number of the Siberian tribes. Krasheninnikoff (1818, as cited in Czaplicka 1914), in commenting on the Kamchadal, says that

> if a child was not desired, there was a widespread custom of causing abortion by shock or by killing the child in the womb. Old women specialists in these matters were found, but they frequently caused the death of the mother. If the undesired infant did not die before birth, the mother strangled it or gave it, living, to the dogs to eat.
>
> (p. 129)

Apparently, the Kamchadal would also kill one twin out of a pair as well as infants who were born during storms.

Similarly, with the Chukchi (Chukchee), Bogoras (1904) reports:

> New-born babes, indeed, after the death of their mothers, are frequently smothered, and carried out with them to the funeral-places, but this is because of the impossibility of raising them. I have heard, too, of women just delivered, who, when feeling very ill, would smother their children as a sacrifice to the spirits.
>
> (p. 48)

And elsewhere he says:

> Sarytcheff says that in his time the Chukchee exposed their misshaped infants . . . Steller mentions that the Kamchadal women of his time had many ways of producing abortion, but that, not satisfied with this, they often also smothered their babes, and then gave the corpses to the dogs, or exposed them alive in the middle of the wood . . . I know of no such practice in modern times. But in the case of a lying-in woman dying in her labors, the babe is often smothered and exposed, together with the mother, in a common funeral . . . D. Crantz says, in his History of Greenland, that, 'with the Greenland Eskimo, a suckling babe which has lost its mother and has no one else to nurse it is soon after buried alive by the desperate father'. . . . The Eskimo of America, moreover, exposed their new-born babies whenever they pleased.
>
> (pp. 513–14)

Bogoras also tells of a starving Yukaghir family who in 1895 resorted to cannibalism of their children. As indicated previously, an infant is in a potentially traumatizing situation if murderous impulses are concretely entertained by the primary caregivers as an actual solution to a problem.

The custom of avoidance which we saw with the Sakha (Yakut) was also practised amongst the Altaians, the Buryat, the Kalmuk (Czaplicka 1914) and the Ket (Ostyak) (Pallas 1788a). As with the Sakha (Yakut), this can place strains on domestic relationships if the mothers, for other reasons, are already experiencing emotional isolation.

Overall, we do not get a positive picture of the position and status of women amongst the main Siberian groups. As with the Sakha (Yakut), there is a possibility in these tribes that these negative factors could so accumulate for certain individuals as to disturb the 'good-enough' mother–infant bond, producing pathological effects on the infants leading to the development of a shaman archetype.

## Conclusions

It needs to be borne in mind that the observations of the early ethnographers were about other things than investigating a connection between difficulties in the early mother–infant relationship and shamanism. That said, it does need to be noted that the historical material overviewed from the Sakha (Yakut) and other Siberian groups supports or is at least in accord with the view that the shaman archetype is a developmentally produced mind/brain structure arising out of intense emotional difficulties experienced by infants in the earliest stages of their preverbal development. Indeed, there is nothing in the material that contradicts this view. Rather, there is evidence of societal practices and customs which could affect the ability of certain mothers to meet the needs of their infants, which would have implications for the efficacy of the early mother–infant dyad. Overall, both the physical and the emotional atmosphere for the Sakha (Yakut) women could be described as harsh and there is a predominance of 'Arctic hysteria' amongst them, including melancholia (depression). There is some evidence that infanticide was practised. The custom of 'avoidance' makes domestic relationships difficult and would work against a sense of inclusion in addition to the effects of the overall low status of the Sakha (Yakut) women in their society. Disputes to do with the bride-price could exacerbate this situation. Again, it needs to be emphasized that none of these customs is necessarily a problem in itself and that a Western criticism of any of them is not implied. Rather, the aim is to see if it is possible for a combination of events to occur whereby the emotional stability of the mother is so disturbed (either in her own early childhood or as an adult at the time of childbirth and immediately following) that emotional mirroring and an attending to her own infant's needs is missing.

What we can see with the Sakha (Yakut), and to some extent with other groups, is the possibility of emotional isolation and victimization of the mother together with distressing childbirth procedures. It is these conditions which in all possibility would produce abnormal affective states from which the mother may want to protect her child; or she may attack her child or use the closeness of the child for her own emotional comfort. In the former circumstance there would be a withdrawal of spontaneous affect so that the mother does 'therapy' with the child rather than parenting (as Winnicott puts it); and in the latter case, the infant becomes narcissistically used (and thus abused) or attacked by the mother. Of course, such response patterns can all occur at the same time, but from the infant's perspective, this would be within a coherent *sib* group with its built-in supports (in fact, the children are owned by the *sib*) so that a situation of 'no other chaos' could quite plausibly be experienced around the central disruption to the mother/infant relationship. This is the recipe (according to Winnicott) for severe psychopathology which, on the one hand, masks itself behind a 'false self' presentation but which, on the other hand, does not slide into full-blown psychosis.

From the ethnography, it does not seem unreasonable to conclude that environmental conditions under which mothering occurs in Sakha (Yakut) society and possibly other Siberian groups, are such as to foment affective states in certain mothers (such as depression and/or anxiety) which could constitute a 'failure of the environment' to such an extent as to be aetiologically implicated in relation to generating a particular kind of psychological development in their infants. I believe it is the intense affectivity of this kind of background which causes a shaman archetype to be developmentally produced and which becomes psychically imbedded as a bio-structural template of response potentials which is later activated in the pre-initiatory illness and which is seen in the resulting shamanic imagery. Ducey (1976) described this psychological construction as 'hysterical psychosis', which is not a current DSM-IV diagnostic category.[5] In the following chapter, a more contemporary model is developed with which to further understand the shaman archetype and the particular wounds in infancy from which it is derived.

# Chapter 9

# The Siberian shaman's wound: A 'borderline type of case'

## Introduction

There would appear to be sufficient evidence from the Sakha (Yakut) Siberian tribe (and to some extent other Siberian groups as well) that the shamanism it displays emerges from an archetypal configuration which has been developmentally produced out of particularly intense emotional woundings that certain individuals have encountered in their early preverbal infant development.

I believe Donald Winnicott's to be the best theories with which to further understand this connection between dysfunctions in the early mother–infant bond and the developmental emergence of a shaman archetype. This is not only because Winnicott combines expertise as both paediatrician and psychoanalyst but also because his theoretical perspective is grounded in infant observation and clinical experience enabling him thereby to formulate a developmental theory of psychopathology which he understands as arising from early infant experience. In particular his concept of 'primary madness' is crucial – the view that the infant initially establishes contact with the environment through hallucinatory illusion and as such cannot be understood to be in contact with reality. Eigen (1986, p. 11) has succinctly pointed out that such ideas originate with Freud's conceptions of the 'id' and 'ego' whereby 'sanity-madness [was made] the basic polarity of human discourse.' He says:

> Freud was able to describe an aspect of the infantile mind as out of contact with the outside world and given to hallucinatory, wish-fulfilling operations . . . [such that] psychotic experience has a certain primacy. . . . A basic madness thus informs human life, and sanity (including neurotic sanity) is a positive and, possibly, a heroic achievement.
>
> (p. 6)

In the same way, Winnicott sees non-madness as a developmental achievement. I believe it is this conception which enables us to understand the 'stable instability' and liminal characteristics of shamans because within an intact personality, they retain pockets of unprocessed emotional dysfunction from this zone of 'primary madness'. Winnicott's is an ideal perspective therefore from which to further explore the particular psychology of the Siberian shaman and the wounds which underpin their wounded healer status.

## Winnicott's formulations

The clearest statements of Winnicott's ideas are in his papers 'Primitive emotional development' (1945), 'Paediatrics and psychiatry' (1948) and 'Psychoses and child care' (1952b). Overall, Winnicott's is a developmental theory of mental illness which argues that

> the emotional development of every infant [involves] complicated processes . . . and that lack of forward movement or completeness of these processes predisposes to mental disorder or breakdown; the completion of these processes forms the basis of mental health. . . . The mental health of the human being is laid down in infancy by the mother, who provides an environment in which complex but essential processes in the infant's self can become completed.
>
> (Winnicott 1948, p. 159)

Winnicott (1945) believed that infants reach a significant stage of development around six months whereby they begin to experience themselves and others as whole persons. Prior to this is the earliest stage of development in which three essential achievements are required. First, an integration out of a primary unintegration; second, personalization (that is, a sense that one's person is in one's body); and third, realization (that is, reality contact).

## The place of environmental impact and the infant

In the earliest stage of development up to six months of age, the infant is not understood to be a unit but rather an 'environment-individual set-up', a kind of somatic-symbiotic interconnection with the mother. What unfolds then for the infant after birth is an ongoing experience of environmental impingement. If this occurs in the context of a good-enough active adaptation to the infant's needs by the mother, then the environment is discovered by the infant (as opposed to being reacted to) and the sense of self is not lost. Alternatively, if the impingement is of a faulty adaptation and thus negative, the infant has to react to it and the sense of self is lost, only to be regained in the return to isolation. As time proceeds this cannot be maintained without more and more defensive organization to try to keep the impingement out and it is this which begins the defensive manoeuvre of splitting which Winnicott (1952b) understands to be the first defensive manoeuvre employed in human experience to deal with the experience of overwhelming feeling states.

Gradually over time through 'good-enough' experiences, the uninte-grated bits come together into an integrated but raw state and 'the individual psyche becomes lodged in the body'. The mother's good care neutralizes the sense of persecution from the outside so that integration and personalization are achieved. Good care is achieved through attention to the bodily needs of the infant and through it being allowed to have its instinctual experiences. However, incomplete integration will lead to the related pathologies of disintegration, depersonalization and dissociation and it is these processes which appear regressively in the psychoses. As Winnicott (1952b) puts it:

> Mental ill-health of psychotic quality arises out of delays and dis-tortions, regressions and muddles, in the early stages of growth of the environment-individual set-up. Mental ill-health emerges imperceptibly out of the ordinary difficulties that are inherent in human nature and that give colour to the task of child care.
>
> (pp. 227–8)

Additionally, a failure at this stage leads to a paranoid potential as the infant is exposed to a sense of persecution from the outside environment. If this situation is extreme, the individual opts to live permanently in their own inner world which is not firmly organized. Consequently, the external persecution is kept at bay at the expense of achieving unit-status. The downside of this scenario is the establishment of a particular inner working model (template) seen in later life as an inability to connect with others in any real relational sense. This is because such individuals oscillate between retreating to a kind of 'living in a bubble' existence when confronted with emotional impingement whilst experiencing a desire/impetus to fuse with love objects so as to close the gap and attain the satisfaction of their needs.[1]

## The infant's 'readiness to hallucinate'

The second aspect of the initial phase of infant development is the readiness for hallucination or illusion as the way of establishing contact between the psyche and the environment. Indeed, from his clinical observations of infants, Winnicott (1941) firmly believed that infant behaviour cannot be accounted for except on the assumption that there are infant fantasies. At this stage the infant is 'ready to believe in something that could exist, i.e. there has developed in the infant a readiness to hallucinate an object' (Winnicott 1948, p. 163). Beginning with the infant approaching the breast with this 'readiness to hallucinate', it conjures up what is actually available, and over time, realization occurs through the progressive build-up of experience of the breast as an actual external reality. As such, the beginning of objectivity is achieved, the converse of which is magical thinking and subjectivity. Winnicott (1952b, p. 224) believed that adult experiences of the arts and religion have their trajectory from this zone which he terms the zone of 'primary madness'.

As indicated previously, 'primary madness' is a crucially important concept because it means that non-madness is actually a developmental achievement. In other words, the foundational human condition is 'madness'; so Santayana's (1926) statement that 'sanity is madness put to good use' is quite a cogent and perceptive comment. Further, though, in relation to shamanism, this concept relativises the debate around the question: is the shaman sane? for shamans are understood to be located on a liminal border zone in relation to their developmental trajectory from 'primary madness' to non-madness.

To return to Winnicott (1952b). In this early 'readiness to hallucinate' stage, the infant is being introduced to actual external reality. Hence, if problems arise at this time the individual will be predisposed to schizoid and schizophrenic states later in life. In other words, emotional development in its earliest stages 'concerns exactly the same phenomena that appear in the study of adult schizophrenia, and of the schizoid states in general and of the organized defences against confusion and un-integration' (p. 222). Thus, psychotic illnesses arise from disruptions and emotional chaos at this stage. In such cases of chaos, splitting defences continue and the end result is a secret inner life (which is truly incommunicable) in which 'magic holds sway' (Winnicott 1948, p. 170), counterpoised with a 'false self' as an adaptive defence (Winnicott 1952b, pp. 224–5).

The idea of the 'false self' is a particular Winnicottian concept and it is understood to be a defensive frontal structure, designed to deal with the dangerously impinging environment, behind which the real individual can hide. It does, however, build itself upon compliance 'with mundane management from outside, convenient because life-giving, but unsatisfactory in the extreme to the infant [because the infant is not actually being its real self]' (Winnicott 1948, p. 170). As Winnicott points out in 'Psychoses and child care' (1952b), the 'false self' can be initially satisfactory and may even acquire a pseudo-maturity, however, the psychotic material behind it is latent and will require attention in the end. Furthermore, the compliance responses associated with the 'false self' can also break down if they are too isolated from the individual's spontaneity. As such, if there is too much routine in such a person's life, external reality lacks meaning and the concomitant feelings of unreality will reveal themselves in a craving for the new. Indeed, problems with reality contact orientate the individual to extreme experiences so as to feel real.

## The infant's use of intellectual processes in development

In so far as normal development is concerned, Winnicott (1952b) maintains that the next major advance by the infant is the use of thinking as a way of dealing with environmental difficulties:

> [The] gap between complete and incomplete adaptation is dealt with by the individual's intellectual processes, by which, gradually, the failures of the environment become allowed for, understood, tolerated, and even predicted. Intellectual understanding converts the not-good-enough environmental adaptation to the good-enough adaptation.
>
> (p. 22)

He goes on to state that this situation is fine if there is no other chaos which causes the environment to behave unsteadily, for unpredictability is traumatic.

In summary then, the earliest phase of personality development requires movement by the infant through a zone of 'primary madness'. If there is a good-enough maternally directed adaptation to the environment then infants achieve reality contact. Infants participate in this unfolding process by way of their intellectual processes, that is, the use of their thinking to overcome the failures in the environment. This healthy line of development can be thwarted in two ways: through inadequate maternally directed adaptation in the first place and/or a situation of 'other chaos' surrounding the mother–infant pair. If the former is primarily the case, then splitting intensifies as a defensive manoeuvre so that a 'false self' is presented to the outside world behind which the individual is caught in the zone of 'primary madness' so that psychotic material lies in the background. If this situation is occurring in an environment of 'no other chaos' then the 'false self' can achieve a pseudo-maturity and the individual is able to function fairly well but the psychotic material in the background will require constant management.

There are two concepts of significance emerging from this overview which need highlighting – the conditions which lead to development of the 'false self' and the possibility of a corresponding and connected situation of 'no other chaos'. For what is suggested is that the addition of 'other chaos' to an inadequate maternally directed adaptation will lead to actual psychosis but that a situation of 'no other chaos' alongside inadequate maternally directed adaptation leads to something else.

It is in his paper on 'Primary maternal preoccupation' that Winnicott (1956) makes more specific the connection between inadequate maternally directed adaptation and a situation of 'no other chaos'.

## Primary maternal preoccupation and the place of 'no other chaos' in infant development

Primary maternal preoccupation is a psychological state which Winnicott (1956) believes mothers enter toward the end of the pregnancy and which lasts for a few weeks after the birth of the child. In it the mother experiences a 'heightened sensitivity, almost an illness' which could be 'compared with a withdrawn state, or a dissociated state, or a fugue, or even with a disturbance at a deeper level such as a schizoid episode in which some aspect of the personality takes over temporarily' (p. 302). Winnicott sees this as a necessary phase because the mother in the first weeks must become absolutely preoccupied with her own infant's needs to the exclusion of other interests. In the ordinary course of events, this situation is temporary and the mother recovers from it. Problems only arise if the life of the infant is threatened or it dies or the mother's anxieties make these a feared possibility or the mother is unsupported to such an extent that she is prevented from going into primary maternal preoccupation.

On the effects of insufficient primary maternal preoccupation with regard to the infant, Winnicott (1956) says that

> without the initial good-enough environmental provision, [the] self that can afford to die never develops. The feeling of real is absent and if there is not too much chaos the ultimate feeling is of futility. . . . *If there is not chaos, there appears a false self that hides the true self . . .* that is only playing for time. . . . [W]hen there has been failure at this first phase, the infant is caught up in primitive defence mechanisms (false self etc.) which belong to the threat of annihilation [italics mine].
>
> (pp. 304–5)

Here we see the nexus between development of a 'false self' and the situation of 'no other chaos' spelled out more succinctly. The situation of 'no other chaos' allows for the development of the 'false self' as a defensive manoeuvre but, as previously indicated, behind the 'false self' is the true self which gets caught in the zone of 'primary madness' and which incorporates psychotic material into its personality organization. As Winnicott (1952b, p. 220) says elsewhere, 'disturbances which can be recognized and labelled as psychotic have their origin in distortions in emotional development arising before the child has clearly become a whole person capable of total relationships with whole persons.' So unlike neurosis, psychosis develops from failure of the individual's environment to satisfy its needs at a very early stage, before emergence of the complete personality. As a result, the individual develops a sense of futility, unrealness and a false self (see Winnicott 1955).

It would appear that pockets of psychotic material can become incorporated into an infant's developing personality because of failures in the maternally directed adaptation to the environment but that it is also possible for this to occur in an environment of 'no other chaos'. It is this situation of 'no other chaos' which aids the emergence of a 'false self' defensive manoeuvre as a way of handling the overall situation. In such a situation we could get the kind of case which Winnicott (1968) describes in his paper on 'The use of an object':

> It is in the analysis of the *borderline type of case* that one has the chance to observe the delicate phenomena that give pointers to an understanding of truly schizophrenic states. By the term 'a borderline case' I mean the kind of case in which *the core of the patient's disturbance is psychotic, but the patient has enough psycho-neurotic organization always to be able to present psycho-neurosis or psycho-somatic disorder* when the central psychotic anxiety threatens to break through in crude form. In such cases the psychoanalyst may collude for years with the patient's need to be psychoneurotic (as opposed to mad) and to be treated as psychoneurotic. The analysis goes well, and everyone is pleased. The only drawback is that the analysis never ends. It can be terminated, and the patient may even mobilize a psychoneurotic *false self* for the purpose of finishing and expressing gratitude. But, in fact, the patient knows that there has been no change in the underlying (psychotic) state and that the analyst and the patient have succeeded in colluding to bring about a failure [italics mine].
>
> (p. 102)

I am proposing that such a situation can occur because the individual's earliest development has had two aspects running in parallel: inadequate maternally directed adaptation to the environment during the early phases of the mother–infant pair but in a situation of 'no other chaos' which prevents the psychotic material from spilling out into (or developing into) full-blown madness. It is this constitution which makes up the 'borderline type of case' where a neurotic 'false self' can be mobilized to counteract the real problem, which is of a psychotic nature. Winnicott's (1952a) conceptions of the 'kernel' and 'shell' components to personality structure shed further light on this process.

## 'Kernel' and 'shell' personality development

In Winnicott's (1952a) paper on 'Anxiety associated with insecurity' he says that without a good-enough technique of infant care the new human being has no chance whatever. With a good-enough technique the centre of gravity of being in the environment-individual set-up can afford to lodge in the centre, in the kernel rather than in the shell. The human being now developing an entity from the centre can become localized in the baby's body and so can begin to create an external world at the same time as acquiring a limiting membrane and an inside. [The converse is of] an environment developing falsely into a human being, hiding within itself a potential individual.

(pp. 99–100)

I believe that by introducing the concepts of 'kernel' and 'shell', Winnicott is indicating the possibility that an infant's earliest experience in the mother–infant dyad across the first six months of life could lead to development of the centre ('kernel') part of the overall personality but further developmental experience could constitute the outer layers ('shell') of personality structure. In such a conception it would be possible for an individual to have a psychotic core to their personality but within outer layers of functioning, if these outer layers have developed in an environment of 'no other chaos'. I believe that it is these conceptions which give us a glimpse into the intrapsychic constitution behind Siberian shamanism and which give us an understanding as to how the shaman archetype is a developmentally produced mind/brain structure.[2]

In aligning these ideas about severe emotional difficulties in the early mother–infant pair alongside a 'no other chaos' situation which enables certain individuals to organize strong enough ego defences around a 'psychotic core', we may be getting a glimpse of what is actually happening within Siberian shamanism given the evidence we have connecting shamanic psychology to early mother–infant difficulties. The suggestion is opened that shamans may be psychologically constructed like a 'borderline type of case' where the outer layers of their personality are functional because they have developed in a situation of 'no other chaos' but this masks psychotic material at the core level of development because of the environmental failures at the time of the 'environment-individual set-up'. Shamans could, thereby, still experience 'primary madness' and it is this which would enable them to access experiences of magic and transpersonal imagery.

Furthermore, the situation of 'no other chaos' could easily be the case with Siberian shamans as they would be surviving their early infant experiences within intact societies and extended family and *sib* groups. It is these latter which would provide an emotional containment of 'no other chaos' alongside the emotional difficulties being experienced in the 'environment-individual set-up' with the mother. This 'no other chaos' would aid their integration as would the mastery inherent in their initiation and training not to mention the ego-strength developed by what they have already been – and will continue to be – forced to overcome.

Given these conceptions, it is no longer a question of 'are shamans mentally ill?' using Western diagnostic categories. Rather it is to assert that all infants go through a stage of 'primary madness' and that non-madness is a developmental achievement as an emergent phenomenon out of this zone where 'magic holds sway'. In other words, the muddles, distortions and traumas experienced by an infant in the earliest stages of development will position them along a normal–abnormal continuum. The extent of derangement and psychotic material will depend on the distortions experienced in the earliest months of life together with the effects of any 'other chaos'. In relation to any individual's position along this continuum, Winnicott's concept of 'no other chaos' being an experiential atmosphere after initial disturbances allows for an explanation as to how individuals who may be quite disturbed can develop sufficient personality organization to present as normal when in fact their earliest layers of development are anything but normal. I believe that Siberian shamans are a variant on these processes – a 'borderline type of case' which enables them to be stable enough to function coherently in their sociocultural group but which also allows them to access psychic material from the zone of 'primary madness' which underpins their magico-religious experiences. However, the 'borderline type of case' being proposed here is something different from the current psychiatric diagnostic category of Borderline Personality Disorder and as such, the term and concept of 'borderline' needs further explication.

## What is a 'borderline type of case' actually like?

The word 'borderline' was first used by Stern (1938) to describe a type of patient who was appearing in consulting rooms displaying both neurotic and psychotic characteristics but who did not fall easily into either diagnostic category. Clinicians soon came to see these patients as characterized by what Schmideberg (1947) described as a 'stable instability'. Grinker (1977, p. 162) concluded from his research that

> the borderline is a specific syndrome with a considerable degree of internal consistency and stability and not a regressive state in response to some internal or external conditions of stress. It represents a syndrome characteristic of arrested development of ego functions. Clinicians have recognized that the borderline syndrome is a confusing combination of psychotic, neurotic, and character disturbances with many normal or healthy elements. Although such symptoms are unstable, the syndrome itself as a process is recognizably stable, giving rise to the paradoxical term 'stable instability'.

As diagnostic clarity emerged over the years, it is the 'stable instability' which has remained as a distinguishing feature of borderline disorders. Peters (1988) concluded that

> the borderline patient is different from the psychotic patient because of the capacity for rapid recovery (often to previous levels of functioning) with nominal therapeutic intervention, relatively good reality testing, ability to establish a therapeutic alliance, more adequate object relations and no residual after-effects of cognitive and affective disorganization that mark the chronic psychoses. However, this stable personality organization remains constricted and impoverished, displaying many of the diagnostic indicators mentioned in DSM III.[3]

(pp. 11–12)

Eventually a particular clinical category of Borderline Personality Disorder was formulated but as with the other personality disorders, it is a psychiatric classification which only became listed in the American Psychiatric Association's *Diagnostic and Statistical Manual of Mental Disorders* in 1980. Gunderson (2001) notes that there are few publications on Borderline Personality Disorder up until and including 1975 with only five books being published on the disorder over the period 1968–74. It is perfectly understandable, therefore, that Ducey (1976), when undertaking his psychoanalytic approach to Siberian shamans, would not have come up with a diagnostic label which included 'borderline' characteristics.

In overviewing the research on Borderline Personality Disorder, Gunderson (2001) indicates that it has virtually no genetic basis but rather arises within a family environment of high conflict and unpredictability and where there are high incidences of sexual abuse. He also cites research showing that the caregivers of many borderline patients are depressed, disturbed or abusive and that this has flow-on effects into the well-being of their infants. Our previous overview of the Sakha (Yakut) tribe reveals a similar kind of environment in which the mother–infant pairs of that tribe could find themselves.

Gunderson (2001, p. 44) elaborates by saying that the 'social conditions needed for BPD [Borderline Personality Disorder] to develop require emotional estrangement from parents' and further that:

> Their family experience often includes marital discord, abandonment, violence, and substance abuse [so that the resulting Borderline Personality Disorder is] marked by broken identities, primitive defenses, and transient failures in reality testing. . . . So disturbed is the development of many BPD . . . individuals that it seems unnecessary to invoke genetic causality.

(p. 54)

In using Ainsworth *et al.*'s (1978) attachment terminology, Gunderson (2001) notes that those with Borderline Personality Disorder display an oscillating maternal attachment pattern around two loci. The first is termed an 'anxious/ambivalent' dimension which is characterized by the need to check for caretaker proximity, signalling need for contact by pleading and other calls for attention and clinging behaviours. The other is a 'disorganized/ disoriented' pattern which denies dependency needs with an apparent absence of separation anxiety and a reluctance or fear of becoming attached. Gunderson indicates that a number of clinicians believe this alternating attachment pattern to be the core psychopathology of Borderline Personality Disorder. This is particularly noteworthy because of the approach/avoidance component as illustrated in Winnicott's model above.

## The Siberian shaman as 'proto-borderline'

It should be noted that it is a questionable exercise to use Western psychiatric diagnostic criteria to look at another culture, although in terms of individuals we know from early research that the major clinical disorders do appear consistently across cultures (Murphy 1976). When cross-cultural surveys of schizophrenia and depression were undertaken, 'core symptomatology' could be detected despite cultural influences (see Murphy *et al.* 1963 and Murphy *et al.* 1967). There would be no reason to suspect the core symptomatology of Borderline Personality Disorder to be any different.

Whilst the DSM-IV clinical category of Borderline Personality Disorder does specify a psychiatric category indicative of gross psychopathology, the kind of 'borderline type of case' I am proposing here in relation to Siberian shamans is indicative of something less 'full-blown' but rather a variant on a continuum toward Borderline Personality Disorder. Its roots arise during early child development when the infant is transitioning the zone of 'primary madness'. Failures in the environment for the infant due to inadequate mothering at this stage predispose the infant to splitting defences so that the core of their personality remains fixed at this primitive level of development. Hence one aspect of their personality structure will be psychotic in nature. For Siberian shamans, it is this psychotic core which underpins their magico-religious experiences. If the developmental environment contains 'no other chaos' then the later outer levels of personality can develop quite functionally but the psychotic core remains active. Whether any individual develops a complete Borderline Personality Disorder or this less severe 'borderline type of case' will depend on the extent and severity of damage in the zone of 'primary madness' plus the quality of the 'no other chaos' experiences. In this way, the 'borderline type of case' can be understood to occupy a place along a continuum, the extreme pole of which would be Borderline Personality Disorder, and so a more apt term which captures the dynamic of the Siberian shaman's psychology would be 'proto-borderline'.

## Summary

I believe that 'proto-borderline' is the best way to describe the psychology of Siberian shamans. Overall, evidence suggests that they do function coherently in their own sociocultural groups which would indicate they do not suffer with gross psychopathology (such as psychiatric Borderline Personality Disorder). In fact, in many Siberian tribes, individuals with gross psychopathology are recognized as quite separate to those who are shamans. As Basilov (1984, p. 26) points out, across Siberia and the Far North 'the shaman was clearly distinguished from the neuropath.'[4]

The proto-borderline model of the Siberian shaman's psychology as proposed here also gives us a clearer understanding as to the particular wounds which underpin their wounded healer status. They are wounded healers because they have been emotionally wounded in the earliest stages of preverbal infant experience – the zone of 'primary madness' where 'magic holds sway'. The intense affectivity during this stage of their development produces a 'shaman archetype' image schema which acts as a scaffold from which later shamanic imagery can emerge. The subsequent experience of the pre-initiatory illness is a later breakout of unprocessed emotional material which underpins the shaman archetype as a mind/brain structure. In many cases this breakout seems to be triggered by the onset of puberty and is similar to a psychotic episode, the mastery of which gives the initiates a capacity and credibility within their tribal group to function as recognized shamans. It is through this mastery that they attain their wounded healer status and this in an ongoing way because the emergence of the developmentally produced mind/brain shaman archetype structure has the capacity to directly influence psychological life. It is this functioning which underpins the later imaginal experiences of these shamans.

There is evidence from the ethnographic records that Siberian shamans exhibit 'borderline' characteristics and this substantially corroborates the proto-borderline model of the Siberian shaman's psychology as presented here.

# Chapter 10

# Evidence that the Siberian shaman is proto-borderline

## Introduction

There are a number of lines of evidence from the ethnographic records pointing to a proto-borderline psychology for the Siberian shaman: there are hints to this feature by some writers; there is almost a universal presence of dismemberment imagery in shamanic initiation; self-mutilating behaviour is widely encountered; the shamanic characteristic of 'liminality' in itself is suggestive of a stable instability; there is evidence of intense and profound anger as well as impulsivity amongst some shamans; and there would appear to be a connection between Siberian shamanism and psychological derangement. In particular, the extensive ethnography gained on the Siberian Chukchi (Chukchee) tribe by Bogoras (1904) during the Jesup North Pacific expedition proves useful. This is because shamanism appears to be a phenomenon spread across the entire tribe in the form of 'family shamanism' and borderline characteristics can be noted to run in parallel with it.[1]

In the following evaluations there will be occasions where I refer to the DSM-IV criteria for Borderline Personality Disorder, this being one of the simplest ways of getting an understanding as to the borderline characteristic noted from the ethnography. The entire criteria appear in Appendix B. However, I do need to emphasize (as I have stated previously) that I am not thereby arguing that Siberian shamans suffer with Borderline Personality Disorder. Rather, their psychology exhibits something less 'full-blown', hence 'proto-borderline', which occupies a place along a continuum, the extreme pole of which would be Borderline Personality Disorder.

## Hints in the literature

Larry Peters seems to be the first to suggest there may be some connection between shamanism and Borderline Personality Disorder but this is only in a very passing way. In his paper, 'Borderline personality disorder and the possession syndrome: An ethnopsychoanalytic perspective', Peters (1988) investigates the relationships between Borderline Personality Disorder and Bourguignon's (1976) 'negative possession trance'. The 'negative possession trance' is defined as an undesired and spontaneous Altered State of Consciousness in which a person's actions are interpreted as being under the influence of an alien spirit. Peters examines these disorders from the perspective of object relations theory and the core symptoms of Borderline Personality Disorder are compared to the 'possession syndromes' reported in certain cultures. Peters concluded that 'negative possession trance' is a cross-cultural variant of Borderline Personality Disorder.

Whilst Peters is particularly interested in the 'possession syndrome', he does in passing note the parallel between shamans' dreams and hallucinatory experiences and those of borderline patients. He sees cultural processes as accounting for the 'creative reconstitution' of the 'psychological states which begin as schizophreniform' but which can be made 'socially beneficial' through group acceptance and affiliation (which militates against isolation), initiation, the positive effects of a shared and agreed upon mythology and the status and role which the neophyte ultimately assumes.

Eight years later in his 'The contribution of anthropology to transpersonal psychiatry', Peters (1996) discussed several cross-cultural and transpersonal principles of healing, particularly psychic healing through shamanic rituals. Peters paralleled these healing principles with rites of passage and then applied these principles to the successful treatment of a case of Western Borderline Personality Disorder. He takes the position that Borderline Personality Disorder is culture-related and on the increase in the West because Western cultures lack 'clear mores and structures for the young' unlike traditional societies, a point he has made previously (Peters 1994). As such, 'rites of passage, like healing rituals, assist people through life crises and have similar transformational structure' (Peters 1996, p. 209) so that '[c]risis, suspension of convention, altered states of consciousness, transcendent symbols, and community can transmute apparent psychopathology into psychological and spiritual growth' (p. 214). In this way Peters does seem to align with Eliade (1964) in thinking that shamans have done something so creative and purposeful with their psychological problems that any psychopathology can ultimately be discounted. Nonetheless, parallels between the shaman's experience and those with Borderline Personality Disorder are implied in his position and as such, the psychology of the shaman could very well be proto-borderline in the way I argue. The wounded healer component in Peters' analysis is also noteworthy.

## The presence of dismemberment imagery in Siberian shamanism

Eliade (1964, 1987) makes the observation that the experience of dismemberment imagery during the shamanic calling/initiation does seem a consistently common theme across a number of Siberian groups. This has been confirmed by later researchers, such as Hutton (2001), who, although questioning the universal aspect for which Eliade argues, does acknowledge that a 'common theme across a swathe of Central Siberia, from the Sagays through the Evenks and Sakha to the Nganasan, was that the novice underwent the terrifying dream-experience of being physically dismembered and then reconstructed' (p. 73).

Such descriptions of dismemberment do raise the question from a psychological perspective as to underlying psychotic tendencies. Over the years, psychiatric researchers have endeavoured to identify typical dreams of various clinical categories such as schizophrenia, depression and Borderline Personality Disorder (see Kramer 1969, Natterson 1980, Oremland 1987, and Richardson and Moore 1963 as examples). However, Friedman (1992) concludes that overall, the results have been disappointing although certain statistical trends can be noted. One such trend amongst those with severe internal pathology such as psychosis or borderline dynamics is dreams that 'depict extreme violence, fragmented and mutilated body parts, cannibalism, and so on' (p. 19) although Friedman also notes that such imagery can occur in the dreams of neurotics and normals. Nonetheless, the trend corroborates Stone's (1979) earlier assertion that dream imagery of dismemberment, death of the dreamer, etc. can indicate extreme psychopathology, often of a borderline nature.[2]

Dismemberment is one aspect of Siberian shamanism which Eliade (1964) particularly uses to illustrate shamanism's universality because it is one thing which occurs in groups so distant from each other that cultural transmission can be ruled out, for example between Siberia, Australia and South America. As he says, 'this likeness [that is, dismemberment] between Australia and Siberia markedly confirms the authenticity and antiquity of shamanic initiation rites' (p. 61). Despite Eliade utilizing this common phenomenon to construct a universal pattern for shamanism, such a common theme across such distant cultures is noteworthy and does support the position being advanced here that the shaman's psychology is proto-borderline. In other words, it is not surprising that dismemberment would be a universal aspect of the shamanic call/initiation because it reflects the proto-borderline type of psychology which is the one predisposed to such a 'call'.

### An example of a Siberian shaman's dismemberment

The most illustrative example of dismemberment imagery among Siberian shamans comes from the case of the Nganasan (Tavgi Samoyed) shaman Sereptie Djaruoskin, as recorded by the Soviet ethnographer Popov (1968, p. 142). In describing his calling to the shamanic vocation, Sereptie Djaruoskin says that at one stage in the process (entering the seventh tent) he 'went in, not as a man but as a skeleton; I don't know who gnawed me off, I don't know how it happened.' Indeed, the inhabitants of the tent 'did not look like real human beings but like skeletons which had been dressed.' As with similar material from Australian aboriginals such an experience was enacted on initiates so that they could be reconstituted. As Sereptie Djaruoskin says: 'When I entered as a skeleton and they forged, it meant they forged me' (ibid.). Whilst the tone of these recollections is thereby positive, it is also of interest that during this process Sereptie Djaruoskin does say: 'This is my fate – to lose my mind' (ibid.).

There is a salient difference between the dismemberment imagery of Westerners and that reported for Siberian shamans – there is a positive outcome in the shaman's case. In current clinical work, such positive outcomes would generally be interpreted as indicative of sufficient internal structure to overcome the psychic fragmentation(s) being experienced. This would again align with the proto-borderline model being presented here because the core part of the personality which has developed in an environment of 'no other chaos' is sufficiently functional to mobilize a degree of transformation of the internal psychotic component and/or sufficient defensive structures which aid functionality have been mobilized.

## The presence of self-mutilating behaviour in Siberian shamanism

Self-mutilation generally indicates psychopathology and it is one of the most noted characteristics in Western Borderline Personality Disorder. DSM-IV specifies its Criterion Five thus: 'Recurrent suicidal behaviour, gestures, or threats, or self-mutilating behaviour (this criterion seems to be the most marked and noted for Borderline Personality Disorder sufferers).'[3]

In relation to Siberian shamans, Basilov (1984) indicates that stabbing and cutting of themselves is not unknown and Bogoras (1904) gives a number of examples of self-mutilating behaviour amongst those from the Chukchi (Chukchee) tribe. The following case of Akɪ'mlʌkê is indicative:

> Among the Reindeer Chukchee on the Wolverene River I knew a man by the name of Akɪ'mlʌkê ('Marrowless'), who gave himself out as a shaman, though the people usually did not pay much attention to his claim. At the times of ceremonials, Akɪ'mlʌkê would pretend that a ke'lɛ had entered his body and was bent on destroying his life. He would usually spend a part of his time crawling about in search of a knife. The women of his house, however, well aware of this holy-day custom of his, usually took care to conceal all knives and other sharp weapons. Once, at a thanksgiving ceremonial at which I was present, he began his usual search, and came to me, among others, explaining with signs his desire for a knife, in order to be able to destroy himself. The 'spirit' who possessed his body could not speak the human language. I

really had a knife on my belt: and a Russian cossack who sat next to me proposed laughingly that I give it to Akɪ'mlʌkê. Hearing this, the women of the house raised a frightened cry. Akɪ'mlʌkê, however, who doubtless was stung by the taunt implied in the words of the cossack, suddenly picked up from the ground a long, sharp-pointed chip of wood, and, baring his abdomen, put one end of the stick on his body, and the other against my breast. Then he made a thrust forward with the whole weight of his heavy body. The chip, of course, was snapped in two. One end flew up and hit me on the brow very near to the left eye, leaving an ugly gash. The other end cut a deep scratch entirely across the abdomen of Akɪ'mlʌkê. I wonder that it had not been driven in. All this was done so quick that nobody had time to interfere.

Akɪ'mlʌkê with much coolness picked up a handful of snow, and, wiping off the blood from his abdomen, quietly went to another tent. In half an hour, when he was no longer thirsty for blood, I asked him about his actions; but he disclaimed all knowledge, and expressed the utmost wonder when showed the bloody scratch on his abdomen.

(ibid., pp. 442–3)

This account of Akɪ'mlʌkê is quite telling because it definitely suggests a connection between shamanic activity and self-mutilating behaviour. Of course, it could be the case that Akɪ'mlʌkê is just more psychologically disturbed than other shamans and it is this which has caused the account to be preserved because of the bizarre nature of the material. It is difficult to determine. However, the fact that Akɪ'mlʌkê experienced complete amnesia in relation to his stabbing attempts is noteworthy in relation to borderline dynamics because amnesia indicates dissociation and dissociation is generally regarded as being connected to the defensive manoeuvre of splitting.

Borderline Personality Disorder sufferers do tend to rely on defences such as splitting because the disorder has arisen from the pre-Oedipal zone of psychological development where splitting is the first defensive manoeuvre of the infant. Of significance in relation to shamanism, Grotstein (1981) argues that splitting can occur to such an extent that separate personalities emerge:

'Split-off' really means that part of one's being has undergone aliena-tion, mystification, and repersonification – in effect has become someone else, an alien presence within . . . splitting is an act of imagi-nation which bequeaths to the split-off portions of the personality a life-support system with a will to live, which repersonifies this creation in a way that it may well be thought of as someone else.

(pp. 11–12)

It is in this way that dissociation would give a psychological explanation to the possession trance phenomena exhibited by shamans.

To return to the Chukchi (Chukchee), Bogoras (1904, p. 446) also noted that 'the exploit of stabbing one's self with a knife is one of the most common achievements of the shamanistic art, and it is so generally practised that the spectators are said to ascribe little importance to it.' In other words, it would appear that cutting and stabbing oneself with knives had become part of shamanic performance. Bogoras relates how Chukchi (Chukchee) tales often recounted stabbing as a shamanistic achievement. For instance, in transferring his power to another, a shaman may stab himself and then the recipient and on several occasions Bogoras says he witnessed shamans trying to stab themselves. Similarly, Scratching Woman (one of Bogoras' shaman informants) showed Bogoras a deep scar which he maintained was produced by stabbing and on another occasion, a young shaman-girl was described in an account of a family feud as a 'woman able to stab herself' with impunity.

Bogoras (1904) relates similar stabbing practices amongst the Yukaghir:

> [I]n the village Pyatistennoye I found . . . an old wooden knife covered with dark spots, which were said by the natives to be the shaman's blood, which flowed down when he stabbed himself through the abdomen.
>
> Krasheninnikoff describes a Kamchadal shaman, who likewise stabbed himself with a knife while having the fur shirt on, and then drew from under its cover handfuls of blood, which he swallowed.
>
> Sarytcheff tells the same of a Yakut shaman, who not only stabbed himself through the abdomen, but even ordered his assistant to drive in the knife with a log up to the handle. After that the shaman came to the hearth, took three burning coals, and swallowed them with much composure and without any visible pain.
>
> (p. 447)

Of course, it could be the case that shamanistic self-cure has enabled self-mutilation to become transformed into a stabbing technique which is then used to indicate shamanistic prowess. Novik (1984) is certainly of the opinion that shamans turn cutting and self-mutilation into a healing iso-morphism on behalf of others rather than themselves. The case of Akɪ'mlʌkê above could be illustrating something at the more primitive end of this transformation process. Dolgikh's (1962, as cited in Novik 1984) example of the Enet shaman, Narzale, precisely illustrates this point:

> I then began to shamanize and did not kill the reindeer. . . . Instead of the reindeer, I cut my own head with the leash, as one chokes a reindeer. I stabbed myself, as though piercing it in this way. It is the

illness that I was stabbing. Had I not stabbed and choked myself, the sick one would not have recovered. Further on in the story it is told how Narzale, after receiving presents, went away, and sometime later . . . [was] . . . killed by a bear. Commenting on his death, the relatives of the cured man came to the following conclusion: 'The bear killed him because he gave up his own soul for the sick man. Did he not choke himself here and give up his soul for the sick man? He said to the *kacha* [spirit of illness] "take my soul instead of the sick one". That is why he died. Why else should a bear come out of its lair in the winter and kill him?'

(p. 201)

It could very well be the case that shamans transform self-mutilating impulses into a healing isomorphism as part of their mastery but its presence in the first place does add corroborating evidence to the view that the Siberian shaman's psychology is of a proto-borderline nature.

## The characteristic of 'liminality' within Siberian shamanism

It is not uncommon for commentators to note that Siberian shamans occupy a zone between psychopathology and normality which is exactly what one would expect if they are proto-borderline, for we have already seen 'stable instability' to be a borderline characteristic. Ducey (1976) puts it this way:

[The shaman] bridges the gap between the known and the unknown, between the cognitively understood and the affectively apprehended, a gap created by suffering, by intrapsychic or interpersonal conflict. Viewed from another angle, he occupies a position in the two realms simultaneously: he functions within his everyday world precisely by going beyond it into the world of fantasy (the supernatural). Hence each group of investigators has been correct but has focused on one extreme of the duality. . . . In other words, the controversy over the relationship of madness and shamanism may be viewed as a variant of, or at least a parallel to, the controversy over the relationship of madness and creativity.

(pp. 175–6)

Consequently, Ducey (1976, p. 177) concludes that with shamans '[h]ealthy and pathological patterns are too deeply interwoven to be meaningfully separated.'

The inherent characteristic of 'stable instability' would explain the divergence of opinion on the psychopathology issue reflected in the literature generally because either the healthy or the psychopathological perspective could be emphasized depending on which aspect of the shaman's psychology one concentrated upon.

## Intense and profound anger amongst Siberian shamans

Intense and profound anger is also an indication of borderline dynamics and this is reflected in DSM-IV's Criterion Four: 'Inappropriate, intense anger or lack of control of anger (e.g. frequent displays of temper, constant anger, recurrent physical fights).'

From Bogoras' (1904) observations amongst the Chukchi (Chukchee) we can find a number of examples of shamans whose behaviour aligns with a tendency toward intense and profound anger. First, there is the shaman Kele'wgi, 'who seeks a quarrel on the slightest provocation' (p. 426) and who on one occasion drew his knife on a Cossack who did not want to pay 'an exorbitant price' for reindeer-skins. Bogoras also says Kele'wgi quarrelled with him over payment for interviews.

Second, of the shaman Scratching Woman, Bogoras (1904, p. 427) says he could not sit long in one place 'but every little while he would jump up with violent gestures.' He also displayed hysterical symptoms of a pain 'somewhere inside his back'. He would quarrel with his neighbours and had an 'exceedingly bad' temper when under the influence of alcohol so much so that Scratching Woman's wife had to keep knives away from him. As he himself said:

> 'Drink really makes my temper too bad for anything. Usually my wife watches over me, and puts all knives out of my reach. But when we are apart, I am afraid.' With this he showed me a long scar on his shoulder, which he said was the result of a drunken brawl when his wife could not watch over his actions.
>
> (p. 428)

Third, the shaman Te'lpīñä, 'according to her own words, had been violently insane for three years, during which time her household had taken such precautions, that she could do no harm to the people or to herself' (Bogoras 1904, p. 428).

The tendency toward violent anger did seem to be a characteristic of many of the shamans Bogoras was able to observe.

## Some evidence of impulsivity in Siberian shamanism

Impulsivity is also an indication of borderline dynamics and this is reflected in DSM-IV's Criterion Two – 'Impulsivity in at least two areas that are potentially self-damaging, e.g. spending, sex, substance abuse, reckless driving, binge eating (do not include suicidal or self-mutilating behaviour covered in Criterion 5).'

Two Chukchi (Chukchee) shamans with whom Bogoras (1904) was familiar could be said to display impulsive kinds of behaviour. He describes Ñïro'n as 'a spendthrift, much given to card–playing, and cared little for his herd and home' (p. 422); and second, Scabby–shaman, who is described as displaying erotomania by running about naked from tent to tent and raping women. Both of these short vignettes could be described as indicating issues to do with impulse control.

## The connection between Siberian shamanism and psychological derangement

It is possible to find in the Siberian anthropological literature examples of those who either become shamans as a result of suffering significant psychological derangement or who during the initiation phase suffer such derangement. Bogoras' (1904) material on the Chukchi (Chukchee) is illustrative here. As he says: 'There are cases of young persons who, having suffered for years from lingering illness (usually of a nervous character), at last feel a call to take to shamanistic practice, and by this means overcome the disease' (p. 421). And he mentions a number of cases that illustrate this theme. For example, Te'lpïñä whom we encountered above and who, 'according to her own words, had been violently insane for three years' (ibid., p. 428).

Elsewhere, Bogoras says:

> [I]t is entirely permissible to abandon shamanistic performances at a more mature age. . . . [One shaman] said that he and his 'spirits' became tired of each other. Most of the cases, probably, were simply the result of recovery from the nervous condition which had made the persons in question fit subjects for the inspiration.
>
> (ibid., p. 419)

Furthermore, it would appear that the very act of shamanizing seems to keep a kind of derangement at bay. Bogoras (1904, p. 419) says that 'while the shaman is in possession of the inspiration, he must practise, and cannot hide his power. Otherwise it will manifest itself in the form of bloody sweat or in a fit of violent madness similar to epilepsy.'

We find similar accounts from the early first-hand ethnography of Jochelson. In his work on the Yukaghir and the Yukaghirized Evenk (Tungus), Jochelson (1926, p. 31) speaks of the 'nervously strained youths who are inclined to become shamans'. In fact, one Yukaghir word for shaman is *i'rkeye* ('the trembling one') which could indicate their 'nervous strain'. Jochelson later describes a performance by the shaman Athanasy. It was so wild it terrified the Yukaghir for 'his performance was like an attack of madness or delirium tremens'. Jochelson describes Athanasy as being 'psychically unbalanced and abnormal' and 'wildly neuropathic' (ibid., p. 199).

Similarly, with the Koryak, Jochelson (1908) says:

> Those that become shamans are usually nervous young men subject to hysterical fits, by means of which the spirits express their demand that the young man should consecrate himself to the service of shamanism. I was told that people about to become shamans have fits of wild paroxysm alternating with a condition of complete exhaustion. They will lie motionless for two or three days without partaking of food or drink. Finally they retire to the wilderness, where they spend their time enduring hunger and cold in order to prepare themselves for their calling.
>
> (p. 47)

In similar fashion in his later fieldwork among the Yukaghir and the Yukaghirized Evenk (Tungus), Jochelson (1926, p. 31) says that '[t]he future shaman complains, in the song, of the spirits that compel him to start the shaman's career, strangle him, and threaten death if he does not consent to follow their call.'

Other accounts indicating the connection between derangement and Siberian shamanism occur in early Russian sources summarized and in part translated by Znamenski (2003). The following is from Anfilov's 1902 account of the séance he witnessed with the Samoyed (Nentsy) shaman Nigalai. The séance began with Nigalai in conversation with his spirits but then it seemed as though the spirit had departed. Znamenski continues:

> The failure of the shaman to attract the attention of his spiritual interlocutor made Nigalai '*totally crazy*'. 'He ran around from one side to another, beating his drum with a wild anger and shouting something that we could not comprehend'. Finally, he . . . 'started to howl in an inhuman and piercing voice. . . . The shaman writhed in convulsions, feverishly tearing away from his chest metal trinkets and cutting his hands with them'. . . .
>
> [T]he Russian observers tried to help the shaman, but the native audience had to evict them literally by force, warning that 'now Nigalai is going to cut everything with his knife!' After they dragged Anifilov . . . out of the dwelling, the Samoyeds themselves scattered away in panic, hiding from the '*crazy shaman*'. . . . [Anfilov] learned from a native who happened to be around that Nigalai indeed ran outside with

a knife and cut the throat of a reindeer, then he cut to death a nearby dog . . . and tried to stab one of the natives. As it turned out, it was not the first time when the shaman '*went mad*'. The Samoyed . . . later told them, 'Last year the same thing happened. If he cannot learn anything [from spirits] during his flight, *Nigalai goes mad*. But if he learns something, he is all right'. Both friends surmised that when spirits did not reveal anything to the shaman, Nigalai lost control of himself and experienced a fit. . . . He is definitely not a charlatan and 'shamanizes' sincerely. Having plunged himself in a 'shamanic trance', *he genuinely loses his mind*. By giving himself up to mysterious spirits, he loses contact with all earthly things. He drives himself to the *extreme of madness* and cuts with his knife whatever he sees [italics mine].

(ibid., pp. 49–50)

In a similar fashion, Anokhin (1910, as cited in, summarized and in part translated by Znamenski 2003) tells of his experiences among the Altaians:

The Altaians are terrified of the power of spirits. . . . 'I believe this feeling of fear was primarily responsible for the spread among the Turkic tribes of a *nervous disease* called *belinchi*. People who are sick with this ailment are called *belinchi-kizhi*, which could be rendered as "possessed"'. *Belinchi-kizhi* usually experience fits and are prone to hypnosis. They frequently run away to woods and wander there for days. *Belinchi-kizhi* are easily [*sic*] to manipulate, and they instinctively imitate the behavior and voices of other people. Anokhin thinks that *belinchi* is a special form of epilepsy. This and similar 'ailments' are considered spirit calls from an internal force called *tös* that signals to a chosen individual to accept the shamanic vocation. . . . An old shamaness named Uituk, from the Chibit village, complained to Anokhin that after Altaian Burkhanists (native religious reformers) burned her drum and shamanic costume, she could not shamanize. As a result, 'satans' (*körmös*) constantly 'pressed' her and forced her to continue her vocation. She added that *when she was alone in her yurt, these spirits attacked her and 'chewed' her legs and hands* [italics, except for native terms, mine]

(pp. 51–2)

From more recent ethnography we find similar accounts indicating the connection between Siberian shamanism and psychological derangement. The Hungarian ethnographer Vilmos Diószegi undertook an ethnographic research expedition through Siberia in 1957–8 and had met the Soyot shaman Suzukpen. After recording him in shamanic performance, Diószegi (1968) enquired as to how he acquired his powers. Suzukpen then related this story: He had been hunting with two of his brothers when they came across a crow in their path. The crow did not move so Suzukpen threw some snow at it but to no avail. He continues:

> Then I hit its beak with my stick. Kok-kok. The knock resounded loudly. What was all this? What was going to happen to me? Because the night before – before seeing the crow – I had already felt miserably. Next day I went back to where I had seen the crow. Not even a trace of it was to be seen, anywhere! Although the others, that is, my brothers, have seen it too. From then on, from the time I hit the beak of that crow, I became very ill. *My mind was deranged.* I have been suffering for as long as seven years. Finally, I began to shamanize, because everybody kept saying all along: *I must shamanize in order to get well again.* Nine years after I became ill, I gave in at last and ordered the drum and the drumstick because I had been urged to take up shamanizing [italics mine].
>
> (pp. 279–80)

In summarizing his findings to Professor Potapov, who was director of the then Leningrad Ethnographic Institute, Diószegi goes on to say of the shamans he had opportunity to observe that

> there were notable individual traits in every single one of them, which were not characteristic of the other members of their ethnic group in general.
>
> The Buryat shaman, Hadi, was an introvert. He was *neurotic.* He had frequent *hallucinations.* Chibadayev, the Beltir, was extremely *misanthropic.* Chibadyakhov was also rather like an introvert person, evidently *neurotic* too. The Sagay, Kizlasov, was of poor physical condition, he suffered from constant headaches. All the time that I was with him, he had cold compresses upon his forehead, daily. Borgoyakhov was *psychopathic.* His mouth was constantly open, his tongue hung out and it kept jerking like that of a dog. The Karagasy Kukuyev was taciturn and shy. His capacity of concentration was poor and failing. At the time of full moon he suffered from headaches. While I was there he had several nose-bleeds.
>
> The Soyot Ak Nitka was a *misanthrope.* Suzukpen Saldzhak had *neurotic convulsions.* His family was affected with hereditary abnormality; the daughter of his sister for instance, about thirty years old, was a harmless idiot.
>
> Those former shamans, whom I have had an opportunity to know personally were, doubtlessly, mostly *nervous, neurotic individuals.* These abnormalcies must have been evidently inherited within the family or the clan. This could explain the belief of the hereditary order of becoming

a shaman. However, this in itself would not be enough to become a shaman: a tendency, a feeling of vocation, must have been another condition. Therefore, those members of a family who were born with a hereditary abnormalcy, could only become shamans if they possessed this tendency, because only such individuals would 'feel' the calling of the spirits, they would 'see' the 'spirits' coming to them. This must be the reason that the aspirants became shamans, only if they were 'chosen' [italics mine].

(ibid., pp. 314–15)

Diószegi's overview in terms of 'neurotic', 'misanthrope' and 'psychopath' is noteworthy because it comes from direct field observation.

A further classic case in the literature is that of the Enet (Entsy/Samoyed) shaman Savone, related by De Prokofyeva (1951, p. 125). When a young girl, Savone had gone with friends to collect cloudberries in the forest but had become separated from them. She recounts that a forest spirit fell upon her and she lost consciousness. She was found a few days later (she believed it to be a month) wandering naked in the forest. She recounted that she had lived with the forest spirit in his forest dwelling. Being found pregnant, she later gave birth to a stillborn 'infant-monster' supposedly fathered by the forest spirit. 'After delivery Savone was in torment for a long time, and acted as one demented.' Shamans from her own group could not heal her so she consulted a renowned Ket shaman who helped her and taught her how to shamanize. However, her nervous condition did not disappear despite her shamanizing. She did not want to be a shaman but eventually reconciled with her fate and accepted the hereditary shamanistic calling of her mother (who was also a shaman). Considering the fact that she possessed a complete shaman's costume (which De Prokofyeva tells us could have been collected by the ethnographer, Verbov, in 1938) meant that she must have been a '"strong", experienced shaman.' Again we see a clear presentation here of the correspondence between psychological derangement and the shamanic calling.

Finally, we have already encountered the case of Sereptie Djaruoskin above in terms of dismemberment imagery but his comment during this process that: 'This is my fate – to lose my mind' (Popov, 1968, p. 142) does suggest a nexus between shamanizing and psychological derangement.

Given the connection between shamanism and psychological derangement it is not surprising that Bogoras (1904) in describing the Chukchi (Chukchee) shamans says:

Nervous and highly excitable temperaments are most susceptible to the shamanistic call. The shamans among the Chukchee with whom I conversed were as a rule extremely excitable, almost hysterical, and not a few of them were half crazy. Their cunning in the use of deceit in their art closely resembled the cunning of a lunatic.

(p. 415)

And Devereux (1980, p. 15) notes that even members of a shaman's community may regard their shamans as 'wretched', 'crazy', 'cowardly', 'rapacious' or 'contaminating'.

Bogoras (1904) elsewhere describes a shaman as having 'a very unsteady, excitable nature' (p. 421), 'often almost on the verge of insanity' (p. 426), so that, overall:

> The Chukchee are well aware of the extreme nervousness of their shamans, and express it by the word nıñı'rkılqin ('he is bashful'). By this word they mean to convey the idea that the shaman is highly sensitive even to the slightest change of the psychic atmosphere . . . The shamans possess this nervous sensitiveness in a still higher degree than other people.
>
> (ibid., pp. 416–17)

This is a telling observation in relation to borderline dynamics because contemporary clinicians are very aware of the highly sensitive nature of Borderline Personality Disorder sufferers who can often be disarmingly accurate in their 'reading' of the thoughts and feelings of the psychotherapist. Similarly, they can be highly aware of minute changes to the physical environment of the consulting room as these seem to activate a sensitivity to environmental impingement from their earliest stage of emotional development.

Two Chukchi (Chukchee) shamans with whom Bogoras (1904) was familiar particularly reflected other aspects of nervousness, for both Ye'tılın and Kı'mıqäi had incessant nervous twitches.

It is not surprising, therefore, that Bogoras (1904) observed the preparation for each shamanistic performance as extremely painful and 'considered almost a peculiar kind of sickness. In conformity to this, most of the shamans show marked nervousness before the commencement of the performance' (p. 432). Of significance, Bogoras goes on to say that 'the [shamanic] performance itself is considered as a recovery from illness. The same shaman who was nervous before the performance regains after it his self-possession, and looks really as if he were braced up by some strong tonic' (p. 433). The healing nature of the séance is being indicated here and this amplifies the wounded healer component to shamanism.

It is the Chukcki (Chukchee) tribe's practice of family shamanism which adds further corroborative evidence to the view that the psychology of the Siberian shaman is proto-borderline.

## Case study: The Chukchi (Chukchee) Siberian tribe

One significant feature of the Chukchi (Chukchee) tribe that we know from Bogoras' (1904) early ethnography is that its members practised family shamanism. As indicated previously, family shamanism is used to describe the situation in some tribes whereby every family has one or more drum of its own which is used by family members for specific ceremonials. As a type of shamanizing, it runs in parallel with individual shamanism where only specific individuals perform shamanic rites. Bogoras notes that unlike most of the other Siberian tribes which practised it, family shamanism was not losing ground amongst the Chukchi (Chukchee).

If shamanism derives from a proto-borderline type of psychological construction as the result of a shaman archetype being developmentally produced through societal conditions which foment emotional difficulties for the mothers and their infants, and if family shamanism is so endemic to the Chukchi (Chukchee) tribe, then it follows that we ought to be able to detect noticeable conditions across the tribe of a borderline nature. Or putting it another way, if the psychological construction of Siberian shamans is proto-borderline then a tribe where family shamanism is practised (that is, where many individuals exhibit the shamanic complex and presumably have the shaman's proto-borderline psychology) should reflect some borderline characteristics. And this is what we do find.

### Evidence for borderline characteristics in the Chukchi (Chukchee) tribe: the propensity to suicide

As noted previously, the most marked borderline characteristic within Western Borderline Personality Disorder is that of 'recurrent suicidal behaviour, gestures, or threats, or self-mutilating behaviour' and as a consequence this characteristic has become included in DSM-IV as Criterion Five.

Particular cases of Chukchi (Chukchee) shamans exhibiting self-mutilating behaviours have already been discussed but Bogoras (1904) is of the opinion that the Chukchi (Chukchee) as a tribe overall are susceptible to suicide ideation. He sees this as arising from the personality characteristic they themselves describe as 'nuthiwi'qin' (which means 'soft to die'). Consequently, Bogoras says the Chukchi (Chukchee) 'generally are highly susceptible to any physical or psychical impressions of a kind to which they are unused' (p. 416). It is the sensitivity of nuthiwi'qin which makes them susceptible to psychic influences. Thus, in relating similar cases of nuthiwi'qin among native guides of Lamut and Yukaghir origin who 'on losing their way in the uninhabited country, run away from fear and despair, and every trace of them thereafter has been lost', Bogoras concludes that 'Suicides are also frequent among the Chukchee' (p. 417).

It would appear that this tendency to suicide is exacerbated by a lack of impulse control to do with rage for Bogoras (ibid., p. 46) notes that when 'thwarted in his purpose, the Chukchee is ready to go to any extreme, even to committing suicide, from uncontrollable rage.' Such a lack of impulse control appeared to Bogoras as a general characteristic of the tribe but it is also a noted criterion in Borderline Personality Disorder. As he says,

> the Chukchee shows a peculiar obstinacy in accomplishing whatever seems of momentary interest to him. In trading, when a Chukchee has set his heart on any trifling object, he is often ready to offer thrice, or even ten times, the price of it. If his offer is not accepted, he will start a brawl rather than desist from his purpose of his own free will.
>
> (ibid., p. 46)

And Bogoras goes on to relate how this tendency toward impulsivity plays into the suicide dynamic:

> I know an instance of a young girl who went out to the herd and hung herself to a tree, out of anger because her mother refused to take her along to the feast in a neighbouring camp.
>
> This motive [suicide] frequently plays a part even in cases of voluntary death among old men. . . . Little-Spoon, having been angered by his sons, requested that he be killed. The Chukchee frequently have a lurking inclination towards suicide . . . well known even to the Chukchee themselves. 'You know our people,' I was told on several occasions. 'For any reason they want to kill another man or themselves.' During the epidemic of influenza on the Wolverine River . . . there occurred two cases of suicide. One was that of a husband vexed at the loss of his young wife; the other, that of a mother who had lost her only son, a child of ten. There are cases of something like *tædium vitæ*. In 1895, at the Anui fair, I spoke with a man named Ka'tık, who declared that he did not want to live any longer. He gave as his reason, that fortune was adverse to him, that all his relatives had died, and that he was afraid that his herd at some time might begin to dwindle away, although at the time of speaking his reindeer were prospering. I did not pay much attention to his words, but the next winter I heard that he really had ordered himself to be strangled.
>
> At the head waters of the river Omolon I met a family four of whose members had taken their own lives within four years without any apparent reason. Their neighbours felt much afraid, and expressed the opinion that the spirits who wanted more prey had treacherously led them on to self-destruction.
>
> (pp. 46–7)

In a later section, Bogoras relates a similar case to that of Ka'tɪk above, where a woman who died by strangulation was motivated more by fear of her herd decreasing and who maintained that 'life held no pleasures for her' (ibid., p. 561).

In his section on 'Birth and Death', Bogoras (1904) relates a number of other incidents. One involves a man who on the second day after his wife's death, because of his grief, took his own life by stabbing himself with a knife. Bogoras also notes that some girls prefer to take their own lives rather than be married against their will. Another incident illustrates the nexus between suicide and the peculiar Chukchi (Chukchee) custom of 'voluntary death'. Bogoras tells of an old man who had taken a second wife for the sake of getting children but was subsequently abandoned by his first wife. After some time he repined and then requested he be killed which was then done by strangulation with a rope. It would appear that voluntary death can be requested for psychological and emotional reasons and is really little different to suicide.

Bogoras devotes a whole section to this custom of 'voluntary death' which he states is still 'of frequent occurrence among the Chukchee'. It tends to be inflicted by a friend or relative upon the express wish of the person who desires to die and Bogoras was aware of about twenty cases during his time with the Chukchi (Chukchee). They considered it better than death by disease or old age and in their folk stories it is presented as praiseworthy. Usually it is done by stabbing with a knife or spear or by strangulation or shooting by rifle and there are ritual ways that it is enacted. Bogoras says that for the elderly, it is due to the 'hard conditions of their life, which make existence almost unendurable for any one unable to take full care of himself. Accordingly, not only old people, but also those afflicted by some illness, often prefer death to continued suffering' (ibid., p. 560).

However, Bogoras goes on to say that the 'most peculiar cause for voluntary death is the wrath, the lack of patience, of the Chukchee. . . . Unable to fight against suffering of any kind, physical or mental, the Chukchee prefers to see it destroyed, together with his own life' (ibid., p. 561). This is suggestive that much in the voluntary death custom is being driven by underlying psychological stress. Hence voluntary death can also be requested in response to intrafamilial problems. Bogoras was told:

> Among our people, when a father is very angry with his lazy and bad son, he says, 'I do not want to see him any more. Let me go away.' Then he asks to be killed, and charges the very son who offended him with the execution of his request. 'Let him give me the mortal blow, let him suffer from the memory of it.'
>
> (ibid., p. 561)

This is a particularly interesting account psychologically for it reveals the use of voluntary death as a means of emotional revenge and also as a way of acting out a splitting polarization of internal emotional states. The father here is using death as a way of escaping a painful situation (caused by the son) but through the custom of the son delivering the blow and being left with the irreversible guilt. As noted previously, such splitting kinds of behaviour have been noted as a borderline characteristic because borderline dynamics have arisen from the pre-Oedipal zone of psychological development where splitting is the first defensive manoeuvre of the infant (Grotstein 1981).

Bogoras (1904) also notes that psychological motives in relation to voluntary death can lead to suicide:

> It must be borne in mind that all these psychical motives lead as often to suicide as to voluntary death. The difference is, that the younger people, especially those not fully grown, when desiring to die, destroy their life with their own hands, while those who are older more frequently ask to be killed. I know of some cases of boys and girls who were not yet twenty, and who killed themselves from spite, shame or sorrow.
>
> (pp. 561–2)

### Evidence for borderline characteristics in the Chukchi (Chukchee) tribe: the propensity for anger

Another notable borderline characteristic is that of intense and profound anger and as such this characteristic has become included in DSM-IV as Criterion Four.

In his section on the Chukchi's (Chukchee's) 'Mental Traits', Bogoras (1904) gives an insightful overview of the Chukchi (Chukchee) tendency to angry and violent outbursts:

> The Chukchee is easily angered; often a trifle will suffice to transform his merry laughter into the most *unreasonable rage*. They themselves are not unconscious of this peculiar feature of their mind. 'I am a tundra wanderer,' one of my Chukchee acquaintances, named Ñiro'n, would say to me. '*My anger rises suddenly*. It comes and goes of its own accord.' Some women bear a special name on account of their violent temper. They are called 'quarrelling women' (mara-ña'us·qattê). These are regarded as nuisances even by their housemates. Among the men, some have the very suggestive epithet 'hasty' (qιvr) prefixed to their names. . . .
>
> The Chukchee, when angry, growls, shows his teeth, and makes a threatening bite on his sleeve or on the handle of his knife, in defiance

of his foe. Some of them, when angered, shed tears of rage, and tear their hair like unruly children.

   Their language is singularly poor in abusive terms, and quarrels are immediately settled by blows or wrestling. *There is no lack of murders*, some of them of a barbarous character. Thus, in a camp near Cape Erri, the son and the nephew of the rich reindeer-breeder Yeku'tku, being goaded to the extreme by constant blows and abuse, cut his throat, and that with the knowledge of his wife, the mother of one of the murderers. In the summer of 1896 on the Poplar River, an affluent of the Small Anui, a young man killed his brother in order to get possession of his flock. The murderer, with his accomplice and their victim, arranged a contest of jumping over a barrier, the loser to pay the forfeit of skipping about for a while with his feet and hands bound together. When the elder brother lost, the other two men accordingly tied his feet, and coolly stabbed him with their knives. I heard the details of both deeds from the murderers themselves.

   In the tale of 'Elendi and his Sons', published in my 'Chukchee Materials', Elendi, to avenge the treachery of his slave, kills him in a most cruel manner. With sharp stakes he fastens the slave's hands, feet, the fleshy parts of his sides, and the skin of his scalp, to the ground, and then makes both of his wives urinate and defecate into his mouth [italics mine].

(p. 45)

In this account, not only is the tendency of the Chukchi (Chukchee) to anger (even to the point of murder) made clear but also a telling characteristic is revealed of certain infantile features; the growling, biting of objects and tearing of the hair. Such regressive states usually indicate unresolved issues from the earliest stages of infant/child development and would align with the proto-borderline disposition argued for here.

   Bogoras (1904) also mentions old Cossack reports of similar situations to the one above, for example, that of Anadyr Cossack Boris Kusnetsky who was captured by the Chukchi (Chukchee) in 1754 and witnessed a son stab his father with a knife and a brother stab his brother out of mere spite.

   Even those Chukchi (Chukchee) with a quiet and good-natured temperament were usually not free from occasional outbursts of anger of quite a severe kind. Bogoras (ibid.) relates the story of Aiñanwa't who, when young, had become so vexed by the unruliness of his reindeer herd that he turned to the setting sun and invited the wolves to come and devour the herd. To the Reindeer Chukchi (Chukchee) this was almost a sacrilege since wolves were classed with evil spirits. Despite Aiñanwa't's attempts to avert the disaster, misfortune did overtake the herd.

   In his overall account, Bogoras mentions on two occasions that mutually destructive violence, sometimes resulting in murder, was common such that 'violent quarrels between father and sons may lead even to murder' (ibid., p. 556). He gives a number of stories illustrating this tendency toward violence. One is the story of two brothers, 'one of whom, at the time of a tobacco famine, killed the other because he refused to share with him his tobacco-supply' (ibid., p. 549). He 'stabbed him from behind with his spear, ripped open his breast, and took out his lungs, which he found covered with soot. He scraped away a part of this, and used it to fill his pipe' (ibid., p. 59).

Particularly relevant is Bogoras' observation that the brutal treatment of women was common so that 'when refused by a woman, they are inclined to violence and rape' (ibid., p. 37). He also observed that:

> The wife is often harshly treated by her husband. I have mentioned the case of a husband killing his wife with a blow of a fire-brand. Blows, though less severe, are not infrequently dealt out to women; but it also happens that a wife ill-treats her husband.
>
> (ibid., p. 551)

Bogoras also relates one case of a wife shooting her husband – although this was purported to be a 'voluntary death' requested by the husband, who was ill.

Similarly, the story of Nuwa't is illustrative of the tendency toward violent anger:

> A man, Čei'pu by name, expelled his eldest son, Nuwa't, who was a very unsatisfactory herdsman, and made his younger son the principal heir . . . The disowned youth wandered from camp to camp, and at last came to a rich reindeer-breeder, Yo'nlɪ. He married Yo'nlɪ's daughter, and lived at his house as an adopted son-in-law. The following spring, when moving to the summer pastures, the father-in-law, who was much displeased with his work, wanted to drive him away. The young wife was with child, but among the Chukchee this forms no obstacle to the rupture of a marriage. The quarrel happened while they were travelling. The young man said nothing; but after a while he sat down on his wife's sledge, embraced her from behind, drew his knife, and cut open her abdomen. Then he jumped from the sledge and cut his own throat.
>
> (ibid., p. 551)

## Conclusions

As indicated previously, it is a questionable exercise to use Western psychiatric diagnostic criteria to look at another culture and it is understood that the DSM-IV criteria for Borderline Personality Disorder could not be used on their own to support the proposal that the Siberian shaman's psychology is proto-borderline. Nonetheless, there seems sufficient evidence from the ethnography to indicate a connection between Siberian shamanism and states of psychological derangement of a borderline kind. Hints have already been made in contemporary assessments as to the parallels between shamans and those who suffer with Borderline Personality Disorder and this is further evidenced through the presence of dismemberment imagery and self-mutilation behaviours. The observed characteristic of liminality of shamans, together with certain indications of impulsivity, further supports this view. Such evidence needs to be taken into account because in all cases it has been gained through direct field observation despite the fact that corroborative in-depth case studies of individual shamans are now impossible. However, the Chukchi (Chukchee) tribe does add material of a further corroborative kind because of the particular emotional atmosphere of a borderline nature exhibited in the tendency toward suicide (including voluntary death) and the propensity toward intense anger. These general tribal characteristics, as with the Sakha (Yakut) previously presented, reflect conditions which could foment difficulties for the 'good-enough' mother–infant relationship and therefore promote the development of a shaman archetype as a mind/brain structure which underpins the family shamanism the tribe exhibits.

Overall, the ethnographic material reviewed here does add evidence to the assertion that the psychology of Siberian shamans is of a proto-borderline kind.

# Chapter 11

# Conclusions

Both shamanism and its wounded healer component have over the years been used as central concepts in Jungian discourse. Guggenbuhl-Craig (1999) understands shamanism to be an archetype connected to the 'good analyst' and von Franz (as cited in Kirsch 1982) uses the concept to articulate the necessary 'breakthroughs' of the collective unconscious during a training analysis. Seeing an archetypal aspect to the phenomenon makes shamanism for many a 'sacred heritage' into which it would be valuable for analysts to tap (Sandner and Wong 1997). Groesbeck (1989, p. 274) goes so far as to say that only the 'true Jungians' are of the shamanic kind because they deal 'directly with the patient's illness.' Understandably, then, Jung's own life has been seen in both shamanic and wounded healer terms (Groesbeck 1975, 1989; Dunne 2000).

Given these important uses to which shamanism with its wounded healer component have been put, it is important to have a clear understanding as to exactly what the phenomenon is but this is an issue which has not been systematically addressed by Jungians.

## The definitional debate about shamanism

An initial difficulty arises here, for in examining shamanism as a field of anthropological study it emerges that there is quite a disparate and at times polarized discourse amongst scholars with a substantial debate as to a clear definition of the phenomenon. Nonetheless, it seems valid to conclude that a sufficient number of reputable scholars agree that there is something significant enough in the phenomenon of shamanism to warrant scholarly investigation. It is possible to arrive at a working definition whilst also recognizing that the debate on definitional issues is far from over. Kraus' (1972) phenomenological summary and skeletal definition highlights the essential features with which most scholars would agree. First, shamans take up their vocation because they are 'chosen'. Second, shamans are involved with powerful spirit familiars whose aim is tutelary and helping. Third, the shaman's initiation is characterized by a period of psychological crisis in which the shaman-to-be withdraws, subsequently experiencing both psychic torment and tutelage. It is this experience of what Eliade (1964) calls the 'pre-initiatory illness' which directly relates to the wounded healer component within shamanism for it is crucial that shamans sufficiently self-cure so as to master this experience. Fourth, the shaman's knowledge is attained through the aforementioned process and (often) the instruction of master shamans; and finally, the end result of these experiences primarily leads shamans into a communal focus around aspects of healing for their sociocultural others attained through a direct engagement with the 'spirits' which cause illness.

It should be noted at this point that Guggenbuhl-Craig (1999) as well as von Franz and other Jungians interprets contact with 'demons, with gods, with other dimensions of human existence' (p. 409) in psychological terms as having to do with unconscious psychic content. Whilst similar imagery and affects could be experienced by shamans on the one hand and analysts on the other, the interpretation of these would reflect cultural differences that do not need to negate any common psychological underpinning.

For the purposes of explicating the nature of the 'true Jungians' and discovering the make-up of the 'good analyst', there are two aspects of shamanism and its wounded healer component in particular which need highlighting. One is the general agreement that Siberia is a *locus classicus* of the phenomenon and the second is the ubiquity across all traditions of the pre-initiatory illness.

## Siberia as a *locus classicus* of shamanism

Siberia as a *locus classicus* of shamanism has significance for a number of reasons. First, it means that the Siberian material can be used centrally in gaining an understanding of the overall shamanic phenomenon with its wounded healer component through the sound ethnographic studies which have been undertaken on it; second, there have been significant psycho-dynamic studies done on Siberian shamanism which evidence a develop-mental side to any apparent archetypal configuration; third, Siberian shamanism displays less dependence on psychedelics to fuel the phenomenal experiences which means the operative psychological dynamics retain a clearer focus; and finally, unlike much Native American experience, the Siberian material argues for the primacy of the 'spontaneous election' to the vocation, that is, those who consciously seek the vocation (as in a vision quest experience) are considered less powerful. Consequently, the sound ethnographic studies done on the Siberian Sakha (Yakut) and Chukchi (Chukchee) tribes prove crucial in an explication of a working model of the shaman's wounded healer component, their particular psychology and how these may relate to contemporary analysts.

## The pre-initiatory illness

The other significant aspect of shamanism is the ubiquity across all traditions of the pre-initiatory illness. This experience not only acts as a sign that an individual has been chosen by the spirits for the shamanic vocation but it is one from which initiates must acquire a self-cure before being recognized by their sociocultural group as functional shamans. This aspect directly relates to the wounded healer component within shamanism because shamans are initially 'wounded' (as evidenced through the states of derangement which overtake them) and then 'healed' through their emerging self-cure. This experience is so imbedded in the shamanic phenomenon that it is reasonable to conclude that shamanism and its wounded healer component reflect aspects of one underlying 'archetypal' pattern and that the study of shamanism can throw further light on the central dynamics of the wounded healer and how these relate to the 'good analyst' and the 'true Jungians'.

Jung's assessment of shamanism does not, however, emphasize its wounded healer aspect.

## Jung's assessment of shamanism

Whilst being aware of the wounded healer component in shamanism Jung particularly concentrated on what he saw as a connection between shamanism and the individuation process. This emphasis on the individuation archetype in relation to shamanism is questionable because shamanism appears to have more to do with the way certain individuals respond to their life situation and attempt to heal it. It is highly likely that the dismemberment/reintegration cycle seen in shamanic initiations is expressing the realization that something is wrong in the original construction of the person and that action needs to be taken to take things apart, correct them and put the person back together. This is a desire for psychic healing (rather than the unfolding of an inbuilt potentiality which individuation would emphasize) so that in the dismemberment/reintegration cycle, a damaged psyche is recognizing its need for reconstitution lest it remain in an initially dismembered, traumatized and suffering state. Nonetheless, because such a process would arise from a deep interior awareness that what is going on is centrally important to the individual, it is quite understandable that this aspect of shamanism would be experienced as a 'biopsychical seizure' with feelings of 'destiny' and a 'calling'. Jung, however, in seeing shamanism with its wounded healer component as an archaic expression of the individuation archetype reflects the common view amongst Jungians that both phenomena derive from archetypes in the classical sense.

## Shamanism and the wounded healer as an archetype

When worldwide shamanism is aligned with Jung's method for determining the existence of an archetype, it can be demonstrated that with its wounded healer component, shamanism does reflect an archetype in the classical sense. It certainly is because of shamanism's ubiquity that we are able to recognize its different manifestations worldwide (both in space and time) as belonging to essentially the same class of things and that scholars can recognize it as a social institution. If shamanism with its wounded healer component is the result then of an archetypal expression in the classical sense, one ought to see attempts at a conscious articulation of it but with a difficulty surrounding precise definition. This is exactly what we do see with shamanism, for the vast literature on it indicates an agreed sense of something similar being investigated by scholars, despite their difficulties in formulating a precise definition. 'Shamanism' as a term may be ill-defined or conceptually flawed to some extent, but this does not invalidate the fact that something of substance is being studied. The recognition of some similar human experience at the same time as discerning different cultural manifestations is exactly what one would expect if an archetypal configuration as conceived by Jung were operative. In this way an archetypal perspective on shamanism and its wounded healer component would bear directly on the definitional debate and could contribute to a further understanding of it. However, current approaches to archetype theory are indicating that archetypes are not innate *a priori* psychic structures and this has implications for the way shamanism and its wounded healer component can be used to explain the work of modern-day analysts.

## Contemporary archetype theory

Whilst it is possible to show from the ethnography that shamanism with its wounded healer component reflects an underlying archetype in the classical Jungian sense, a difficulty arises when contemporary views of archetype theory are taken into account. Over recent years classical archetype theory, and especially that part which sees archetypes as innate *a priori* inherited psychic structures which can spontaneously influence psychological life, has been under considerable review given the research findings from early infant and neonate neuroscience. This research suggests that mind/brain structures, as in those which underpin complex imagery of an archetypal nature, are developmentally produced out of intense affective experiences during early infancy. This is an utterly new and radical way of conceiving archetypes and Jean Knox's (2003) model, which utilizes the 'image schema' concept of attachment theory, combines emergentism and a developmental perspective as reflected in the neuroscience research, which was not available to Jung when he wrote. The critical point is that in this model, archetypes are not understood to be innate, predetermined psychic structures but are developmentally produced even though once present, they can directly influence psychological life.

This means that to some extent our understanding of shamanism, its wounded healer component and their connection to the 'good analyst' and the 'true Jungians' comes down to a debate about archetype theory. But this is a necessary debate because if the phenomena reflect an archetype that is, in the classical Jungian sense, centrally connected to being a 'good analyst', then quite different implications are suggested in relation to the selection, training and work of analysts than if apparent 'archetypal' experiences derive from a developmentally produced mind/brain structure.

The emergent/developmental model of archetype as proposed by Jean Knox (2003) does seem the most plausible of all for the following reasons: First, it aligns with current neuroscience in terms of the bidirection of structure and function. In relation to shamanism, the model sees a shamanic mind/brain structure as arising from particular developmental experiences rather than an innate shaman archetype predetermining experience. Second, such a model retains a biological perspective which, as Stevens (1998) points out, is epistemologically important for archetype theory beyond the face validity that there must be a biological underpinning to archetypal imagery. Significantly, the developmental aspect of this biological perspective means that a position can be taken on archetypes without adhering to preformationism or innatism. Third, such a model has significant explanatory power as it can incorporate all other theoretical positions up until this point in time. Specifically, it is able to explain all aspects of shamanism and its wounded healer component (see following discussion). Fourth, it can explain why archetypes will appear *as if* innate and why Jung could conclude, though I believe erroneously, that they operate with 'autochthonous revival'. Fifth, it re-asserts the environment/archetype nexus but in a bidirectional way, that is, it is early infant environmental experience which leads to the initial construction of archetypes but these psychic structures do not become activated later in life without particular environmental triggers to do with intense affectivity of a similar kind which led to the original formation of the 'archetypal' mind/brain structure in the first place. In relation to shamanism, this would explain why the shamanic calling can be experienced not only in adolescence but also later in life. Further detail on these issues is covered in Appendix A.

When a review of classic archetype theory is undertaken as suggested by the assertions of a contemporary emergent/developmental model of archetype such as that proposed by Jean Knox (2003), I believe Jung supplies insufficient evidence for a central component of his theory – the spontaneous activation of archetypes, that is, the concept of 'autochthonous revival'. Rather, on all occasions, archetypes appear to become activated in response to intense affectivity which has come about through a person's subjective life experience. My point is not that this critique invalidates Jung's overall theory of archetype but that archetypes need to be understood in a different way. Whilst still being psychic structures which have the capacity to directly influence psychological life, they are not innate but have arisen in the first instance out of developmental experience. Their later activation in a person's life in terms of imagery and numinous affect is due to the similarity of the person's current emotional experiences with those which formed the 'archetypal' mind/brain structure in the first place. In other words, unconscious imaginal and affective content always occurs in a context and in response to something and this will be the case even when images apparently unknown to a person appear.

Given this situation it is not surprising that the imagery which archetypes activate can appear primitive, archaic and often mythological. This is because such images are related to early (and thus more primitive and 'primary process') levels of psychic functioning at the time of the 'archetypal' mind/brain structure's construction. Mythic imagery points to the 'earlyness' of psychic experience since early infant experience coincides with a time when the psyche and the affects it experiences are 'primitive'. In fact, mythological motifs may be the best way for the unconscious to articulate deep and early affective states (as if they are coming from another world). As such, 'archetypal' imagery cannot be said to be arising spontaneously and autonomously. It is more plausible to understand it as a way of expressing something 'psychically primæval'. It does need to be noted, however, that there will always be difficulty in explaining the specifics of any individual's 'archetypal' imagery without knowing every detail of their developmental life experience.

There is, however, quite a profound implication which flows on from this – Jung's classical view that the collective unconscious is unaffected by personal history requires substantial revision because in an emergent/developmental model, archetypes are understood to be developmentally produced structures arising out of the intense affective experiences of early infancy and are not innate or *a priori*. As such, the conceptual division between the collective and the personal unconscious collapses, for if archetypes are constructed out of early infant affective experience in the first place and are not preformed structures, there need be only one unconscious. This possibility demands serious consideration by all those who advocate for a shaman archetype within a 'sacred heritage' viewpoint for there is no separate wellspring of pristine collective psychic content which is healing and guiding. Rather, the 'good analyst' and 'true Jungians' are defined by their developmental experiences and their own psychotherapeutic self-cure.

## A contemporary model of the shaman archetype and its wounded healer component

All of the aforementioned bears directly not only on our understanding of shamanism and its wounded healer component but also on the connection between these, the 'good analyst' and the 'true Jungians', for once an emergent/developmental model of archetype such as that proposed by Jean Knox (2003) appeared in the Jungian literature, a serious examination of *locus classicus* shamanism was required to see if the pre-initiatory illness was underpinned by early infant trauma leading to the ultimate development of a shamanic mind/brain structure. I believe it to be the case that the Siberian *locus classicus* ethnographic records do provide sufficient evidence to conclude that the presence of societal practices and customs which could affect a mother's ability to meet the needs of her infant would have implications for the efficacy of the early mother–infant dyad. It is plausible then to understand Siberian shamanism and its wounded healer component as expressions of a developmentally produced 'archetypal' mind/brain structure, the critical experience being trauma in the early mother–infant dyad before the achievement of unit status and in an environment of 'no other chaos' so that a particular psychology akin to Winnicott's (1968) 'borderline type of case' emerges – what I have termed 'proto-borderline'. Consequently, in the mythic representation of the wounded healer, the borderline constitution of Chiron as centaur may be more significant than is initially apparent.

Specifically, Siberian shamanism reflects a particular kind of psychological structure along the normal–abnormal continuum of 'borderline states' so that on the one hand, shamans cannot be described as 'mentally ill' – which, as Hutton (2001) points out, is 'patently untenable' – whilst on the other hand, they have suffered real psychological derangement as a result of traumas and difficulties arising from their early mother–infant experience but from which they have actualized some healing. It is just such an experience of the 'recycling of . . . wounds and madnesses', as Giles Clark (2006, p. 81) puts it, which not only enables shamans eventually to occupy a place of sociocultural significance in being the communication channels between the known sense world and that of the transpersonal but also confirms their status as wounded healers *par excellence*.

## Specific implications of the proto-borderline model of shamanism

### The proto-borderline model explains the pre-initiatory illness

The proto-borderline model of the Siberian shaman's psychology does have the capacity to explain the phenomenon of shamanism and its wounded healer component as we see it. The pre-initiatory illness noted in the ethnographic records as usually occurring in adolescence becomes under-standable as a breakout of deranged psychic material from the psychotic core of the developmentally produced shaman archetype which is already present in the initiate's psyche having arisen from ruptures and traumas experienced in the earliest stages of infancy. Presumably, the emotional changes to do with adolescence and the onset of puberty create affective states of such intensity as to foment activation of this underlying mind/brain structure. The concurrence of dismemberment/reconstitution imagery during the pre-initiatory illness also becomes understandable in terms of psychic content expressing both the realization that something is wrong in the original construction of the person and that action needs to be taken to take things apart, correct them and put the person back together.

In a similar way, the model can explain the experience of modern-day analysts in terms of those 'breakthroughs of the collective unconscious' (as von Franz calls them) which either led these persons into their own analysis in the first place and/or occurred during their training, especially any 'breakthroughs' generated by a re-experience of early infant states evoked in the transference.

### The proto-borderline model explains why some are 'called' and others are not

Seeing shamanism in its Siberian expression as derived from a develop-mentally produced mind/brain structure having arisen from ruptures in the early mother–infant dyad before the achievement of unit status actually explains why some individuals receive a shamanic 'calling' and others do not. The archetypal mind/brain structure's construction is dependent on particular early infant experience which only certain individuals will have. The reification of shamanism and the wounded healer as archetypes in the classical sense explains far less because no reason can be given for the 'autochthonic revival', that is, the apparent spontaneity of the experience. The model of the shaman's psychology as proposed here can actually explain why certain individuals are 'chosen'.

Similarly, the model can explain the sense many analysts have of being 'compelled' to do the kind of work they do. This would be because, like shamans, they have experienced early infant trauma resulting in a similar proto-borderline psychological construction that leads to dysfunctions, prompting their own personal analysis. For many, then, their ongoing work demands an engagement and re-engagement with the 'spirits' (that is, complexes) which underpin their life experience and this can be experienced as a destiny/calling. The analyst Joe Wheelwright (1989), who trained with Jung in Zurich, puts it this way: 'We didn't choose our profession, our profession chose us but what we knew was that we were as neurotic as hell and we better run not walk to the nearest analyst.'

### The proto-borderline model explains why some can be 'called' later in life

The ethnographic records also indicate that there are times when people become shamans later in life following accidents or highly unusual events of a bizarre or life-threatening nature. This experience of a later call to the shamanic vocation can also be explained by the view of the shaman's psychology presented here, for such experiences coincide with intense affectivity which presumably reactivates states of early infant vulnerability thereby constellating a pre-existing shamanic mind/brain structure.

A parallel occurrence can occur with modern-day analysts who feel 'called' to their vocation later in life as a result of early infant vulnerabilities which, though masked and managed for many years, have become evoked and demand attention.

### The proto-borderline model explains the self-cure aspect of the pre-initiatory illness

Mastery of the pre-initiatory illness, so essential to shamanic initiation, is also explained by this proto-borderline model of the shaman's psychology. The degree of mastery would depend on the functionality arising in the 'outer layers' of personality development beyond the mother–infant dyad. These layers are actually functional because they have developed in an ongoing environment of 'no other chaos'. It would be from these functional layers that transformation of the 'psychotic core' components would be mobilized, for in current clinical work, such positive outcomes generally are interpreted as indicative of sufficient internal structure overcoming the psychic fragmentation(s) originally experienced.

In a similar way the proto-borderline model of the psychological construction of modern-day analysts can account for the self-cure they attain in their personal analysis. Mastery of their core dysfunctions is possible because the outer layers in their personality structure are functional enough to enable sufficient repair. And this is because these outer layers have arisen in an environment of 'no other chaos'. I believe then that this shamanic kind of initial wounding and subsequent re-constitution/mastery through their personal analysis is foundational to those wounded healers who are the 'true Jungians'.

### The proto-borderline model explains the debate as to the shaman's psychopathology

Overall, the differential aspects of the 'core' and 'outer layers' of the shaman's personality structure can explain both the shaman's experience of derangement in the pre-initiatory illness (especially the presence of dismemberment imagery) and the reason why they can attain eventual mastery, with its all-important self-cure. These differential aspects can also explain the divergent debate in the literature that has gone on in terms of the psychopathology of shamans. It can be very easy to emphasize one aspect of the shaman's personality structure over another, seeing them as either 'supernormal' when the effects of the 'outer layers' are stressed or, alternatively, pathological if the effects of the 'core' component are stressed. The proto-borderline model of the shaman's psychology as proposed here maintains that both positions are accurate but that they must be held together, not separated, a position which Ducey (1976, p. 177) so aptly recognized when he said that the 'healthy and pathological patterns [in the shaman's psychology] are too deeply interwoven to be meaningfully separated.' Little wonder that researchers can detect characteristics of 'betwixt and between' liminality and a 'stable instability' amongst shamans because the latter would always be mediating between their functional outer layers and the dysfunctional core zones within themselves. It is this which constitutes the wounded healer – a cyclical experience of healing whilst being ongoingly unhealed and wounded oneself, or, as Kerényi (1959, p. 99) puts it, 'the knowledge of a wound in which the healer forever partakes.'

It does have to be noted that the proto-borderline model of the Siberian shaman's psychology as argued here does somewhat re-open debate around the question: 'is the shaman psychopathological?', although it has not been my direct intention to do so. I do think that the question to do with the psychopathology of shamans has been ill-conceived, revealing earlier and outmoded views of psychopathology. Simply put, shamans will have a psychology as everyone has a psychology and I prefer to articulate this in terms of the uniqueness of their psychology rather than necessarily arguing for a psychopathology with its over-reliance on Western psychiatric categories. Besides, it is virtually impossible now to get any case study evidence by which to affirmatively answer the psychopathology question. Nonetheless, the psychopathology issue does still appear as a point of discussion with those researchers who approach shamanism from a psychological orientation despite Hutton (2001) asserting that by the 1950s it had become untenable to view Siberian shamanism as a form of mental illness (see deMause 2002, Krippner 2002, Noll 1983, Peters 1982, 1989, 1996 and Peters and Price-Williams 1980).

Questions to do with the psychology of shamanism are highly significant, however. Ränk's (1967) observation has been previously noted – that once a psychopathology can be determined, the whole definitional debate around shamanism reduces as the difficulties become collapsed and a psychological universalism is introduced which has the capacity to simplify. I believe that the proto-borderline model of the shaman's psychology that I am proposing does have that capacity to simplify the definitional debate in relation to shamanism.

As for modern-day analysts, the proto-borderline aspect to their psychology highlights the differential aspects of the 'core' and 'outer layers' of their personality structure, explaining both the internal dysfunctions which have drawn them to their personal analysis in the first place and the self-cure they have ultimately been able to achieve. What the model highlights, however, is not just that analysts are wounded, which, as Samuels (1994, p. 187) notes, is 'scarcely to be doubted' but that the zone of wounding can be specified, that is, the zone of pre-verbal infancy. This is highly significant for it begins to answer Steinberg's (1989, p. 11) observation that 'little appears in print or public discussion about the specific wounds the healer has to contend with and how they affect treatment.' We are now in a position to say that it is the activation of wounds in the zone of pre-verbal infancy which explains the 'psychic infection' kind of embodied counter-transference experience which underpins the 'true Jungian' way of working – a point I will take up below.

### The proto-borderline model can explain the shaman's transpersonal imagery

This proto-borderline model of the shaman's psychology can also explain other aspects of shamanism, such as transpersonal imagery and experiences. Since the shaman's core complexes are understood to reside in the developmental zone where 'magic holds sway', it would be through projection that these complexes are experienced outwardly as spirits and inwardly as visions. Such an understanding does rely on accepting Jung's position that projection is the natural way that the psyche functions and that the experience of spirits is a projection of unconscious complexes. Jung (1902/1993) initially proposed this idea in 'On the psychology and pathology of so-called occult phenomena' and developed it in detail in 'The psychological foundations of belief in spirits' (Jung 1948/1991a). It has not been uncommon for later commentators on shamanism, such as Vitebsky (1995), to take a similar view. It is quite plausible that the proto-borderline model could also explain transpersonal imagery experienced by many modern Westerners.

### The proto-borderline model can explain the shaman's female imagery and deviance from cultural norms

Specifically in relation to shamanism, the centrality of feminine imagery in the shaman's visions and regalia is also explained by the proto-borderline model of their psychology. Since the dysfunctions in the shaman's personality structure go back to the earliest months of life, when the infant is primarily dependent on the mother, the feminine imagery represents a mother identification as an attempted cure.

Similarly, the model has the capacity to explain the noted deviance of shamans even within their own tribal groups. This is because their psychological construction is actually different to their sociocultural others – they are proto-borderline – and this explains the over-representation of suicide and the unusual custom of 'voluntary death' in certain Siberian tribes where shamanism predominates.

## Analysts and shamans

Given that the Siberian expression of shamanism and its wounded healer component is understood to derive from a developmentally produced mind/brain structure, it is not unreasonable to assume that similar developmental experiences could lead to its expression in modern persons. Guggenbuhl-Craig (1999) could very well be correct to conclude that contemporary Western 'healers' such as analysts have this psychic structure within them since they undertake healing roles within their sociocultural group in the same way that shamans do. However, it is then not so much that being a good Jungian analyst is 'a talent with which, if you are lucky, you are born' (p. 408), as Guggenbuhl-Craig asserts, but rather that being 'good' has more to do with an individual's capacity to process and use the early infant traumas associated with the development of a 'shamanic' mind/brain structure. In other words, 'good analysts' are actually 'made' in more ways than one.

Overall, the proto-borderline model when applied to analysts has the capacity to explain why they are drawn to their own psychotherapy in the first place, what kinds of wounds are predisposing them to the analytic vocation and why they are then selected as analysts. I believe that the 'good analyst' must have (at least) a similar proto-borderline kind of psychological structure to shamans, that is, sufficiently wounded at the core level of their personality but without gross psychopathology deriving from 'other chaos' in their developmental history which would impede the all important self-cure. This proto-borderline model can then explain how 'good analysts' use this psychological construction in the countertransference. Embodied countertransference experiences of the 'psychic infection' kind to which Jung (1937/1993) alludes occur because the analyst's own pockets of early infant damage have become activated by, and resonate with, that of their patients. Their self-cure through their own analytic work enables them to re-engage with these 'spirits' (that is, complexes) without being possessed by them, thereby enabling a read-out of their patients' unconscious psychological states. Putting things another way, it is only those analysts who have been wounded in the earliest stages of infancy who will have the porosity and susceptibility to the 'psychic infection' kinds of embodied countertransferential experiences. Of course, this is not to say that the analyst has to be wounded in this early infancy zone in exactly the same way as their patients. Giles Clark (2006) alludes to this:

Of course the analyst's particular emotional and/or physical pains and other reactive symptoms do not necessarily reflect or reproduce exactly the patient's symptomatic points of psychosomatic pain and disturbance. It is the analyst's own zones and forms of psychosomatic vulnerability that are affected; so my idiosyncratic emotional and physical sensitivities are open to being disturbed and moved. Counter-transferential information is received through my psychosomatically 'weakest' and most problematic areas. These are my 'strongly' reactive areas and so are where I am made to work from.

(p. 81)

It is more a case of being wounded in the same zone – that is, early infancy – which underpins the porosity required to experience the embodied coun-tertransference. I believe that it is those who work in this kind of countertransference who are the 'true Jungians' because this way of work-ing entails, as Groesbeck (1989, p. 274) highlights, 'dealing directly with the patient's illness in order to produce a transformational healing experience' – which is what shamans do in their cultures.

### Selection and training issues

Definite selection and training issues to do with Jungian analysts are implied by the proto-borderline model of the shamanic wounded healer being presented here, for if shamanic and wounded healer phenomena derive from an emergent/developmental psychic structure, and its presence is critical for being an effective analyst, then its detection at the time of selection of trainees and its activation during the training process are critical. Selection of trainees would need to include the detection of par-ticular early infant states which have led to a shamanic mind/brain struc-ture in the first place. Moreover, the aspect of shamanic mastery becomes highlighted because it would be important in the selection of trainees to detect those individuals whose outer layers of personality structure are sufficiently developed and non-chaotic to be able to contain and aid reconstitution of the underlying psychotic material in the core of their personality.[1] Furthermore, the nature of the training analysis comes into clearer focus for if the presence of an activated shamanic mind/brain structure is required for psychotherapeutic effectiveness, and this mind/brain structure has arisen from ruptures and difficulties in the early mother–infant bond, then the training analysis would need to be more than supervision or the observation of an analyst-in-training's psychic processes. It would need to be of a developmental and reductive nature as opposed to synthetic analysis alone, so that the early infant traumas in the core of the personality could be reconstituted as resonance points for later use in the countertransference.

It is because of the connection which I see between early infant states and the psychic porosities associated with countertransferential phenomena experienced as 'psychic infections' that I believe it is even more critical for training analyses to be reductive. The analyst-in-training must get back to their bedrock early infancy complexes which underpin their embodied countertransference porosities so that they can be sufficiently processed (that is, self-cured). The final aim of this experiential training is for the analyst not to be 'possessed' by these complexes when they get activated but rather to establish a dialogue with them so that they can inform the analyst as to what is operating in their patient unconsciously. Without this training the analyst could easily succumb to the negative aspects of 'psychic infection' in the way to which Jung (1937/1993) alludes.

I believe that the emergent/developmental model of shamanism with its wounded healer component substantially adds to our understanding of the way the embodied countertransference actually operates and can thereby provide an explanation for Jung's 'psychic infection' model of psychotherapeutic work. Shamanism then is not just a metaphor and Groesbeck (1989) is correct in saying that the 'true Jungians' are of the shamanic type.

As a consequence I believe that it is imperative that Jungians do not deviate from the model of training where an unimpeded and open-ended personal analysis is central. It is noteworthy that the experiential nature of the personal analysis actually parallels the 'ecstatic' aspect of shamanic initiation which Eliade (1964) highlights. Of further significance in relation to processing the pre-initiatory illness is the fact that shamanic societies have discovered the importance of a 'didactic' and 'ecstatic' training structure under the oversight of a 'master shaman'. For modern-day training programs this would parallel the use of theoretical seminars alongside personal analysis under the oversight of an analyst and supervisor(s). Given the proto-borderline parallels in psychological structure between analysts and shamans as presented here, the validity of the training models Jungian societies have developed is highlighted as the most appropriate way to prepare candidates to be 'true Jungians'.

It would appear that shamanism with its wounded healer component is far from being an ethnographic romance. Rather, since it is derived from an emergent/developmentally produced mind/brain structure it has explanatory and hypothetico-deductive potentialities which relate to the characteristics of the type of mastery required for psychotherapeutic work, the selection and training issues for analysts and the countertransferential aspects of Jung's 'psychic infection' model of psychotherapeutic healing. As such, the proto-borderline model of the shamanic wounded healer as presented here goes some way towards addressing Walsh's (1990, p. 270) observation about shamanism that '[at] the present time, psychological studies are almost non-existent.'

# Appendix A

## The implications of Knox's emergent/ developmental model of archetype

Much of the following material is adapted from Merchant (2006) and has been included as an appendix because it primarily relates to the ongoing debate to do with archetype theory and the significant position which Knox's (2003) model occupies in it. Whilst this material does not directly relate to shamanism and the wounded healer, which this book is addressing, Knox's concepts provide the underpinning to the model of the shamanic wounded healer presented.

### Implication 1: An emergent/developmental model of archetype has substantial explanatory power

This point has been substantially covered in Chapters 5 and 6 where it was stated that an emergent/developmental model can incorporate all positions on archetype up to this point in time for it is in disagreement with neither other emergentism positions nor the cultural perspective put forward by Pietikainen (1998a, 1998b). Furthermore, if innate biological start points coinciding with developmental experience lead to mind/brain structures which initially operate implicitly and which underpin the emergence of complex human archetypal imaging as Knox (2003) suggests, then the observations of those such as Stevens (1998), who detect a correspondence between archetypes and brain locations, is not that unexpected. The main difference is in the explanation as to how the bio-structural components which throw up archetypal imagery get there in the first place. For Stevens, they arise from the encoded genetic make-up of the individual, whereas for Knox, they are arising out of developmental experience.

An emergent/developmental model of archetype also enables us to explain instinct as we observe it because these response patterns are understood to arise within species-typical environments from automatic subcortical innate biological start points. As indicated in Chapter 6, this is important for archetype theory because Jung from his earliest years was drawing a connection between instinct and archetype – 'the archetypes are simply the forms which the instincts assume' (Jung 1931/1991a, p. 157).

Whilst it is beyond the scope of this appendix to critique instinct theory, given Jung's adherence to it in relation to archetype theory, it is important to note that Knox's (2003) model does contribute an explanation as to the way instinct functions.

Finally, because an emergent/developmental model of archetype contains a place for biological start points which underpin the emergence of complex archetypal imagery, an explication of the psychoid (psychophysical) nature of archetypes as postulated by Jung (1954/1991a) is enabled. The physical side would coincide with the developmentally produced bio-structures and the psychological side with the emergent archetypal imagery.

## Implication 2: An emergent/developmental model of archetype leads to a new perspective on innatism

All the emergentist theorists seem to be against anything genetically speci-fied in relation to archetypes and it is from this position that they argue against innatism. However, a model such as Knox's (2004, p. 4) posits not only 'developmental processes out of which early psychic structures reliably emerge' as the foundation of the experience of archetypal imagery but also that once present, such structures have the capacity to influence psycho-logical life. It is not unreasonable to conclude then that archetypes will be experienced as if innate because they have become present through early life experience before the emergence of consciousness. They are present before we become aware of their activity but they have not been present from birth. To the adult they will appear to be spontaneous and not as having arisen from conscious awareness. This is because the underpinning bio-structure was imbedded when the infant psyche was still unconscious and developing so that archetypal imagery will be experienced as if arising from something innate. The whole way that our subjective experience of innatism has been conceived of until now will need revision.

## Implication 3: An emergent/developmental model of archetype always implies an archetype–environment nexus

In a model of the archetype such as that proposed by Knox (2003), archetypes are the result of a developmental interaction between the human organism and the environment. Without the environment, archetypes would not emerge into being. It follows that since any archetype emerges in the first place because of particular environmental experience then the emergent imagery will be environmentally specific. Species-typical environ-ments would lead to the norm but other environmental input could lead to different and specific archetypal clusters. I believe that this implies that there will always be a nexus between archetypal imagery and particular environmental experience so that a vector is established in the opposite direction, akin to Gottlieb's (2001) 'bidirectional' hypothesis and supported by Schore (2005) and Fonagy's (2002) observations that once neural structures are in place, they can modulate subsequent psychological responses. Specifically, then, the environment will not just lead to the original developmental emergence of any one archetype but once some kind of bio-structure has been forged, similar environmental conditions will always be necessary for that archetype's constellation. In other words, the emergence of particular archetypal imagery in a person's life will be connected to a similarity in the current environment with the original environment during the archetype's original developmental emergence. It is the interactive resonance between these two states (the 'then' and the 'now') which will constellate the emergence of archetypal imagery in the present, for this interaction between the environment and the structure will formulate imagery out of 'then' (early experience) and 'now' (current affect) so long as there is a correspondence between the two which has been forged through the developmental process. In this model, archetypes are not understood to operate autochthonously but always in connection with specific environmental conditions because they have developmentally emerged from, and cluster around, particular environmental inputs. This means that for ongoing research of any particular archetype, the specific environmental input which has led to its bio-structural underpinning will need explication.

Examples which illustrate this implication are the phenomena of transference love and the repetition compulsion which are covered in Chapter 6.

## Implication 4: An emergent/developmental model of archetype collapses the nature/nurture debate in relation to archetype theory and possibly the division between the Classical and Developmental schools

The nature side of the debate in archetype theory emphasizes a genetic basis to archetypes and this view is primarily represented by Stevens (1982, 1998, 2002). The nurture view sees archetypes as entirely cultural phenomena without needing any reference to biology or anything innate and is mainly represented by Pietikainen (1998a, 1998b).

We have already seen that by connecting her model with Schore (1994) and Fonagy's (2002) research and asserting that emotional experience directly influences brain development, Knox (2003) is aligning herself with the whole biological perspective which sees structure as only fully realizing itself through function. This is an extremely important consideration for, as Gottlieb (2001) so succinctly points out, if this is the case the nature/nurture controversy all but evaporates. In the same way, emergent/developmental models of the archetype have the potential to collapse the nature/nurture debate in relation to archetype theory.

In relation to the different schools within analytical psychology, it was Samuels (1994) in his *Jung and the Post-Jungians* who proposed that within the Jungian world there was from 1950 to 1975 a London (Developmental) School, which emphasized a clinical perspective, and the Zurich (Classical) School, which emphasized a symbolic approach to the psyche. During the 1970s, a third school, the Archetypal School, emerged. Now if archetypes emerge from developmentally produced bio-structures which initially operate implicitly and which underpin the emergence of complex human imagery then such an emergent/developmental model of archetype has the capacity to draw the Developmental, Classical and Archetypal schools together.

First, the 'other worldly' and 'numinous' aspect of archetypal experience emphasized by the Classical and Archetypal schools is understandable because the emergent imagery is arising from deep unconscious layers of the psyche where the underpinning bio-structures having been forged during the intense affectivity of early infant life. The experience will appear to be of something spontaneous, innate and not related to conscious knowing.

Second, the 'structural components of the psyche' perspective of the Classical School is retained because archetypal imagery is underpinned by actual bio-structures. It is just that these bio-structures are developmentally produced and not preformed by any connection to a genetic code.

From the Developmental School's perspective, if the bio-structures which underpin the emergence of complex human archetypal imagery have originally arisen through developmental experience, then this school's emphasis on the importance of environmental experience in the development of the psyche is satisfied.

## Implication 5: An emergent/developmental model of archetype collapses the 'sacred heritage' view of archetypes

Generally, it is the received position in classical archetype theory to view the archetypal level as a wellspring of health that is available to humanity because, as Jung (1931/1991a) says, it is 'untouched' by personal experience and therefore tends to remain pristine. An emergent/developmental model of archetypes has the capacity to collapse this kind of perspective because emergence of the archetypal is a developmental outcome connected to particular environmental experiences and is not the result of preformationism. As Knox (2004, p. 9) says, archetypes are 'reliably repeated early developmental achievements.' In other words, because the archetypal world is built up through developmental experience there is unlikely to be any separate collective unconscious divorced from personal experience into which individuals can tap for their healing. This raises a much larger theoretical issue, as discussed below.

## Implication 6: An emergent/developmental model of archetype collapses the conceptual division between the collective and personal unconscious

The logical consequence of the foregoing implication means there need be no division between a collective and a personal unconscious. There would only be differential layers of unconsciousness depending on the age of a person when the bio-structural start points became imbedded through developmental experience.

In other words, it is possible to conceive of archetypes as (developmentally acquired) structural components of the psyche but without the additional concept of the collective unconscious.

## Implication 7: An emergent/developmental model of archetype aligns with Developmental Systems Theory from contemporary biology

Developmental Systems Theory is an attempt to do biology without the dichotomies of nature/nurture, genes/environment or biology/culture, and Oyama *et al.* (2001) provide a comprehensive overview of this approach. In particular, it criticizes the current trend toward conventional interactionism and the concept of 'genetic predisposition'. It prefers to approach matters from a developmental perspective that does not rely on a distinction between 'privileged, essential causes and merely supporting or interfering ones.' The life cycle of an organism is understood to be developmentally constructed, not programmed or preformed. It comes into being through interactions between the organism and its surroundings as well as interactions within the organism. As such, this approach is especially critical of the concept of the 'genetic blueprint' with its implied preformationism. Oyama *et al.* go on to outline the six main themes of Developmental Systems Theory.

### Theme 1: Joint determination by multiple causes

Developmental Systems Theory argues that a wide range of developmental resources goes into producing any trait and that the gene/environment division is only one way to describe what goes on. Phenocopying (that is, where mutation as well as environmental change alters an organism in the same way) would be an example in point. Hence Developmental Systems Theory argues for causal parity between genes and other factors of development. The emergent/developmental model of archetype as proposed by Knox (2003) has a similar emphasis on multiple causes. As Knox (2004, p. 1) says, hers is 'a developmental model in which mental contents emerge from the interaction of genes, brain and environment'.

## Theme 2: Context sensitivity and contingency

For Developmental Systems Theory, 'the significance of any one cause is contingent upon the state of the rest of the system' (Oyama *et al.* 2001, p. 2). Thus, calculated coefficients of heritability can say nothing about the extent to which a trait can be modified by environmental change. They note that once information metaphors are used in relation to DNA so that an outcome is seen as an expression of this genetic information that is somehow controlling development, then it acquires a special status, it 'represents what the organism is meant to be . . . its "inner essence", which was conferred on it at the moment of conception' (p. 3). Context sensitivity is then often treated as interference to a basic pattern. How much of Jungian thinking about the Self archetype has been cast in such terms?

These biologists demonstrate that development is indeed very environmentally sensitive so that context sensitivity can operate at micro-levels. This is evidenced through what they call 'noise' effects. In arguing against the view that organisms are '"lumbering robots" created by their genes, "body and mind"', Lewontin (2001) refers to Waddington's (1957) foundational research on 'developmental noise' which showed that an organism's phenotype is not necessarily given even when the genotype and environment are completely specified. Lewontin (2001, p. 62) concludes:

> The two sides of *Drosophila* [the fruit fly often used in genetic experiments] have the same genotype, and no reasonable definition of environment will allow that the left and right sides of a pupa developing halfway up the side of a glass milk bottle in the laboratory are in different environments. Yet, the number of sterno-pleural bristles and the number of eye facets differ between the two sides of an individual fly. Small events at the level of thermal noise acting during cell division and differentiation have large effects on the final developmental outcome.

Flow-on research over later years was able to show that 'by selection, an organism can be made developmentally insensitive or highly sensitive to perturbations of its genotype, its environment, developmental accidents, or any combination of these' (Lewontin 2001, p. 62).

Whilst it is beyond the scope of this appendix to give full treatment to the findings from developmental biology and recognizing that the sterno-pleural bristles of *Drosophila* are a far cry from archetypal imagery, there are important implications from this ongoing research in developmental biology for it suggests that during development, even slight micro differences in environmental conditions can have observable effects at the phenotypic level. The observable differences between monozygotic twins would be a case in point. It stands to reason that such effects would be even more the case for human individuals when in their early life they are imbedded in intense emotional experiences that are likely to be anything but 'micro'. In Knox's (2003) emergent/developmental model of archetype, it is from this level of early infant experience that image schemas leading to archetypal imagery develop. Hence, when considering any particular archetype, the macro and micro environmental conditions related to its emergence will require careful consideration.

## Theme 3: The place of extended inheritance

In Developmental Systems Theory, organisms are understood to inherit much more than their genetic constitution, including things such as 'chromosomes, nutrients, ambient temperatures, childcare' (Oyama *et al.* 2001, p. 4) and other resources from epigenetic inheritance, such as the chromatin marks that regulate gene expression, cytoplasmic chemical gradients, gut and other endosymbionts, a niche and physical environment. Such things do not fall neatly into gene/environment categories. In a similar way, an emergent/developmental view of archetypes sees them as arising from a range of developmental experiences and the influences from genes, brain and environment.

## Theme 4: Development as construction

Developmental Systems Theory understands development in terms of construction so that '[t]he life cycle of an organism is developmentally constructed, not programmed or preformed. It comes into being through interactions between the organism and its surroundings as well as interactions within the organism' (Oyama *et al.* 2001, p. 4). Developmental Systems Theorists are quite critical of the implicit and at times explicit preformationism within neo-Darwinism, that is, the view that the information for producing an organism is contained in the zygote and becomes 'read-out'. Rather, they see things in terms of what Gottlieb (2001) calls a 'bidirection between structure and function'. Research has now overwhelmingly shown that over the lifespan of an organism, feedback continually occurs bidirectionally between function and structure to the extent that structure only fully realizes itself through function. The critical point from these findings in developmental biology is that the end product of development leads to actual neural bio-structure as a result of the dynamic interaction which goes on bidirectionally between structure and function (experience in the environment) and that this occurs from the earliest stages of development, even prenatally.

Knox's (2003) emergent/developmental model of archetype relies on a similar neuroconstructivist position in terms of the bidirection between structure and function. When commenting on Schore's (1994) foundational research on the neurobiology of emotional development, she says that 'the intense relationships of early life directly influence the development of key parts of the brain' (Knox 2004, p. 6).

### Theme 5: There is distributed control of development

Developmental Systems Theory understands that no one factor can be said to completely control developmental outcomes. There is a vast and hetero-geneous assembly of interactants which are system-dependent and change over time so that attention needs to be given to ways the developing organism functions as a resource for its own further development. As such, Developmental Systems Theorists are especially critical of the concept of the 'genetic blueprint', Moss (2001, p. 85) concluding that there is ample evidence we are dealing with 'self-organizing, causally reciprocal systems of interactants.' In a similar way, an emergent/developmental view of arche-type is opposed also to any notion of a 'genetic blueprint'. As Knox (2004, p. 6) says, 'this model refutes any possibility of innate (genetically-specified) archetypal imagery.'

### Theme 6: Evolution is understood in terms of construction

Organisms and their environments are seen to be one system by Devel-opmental Systems Theory and it is this which is understood to co-evolve over time so that outcomes are not imposed but emerge. Whilst the process of evolution is not really the focus of emergent/developmental approaches to archetype theory, it should be noted again that this issue has been addressed by Hogenson (2001) when he argues that many of Jung's state-ments about the transmission of archetypes can be understood in terms of the 'Baldwin Effect', that is, psychological factors played out in cultural contexts can be central to the overall evolutionary process.

### Summary

Whilst parallels between Developmental Systems Theory and an emergent/ developmental model of archetype such as that proposed by Knox (2003) can be noted, the overall significance of Developmental Systems Theory for archetype theory has not yet been developed by Jungians. There has only been one passing reference to Oyama's (2000) work by Hogenson (2004a) because she criticizes innatist models in biology. What this overview of Developmental Systems Theory suggests is that a line of mutual and fruitful interchange is possible between the research findings of these biologists, emergent/developmental positions on archetype and archetype theory gener-ally. What Developmental Systems Theory indicates in particular is that one can retain a biological perspective on archetypes without having to accept innatism or preformationism so long as a developmental focus is maintained.

# Appendix B

## Borderline personality disorder

The current criteria for Borderline Personality Disorder follow from the American Psychiatric Association's (1994) *Diagnostic and Statistical Manual of Mental Disorders*.

*Criterion 1*: A pattern of unstable and intense interpersonal relationships characterized by alternating between extremes of idealization and devaluation.

*Criterion 2*: Impulsivity in at least two areas that are potentially self-damaging, e.g. spending, sex, substance abuse, reckless driving, binge eating (do not include suicidal or self-mutilating behaviour covered in *Criterion 5*).

*Criterion 3*: Affective instability due to a marked reactivity of mood, e.g. intense episodic dysphoria, irritability, or anxiety, usually lasting a few hours or only rarely more than a few days.

*Criterion 4*: Inappropriate, intense anger or lack of control of anger (e.g. frequent displays of temper, constant anger, recurrent physical fights).

*Criterion 5*: Recurrent suicidal behaviour, gestures, or threats, or self-mutilating behaviour. [It is this criterion which seems to be the most marked and noted for BPD sufferers.]

*Criterion 6*: Identity disturbance; markedly and persistently unstable self-image and/or sense of self. [Note: he or she may feel that he or she does not exist or embodies evil.]

*Criterion 7*: Chronic feelings of emptiness.

*Criterion 8*: Frantic efforts to avoid real or imagined abandonment (do not include suicidal or self-mutilating behaviour covered in *Criterion 5*).

*Criterion 9*: Transient, stress-related paranoid ideation or severe dissociative symptoms. [Note: or depersonalisation, derealisation, or hypnagogic illusions.]

# Notes

## 2 The wounded healer

1 There is now a vast literature to do with the countertransference and Sedgwick (1994) gives a comprehensive overview from a Jungian perspective of the psycho-analytic views on the subject as does Samuels (1985a) in his succinct introduction to his countertransference research project. Further Jungian explications can be found in Clark (2006, 2010) and Samuels (1993, 2006).
2 See also Bloom (2006), Corrigall *et al.* (2006), Shaw (2003) and Stone (2006) on this type of countertransference.
3 Mander takes this idea from Heimann (1967/8). See also Barnett (2007), Dryden and Spurling (1989), Ellenberger (1970) and Kottler (1986) on this issue.
4 Steinberg (1989) also introduces another important issue which he is not able to discuss – the use analysts can make of countertransference reactions in under-standing their own personality, that is, 'why do these particular countertrans-ference reactions occur now and in relation to this particular person?' (pp. 11–12).
5 The significance of early infant material can be noted in many of the Greek myths. For example, Oedipus was both abandoned and the object of attempted infanticide so that from a psychological point of view it is quite understandable that he would want to kill the killer (as in father), get back to mother and have everything repaired. Similarly, Narcissus' conception is in rape trauma and he is then reared by an abandoned mother.
6 Eliade (1964) does also indicate that hereditary transmission of shamanism within Siberian families can occur although this is still seen as a gift from the gods or spirits who must accept and approve the candidate through some initiatory experience. As he says, in 'Siberia the majority of shamans are "chosen" by the spirits and gods' (p. 50) and this is evidenced through some form of initiatory illness/derangement.
7 The shamanic aspects of the countertransference have been explored further by Stein (1984).
8 It is in 'The Philosophical Tree' (Jung 1954/1981) and 'Transformation Sym-bolism in the Mass' (Jung 1954/1991b) that shamanism in the context of individuation is most explicitly addressed. Summaries of Jung's theory of individuation can be found in McNeely (2010) and Stein (2006) whilst Downton (1989) overviews shamanism in terms of individuation.
9 Jung (1954/1981, p. 272) says: 'Like all archetypal symbols, the symbol of the tree has undergone a development of meaning in the course of the centuries. It is far removed from the meaning of the shamanistic tree, even though certain basic features prove to be unalterable. The psychoid form underlying any archetypal

image retains its character at all stages of development, though empirically it is capable of endless variations. The outward form of the tree may change in the course of time, but the richness and vitality of a symbol are expressed more in its change of meaning.' Jung is making use here of his concept of the 'psychoid unconscious' which he explains elsewhere in 'On the nature of the psyche' (Jung 1954/1991a).

## 3 What is shamanism?

1 In an endeavour to avoid confusion with previous publications, when the various tribal groups are specified I will spell their name in the way they currently prefer but with the old designation following in brackets.
2 Mikhailowski (1892, as cited in Czaplicka 1914), Lowie (1948) and Radin (1914, 1937) also hold that shamanism is a universal primitive religious expression.

The indebtedness of shamanic studies to the Jesup North Pacific Expedition needs to be noted because of the extensive fieldwork it undertook in Siberia. Franz Boas from the American Museum of Natural History initiated the expedition over 1900–2 after preliminary work along the Canadian and north-west coast of the USA. It traversed the Pacific coast of Alaska across to Siberia and made contact with various tribal groups, the principal investigators being Bogoras (1904) and Jochelson (1908). Before involvement in the expedition, both these men had spent previous time in Siberia as political prisoners. From 1889–98, Bogoras had been in exile in the Kolyma region of north-east Siberia among the Chukchi (Chukchee) tribe and he returned there with the Jesup North Pacific Expedition. Through extensive fieldwork and observation, he was able to describe the séance, role and initiation of Chukchi (Chukchee) shamans. Jochelson made similar fieldwork observations amongst the Sakha (Yakut), Yukaghir and Koryak groups. Both Bogoras and Jochelson were of the firm belief that shamanism originated in North Asia and that parallels with North America were due to earlier migrations. They not only formed a view about the religious aspect to shamanism but also believed shamanism to be expressive of a particular kind of psychopathology.
3 The Tamang are a minority Nepalese ethnic group and Peters spent a considerable amount of time living with them, eventually undergoing initiation as one of their shamans.
4 For the Siberian ethnography see Bogoras (1904), Castagné (1930), Chichlo (1981), Jochelson (1908, 1926, 1933), Lopatin (1940–1, 1946–9), Lot-Falck (1953, 1970), Mikhailowski (1894), Montefiore (1894–5), Murphy (1964), Pallas (1788a, 1788b), Shirokogoroff (1923, 1929, 1935), Sieroszewski (1902), Siikala (1978, 1980, 1984, 1987a, 1987b, 1989) and Sumner (1901).
5 The centrality of the Siberian *locus classicus* raises another important point as to the place accorded Native American material and why it should be given less prominence in explicating the wounded healer dynamics within a shaman archetypal configuration. Eliade (1964) indicates there is an issue to do with those shamans who choose the profession for themselves – they are considered less powerful – and there is significant self-selection in the Native American context. For instance, the Ghost Dance rituals and Vision Quest are phenomena which have been consciously reconstructed by Native Americans and in which participants choose their involvement (see La Barre 1970). Since this book's purpose is to explicate the unconscious (as in archetypal) side of the wounded healer component within the shamanic phenomenon, that is, the side which is more psychically pristine, it is more judicious to concentrate on those cultures

where shamanism is experienced as a spontaneous 'calling' especially where this may go against the neophyte's rational will. There is abundant evidence of just this sort of experience in the Siberian material.

## 4 Shamanism and the wounded healer as an archetype

1 Jung's ideas about archetypes seem to have emerged in three stages but it is generally agreed that he gives an extensive treatment of the theory in 'The structure of the psyche' (Jung 1931/1991a) and 'On the nature of the psyche' (Jung 1954/1991a) with specific examples being elaborated in 'The archetypes and the collective unconscious' (Jung 1959/1990).
2 'Archetype' was a word Jung re-interpreted from earlier usages in the *Corpus Hermeticum* (Scott 1985) by Dionysius the Areopagite (Rolt 1920) and Irenaeus (Keble 1872). Samuels, Shorter and Plaut (1993) in their *Critical Dictionary of Jungian Analysis* define an archetype as the 'inherited part of the psyche; structuring patterns of psychological performance linked to instinct; a hypothetical entity irrepresentable in itself and evident only through its manifestations' (p. 26).
3 Jung also discusses the 'solar phallus' case in *Symbols of Transformation* (1912/1986) and 'The concept of the collective unconscious' (1936/1990).
4 An extended example of Jung's approach would be his analysis of Wolfgang Pauli's dream series in 'Individual dream symbolism in relation to alchemy' (Jung 1952/1992).
5 Campbell (1976), Drury (1996), Eliade (1964), Halifax (1982), Haydu (1970), Kirchner (1952, as cited in Eliade 1964), La Barre (1972), Leroi-Gourhan (1977), Lommel (1967), Makkay (1953) and N. Smith (1992) all comment on the French palaeolithic caves as representing something shamanic.
6 See also Clottes and Lewis-Williams (2001).
7 See Eliade's (1964) Chapter 8 in particular as well as Grim (1983), Ryan (2002), Siikala (1978), C. M. Smith (1997) and Peters (1989) on this issue.
8 See Noll (1985) on shamanic imagery and for particular themes see Eliade (1964), Groesbeck (1989) and Siikala (1978).

## 5 Contemporary archetype theory

1 Contemporary approaches to archetype theory and counter-arguments can be found in Cambray (2002, 2006), Goodwyn (2010), Hogenson (1998, 2003a, 2003b, 2004a, 2004b, 2005, 2010), Jones (2003), Knox (2003, 2004, 2010), McDowell (2001), Merchant (2006, 2009, 2010), Mogenson (1999), Pietikainen (1998a, 1998b), Roesler (2010), Solomon (1998), Stevens (1998), Tresan (1996) as well as in Stevens' (2006) summary.
2 On the general issue Hogenson (2004a, p. 70) says: 'This argument [by Saunders and Skar] is based in a dynamic systems mode of thinking, but I do not believe most Jungians have recognized its radical nature.' The application of Developmental Systems Theory and emergentism to archetype theory has led Hogenson (2004b) to a similar view to that of Saunders and Skar (2001) that archetypes are later levels of emergence preceded by complexes and as such 'the archetype does not exist, in the sense of being a discrete ontologically definable entity with a place in the genome or the cognitive arrangement of modules or schemas in the brain' (p. 13).
3 Stevens (2002) in his updated publication *Archetype Revisited: An Updated Natural History of the Self* gives a comprehensive overview of the many

statements by Jung to do with the biological base to archetype theory. See also Stevens and Price (1996).
4 Stevens (1982) says he was initially introduced to the idea of the biological underpinning to Jung's theory by Champernowne who asserted that Jung was more biological than Freud. 'Archetypes, she declared, are *biological entities* . . . Like all biological entities they have a natural history: they are subject to the laws of evolution. In other words, *archetypes evolved through natural selection*' (p. 17). Stevens believes inherited innate capacities of mind are evidenced through the research of Cosmides and Tooby (1989) in the field of evolutionary psychology; Mithen (1996) from evolutionary archaeology; Sperber (1996) from the field of cognitive science; and Stevens and Price (1996) from the field of evolutionary psychiatry.
5 All the implications of Knox's emergent/developmental model are substantial for archetype theory and are dealt with in Appendix A.
6 Neumann's (1955) classic use of the concept of the Great Mother archetype is the alternative archetypal way of explaining the kind of ubiquity which Skar (2004) highlights.

# 6 A re-evaluation of Jung's classic theory of archetype

1 Hogenson (2001) has considered this claim that Jung used a Lamarckian model of evolution to underwrite his theory of archetypes. He is able to demonstrate that Jung is not only familiar with, but uses the writings of Baldwin and Morgan, both of whom were noted and forceful opponents of neo-Lamarckian theory from within a neo-Darwinian framework and that Jung's statements need to be understood from this perspective. The Baldwin and Morgan model, now known as the 'Baldwin Effect', explicitly views psychological factors as central to the evolutionary process and Hogenson makes an argument that Jung's statements can be read this way rather than as representing anything Lamarckian.

# 7 The developmental side to the shamanic wounded healer

1 The concept of the paranoid-schizoid position refers to those anxieties experienced by infants in the earliest preverbal stage of development. The fears are understood to be around persecution and attack (hence, 'paranoid') so that the defensive manoeuvre is to split the persecuting object (hence, 'schizoid') into 'good' and 'bad' components so as to retain the good and remove the bad.
2 Ducey cites Brill (1913), Shirokogoroff (1935) and Gussow (1960) in constructing his list of dissociative symptoms. See also Eliade (1964, 1987).
3 Conversion disorders occur where a distressing psychological complex is replaced by a physical symptom and these were originally termed by the early researchers as 'hysteria'. *La belle indifférence* [the beautiful indifference] was one of the first characteristics noticed in some sufferers with conversion disorder by Charcot at the Salpêtrière in Paris at the end of the nineteenth century. It was as if the patients were emotionally indifferent to their condition. Freud concluded that this was because the neurotic symptoms were providing actual benefit to the patients (if only in a secondary way) because they were partly resolving a more profound but unconscious conflict.
4 In Klein's (1946) conception, the depressive position follows on from the paranoid-schizoid position in infant development where splitting tendencies are

resolved through the recognition that love and hate are being directed toward the same object.

5 Legends could be problematic material here because they are constructed stories, each aspect of which is intended to communicate something specific. Jung (1940/1990) notes in his analysis of 'The child archetype' that the child-hero is usually presented as both special/divine on the one hand and vulnerable/attacked on the other. This is to emphasize a number of important attributes – the divine-child-hero's manifest detachment from its background (the mother), its 'vocational specialness' and its capacity to transcend misfortune. Being so symbolically dense, it is not necessarily the case that orphanhood in the shamanic legends reflects actual life experience. It may be more about asserting the 'vulnerable' side of the special/divine–vulnerable/attacked nexus. Furthermore, as the orphaned 'Divine Child' is seen in the mythology of many world groups irrespective of shamanism, deductions from such legends should not be over-emphasized.

6 See Chapter 9 for a more detailed description of Borderline Personality Disorder.

## 8 Case study: The Siberian Sakha (Yakut) tribe

1 See the description of Arctic hysteria in Chapter 7 under the heading 'The Siberian shaman's pre-initiatory illness: Stage One' (pp. 90–1).

2 Since the statistical question being asked by Ducey is: 'are the other cultures' average (mean) scores on Item 9 (diffusion of nurturance) different from the Sakha (Yakut) score?' a one-sample $t$ test is appropriate. When this is done, the Sakha (Yakut) are definitely significantly different to all other cultures on Item 9 ($t_{100}$ = 11.94, $p<0.05$), the average (mean) for the other cultures being 7.75 (see *Table 8.1*).

3 As above, the statistical question being asked is: 'are the other cultures' average (mean) scores on all the items different from the Sakha (Yakut) score?' so one-sample $t$ tests were performed in which the rating given to the Sakha (Yakut) on each scale was used as the comparison score against the average (mean) for the other cultures. The results are listed in *Table 8.1*.

4 As above, one-sample $t$ tests were performed in which the rating given to the Sakha (Yakut) on each scale was used as the comparison score against the average (mean) for the other cultures. The results are listed in *Table 8.2*.

5 DSM-IV is the American Psychiatric Association's *Diagnostic and Statistical Manual of Mental Disorders*, which is one of the most widely used instruments by which clinicians diagnose mental disorders.

## 9 The Siberian shaman's wound: A 'borderline type of case'

1 Balint's (1992) 'ocnophile' and 'philobat' would experience a similar oscillation.

2 There may be a connection between Winnicott's 'kernel/shell' idea and Wisdom's (1961, 1964) ideas of 'nuclear' and 'orbital' aspects of personality structure. Wisdom primarily uses his terms in relation to psychoanalytic introjects and their place in personality development. Nonetheless, a crude nosology of personality 'disease' could then result as in *Table N.1* (p. 179). The use of the term 'dysfunctional' in the 'kernel' (centre) part to the personality is equivalent to 'psychotic' as it would align with Winnicott's zone of 'primary madness' and probably that of Eigen's (1986) concept of the 'psychotic core'.

3 Peters is referring here to the third edition of the American Psychiatric Associ-

*Table N.1* A crude nosology of personality 'disease'

| Kernel (Centre of the personality) | Shell (Outer layers of the personality) | Result |
| --- | --- | --- |
| If functional | If dysfunctional | Then neurosis |
| If dysfunctional | If dysfunctional | Then psychosis |
| If dysfunctional | If functional | Then personality disorder |

ation's *Diagnostic and Statistical Manual of Mental Disorders*. The current fourth edition is generally designated as DSM-IV.
4 The fuller quote from Basilov (1984, p. 26) is instructive: 'Is the shaman sane? To fellow tribal members, there was no doubt. Of course he is. The "shamanic illness" was regarded as an ailment, but the shaman then recovered, in the opinion of those around him. Everywhere the shaman was clearly distinguished from the neuropath, and this must be emphasized to avoid distortion in evaluating the traditional culture of the native peoples of Siberia and the Far North.'

## 10 Evidence that the Siberian shaman is proto-borderline

1 Family shamanism is used to describe the situation in some tribes whereby every family has one or more drums of its own which are used by family members for specific ceremonials. As a type of shamanizing, it runs in parallel with individual shamanism where only specific individuals perform shamanic rites. There is debate in the literature as to the nature of the relationship between family shamanism and individual shamanism. Bogoras (1904) was of the view that 'Family shamanism, being quite simple and primitive, probably antedated the shamanism of individuals having special skill and vocation, and the latter seems to have grown up based on the former' (p. 413). This was also the view of Jochelson (1908) through his work on the Koryak. Eliade (1964), on the other hand, takes an opposing position and considers family shamanism among the Chukchi (Chukchee) to be a 'plagiaristic aping of the ecstatic technique of the professional shaman' and a 'hybrid phenomenon' (p. 253). Nonetheless, whilst family shamanism is encountered amongst other tribes, such as the Koryak, the Asiatic Inuit (Eskimo) and probably the Yukaghir and the Kamchadal, Bogoras (1904) does note that in 'modern times the importance of family shamanism is losing ground among all the tribes named, with the exception of the Chukchee' (p. 414). This would suggest that it is defensible to use the Chukchi (Chukchee) as a special case in relation to family shamanism.
2 Some illustrative examples from the clinical literature include Stone's (1979, p. 12) report of a woman who attempted suicide and was diagnosed with psychotic depression which was preceded by the dream image: 'One of my arms was torn off and my heart was exposed.' Similarly, Boss (1959, p. 170) reports this dream image: 'I fell into a large heap of skulls and my body disintegrated', which preceded a schizophrenic episode. One of Friedman's (1992, p. 23) cases involved a patient who presented with depression and anxiety but this masked more severe underlying pathology revealed in this dream image: 'A dead woman is hanging on the wall of a shed with hooks and her legs are cut off at the knee.'
3 See Appendix B.

## 11 Conclusions

1 The way selectors use their own countertransferential experiences in trainee selection is a topic insufficiently explored in the literature despite its importance far outweighing assessment of an applicant's formal qualifications. And a flow-on question would be: how do selectors become trained in this?

# References

Ackerknecht, E. H. (1943) 'Psychopathology, primitive medicine and primitive culture', *Bulletin of the History of Medicine*, *14*: 30–67.
—— (1971) *Medicine and Ethnology. Selected Essays*. Baltimore, MD: Johns Hopkins Press.
Ainsworth, M., Blehar, M. and Waters, E. (1978) *Patterns of Attachment: A Psychological Study of the Strange Situation*. Hillsdale, NJ: Erlbaum.
Alekseev, N. A. (1987) 'Shamans and their religious practices', trans. R. Radzai. In M. Balzer (1997) *Shamanic Worlds: Rituals and Lore of Siberia and Central Asia*. New York, NY: North Castle Books.
American Psychiatric Association (1994) *Diagnostic and Statistical Manual of Mental Disorders* (4th edn). Washington, DC: American Psychiatric Association.
Anfilov, V. (1902) 'Christian Shaman: Notes from the trip to the "Big Land Tundra"', summarized and part translated by A. Znamenski. In A. Znamenski (2003) *Shamanism in Siberia: Russian Records of Indigenous Spirituality*. Dordrecht, The Netherlands: Kluwer Academic Publishers.
Anokhin, A. V. (1910) 'Shamanism of Siberian Turkic Tribes', summarized and part translated by A. Znamenski. In A. Znamenski (2003) *Shamanism in Siberia: Russian Records of Indigenous Spirituality*. Dordrecht, The Netherlands: Kluwer Academic Publishers.
Atkinson, J. (1992) 'Shamanisms today', *Annual Review of Anthropology*, *21*: 307–30.
Atwood, G. and Stolorow, R. (1977) 'Metapsychology, reification and the representational world of C. G. Jung', *International Review of Psychoanalysis*, *4*: 197–214.
Balint, M. (1992) *The Basic Fault*. Evanston, IL: Northwestern University Press.
Barnett, M. (2007) 'What brings you here? An exploration of the unconscious motivations of those who choose to train and work as psychotherapists and counsellors', *Psychodynamic Practice: Individuals, Groups and Organisations*, *13*: 257–74.
Baron-Cohen, S. (1998) 'Does the study of autism justify minimalist innate modularity?', *Learning and Individual Differences*, *10*: 179–91.
Barry, H., Bacon, M. K. and Child, I. L. (1955) 'Definitions, ratings and bibliographic sources for child-training practices of 110 cultures'. In C. S. Ford (ed.) (1967) *Cross-cultural Approaches*. New Haven, CT: Human Relations Area Files Press.

Basilov, V. (1984) 'Chosen by the spirits'. In M. Balzer (1997) *Shamanic Worlds: Rituals and Lore of Siberia and Central Asia*, trans. R. Radzai. New York, NY: North Castle Books.

Batchelor, J. (1901) *The Ainu and Their Folklore*. London: The Religious Tract Society.

Bloom, K. (2006) *The Embodied Self*. London: Karnac.

Bogoras, W. (1904) 'The Chukchee', The Jesup North Pacific Expedition, vol. 7. In F. Boas (ed.) *Memoirs of the American Museum of Natural History, 1904–1909*, vol. 11. Leiden: E. J. Brill.

Boss, M. (1959) 'The psychopathology of dreams in schizophrenia and organic psychoses'. In M. DeMartino (ed.) *Dreams and Personality Dynamics*. Springfield, IL: Charles Thomas.

Bourguignon, E. (1976) *Possession*. San Francisco, CA: Chandler & Sharp.

Brill, A. A. (1913) 'Pibloktoq or hysteria among Peary's eskimos', *Journal of Nervous and Mental Disease*, *40*: 514–20.

Bullock, A. and Trombley, S. (eds) (2000) *The New Fontana Dictionary of Modern Thought*. London: Harper Collins.

Cambray, J. (2002) 'Synchronicity and emergence', *American Imago*, *59*: 409–34.

—— (2006) 'Towards the feeling of emergence', *Journal of Analytical Psychology*, *51*: 1–20.

Campbell, J. (1976) *The Masks of God: Primitive Mythology*. New York, NY: Penguin Books.

Casia, V. M., Turati, C. and Simion, F. (2004) 'Can a non-specific bias toward top-heavy patterns explain newborns' face preference?', *Psychological Science*, *15*: 379–83.

Castagné, J. (1930) 'Magie et exorcisme chez les Kazak-Kirghizes et autres peuples turcs orientaux', *Revue des Études Islamiques*, *4*: 53–156.

Chichlo, B. (1981) 'L'Ours-chamane', *Etudes Mongoles et Sibériennes*, *12*: 35–112.

Chomsky, N. (1968) *Syntactic Structures*. The Hague: Mouton.

Clark, G. (2006) 'A Spinozan lens onto the confusions of borderline relations', *Journal of Analytical Psychology*, *51*: 67–86.

—— (2010) 'The embodied countertransference and recycling the mad matter of symbolic equivalence'. In G. Heuer (ed.) (2010) *Sacral Revolutions: Reflecting on the Work of Andrew Samuels – Cutting Edges in Psychoanalysis and Jungian Analysis*. New York, NY: Routledge/Taylor & Francis.

Clottes, J. (ed.) (2003a) *Return to Chauvet Cave. Excavating the Birthplace of Art: The First Full Report*, trans. P. Bahn. London: Thames & Hudson.

—— (2003b) 'The end chamber'. In J. Clottes (ed.) *Return to Chauvet Cave. Excavating the Birthplace of Art: The First Full Report*, trans. P. Bahn. London: Thames & Hudson.

—— (2003c) 'Conclusion'. In J. Clottes (ed.) *Return to Chauvet Cave. Excavating the Birthplace of Art: The First Full Report*, trans. P. Bahn. London: Thames & Hudson.

Clottes, J. and Courtin, J. (1996) *The Cave Beneath the Sea: Paleolithic Images at Cosquer*, trans. M. Garner. New York, NY: Harry N. Abrams.

Clottes, J. and Lewis-Williams, J. (1998) *The Shamans of Prehistory: Trance and Magic in the Painted Caves*, trans. S. Hawkes. New York, NY: Harry N. Abrams.

—— (2001) *Les chamanes de la Préhistoire. Texte intégral, Polémique et Réponses.* Paris: La Maison des Roches.

Conti-O'Hare, M. (2002) *The Nurse as Wounded Healer: From Trauma to Transcendence.* Sudbury, MA: Jones & Bartlett.

Corrigall, J., Payne, H. and Wilkinson, H. (eds) (2006) *About a Body: Working with the Embodied Mind in Psychotherapy.* London: Routledge.

Cosmides, L. and Tooby, J. (1989) 'Evolutionary psychology and the generation of culture, Part 1: Case study: A computational theory of social exchange', *Ethology and Sociobiology, 10*: 51–97.

Czaplicka, M. (1914) *Aboriginal Siberia: A Study in Social Anthropology.* Oxford: Clarendon Press.

deMause, L. (2002) 'The evolution of psyche and society', *Journal of Psychohistory, 29*: 238–85.

De Prokofyeva, Y. (1951) 'The costume of an Enets shaman'. In H. Michael (1963) (ed.) *Studies in Siberian Shamanism.* Toronto: Toronto University Press.

Devereux, G. (1956) 'Normal and abnormal: The key problem of psychiatric anthropology'. In J. B. Casagrande and T. Gladwin (eds) *Some Uses of Anthropology: Theoretical and Applied.* Washington, DC: Anthropological Society of Washington.

—— (1961) 'Shamans as neurotics', *American Anthropologist, 63*: 1080–90.

—— (1980) *Basic Problems of Ethnopsychiatry.* Chicago, IL: University of Chicago Press.

Diószegi, V. (1968) *Tracing Shamans in Siberia.* New York, NY: Humanities Press.

Downton J. (1989) 'Individuation and shamanism', *Journal of Analytical Psychology, 34*: 73–88.

Drury, N. (1996) *Shamanism.* Rockport, MA: Element Inc.

Dryden, W. and Spurling, L. (1989) *On Becoming a Psychotherapist.* London: Routledge.

Ducey, C. (1976) 'The life history and creative psychopathology of the shaman: Ethnopsychoanalytic perspectives', *Psychoanalytic Study of Society, 7*: 173–230.

Dunne, C. (2000) *Carl Jung: Wounded Healer of the Soul.* New York, NY: Parabola.

Edsman, C. (ed.) (1967) *Studies in Shamanism.* Stockholm: Almquist & Wiskell.

Eigen, M. (1986) *The Psychotic Core.* Northvale, NJ: Jason Aronson.

Eliade, M. (1964) *Shamanism: Archaic Techniques of Ecstasy.* Princeton: Princeton University Press.

—— (1987) 'Shamanism: An overview'. In M. Eliade (ed.) *The Encyclopedia of Religion*, vol. 13. New York, NY: Macmillan.

Ellenberger, H. (1970) *Discovery of the Unconscious: The History and Evolution of Dynamic Psychiatry.* New York, NY: Basic Books.

Fairbairn, W. R. D. (1952) *Psychoanalytic Studies of the Personality.* London: Tavistock.

Federn, P. (1940) 'The determination of hysteria versus obsessional neurosis', *Psychoanalytic Review, 27*: 265–76.

Fonagy, P. (2002) 'Introduction to the colloquium of neuroscience and psychoanalysis'. Paper presented at the Anna Freud 50th anniversary conference, London, Anna Freud Centre.

Freud, S. (1910/2001) 'The future prospects of psycho-analytic therapy'. In *The*

*Complete Psychological Works of Sigmund Freud*, vol. 11, trans. J. Strachey. London: Vintage.

—— (1912/2001) 'Recommendations to physicians practising psycho-analysis'. In *The Complete Psychological Works of Sigmund Freud*, vol. 12, trans. J. Strachey. London: Vintage.

—— (1914/2001) 'Observations on transference-love (further recommendations on the technique of psycho-analysis III)'. In *The Complete Psychological Works of Sigmund Freud*, vol. 12, trans. J. Strachey. London: Vintage.

Friedman, R. (1992) 'The use of dreams in the evaluation of severely disturbed patients', *American Journal of Psychoanalysis*, *52*: 13–30.

Geertz, C. (1977) 'Religion as a cultural system'. In M. Banton (ed.) *Anthropological Approaches to the Study of Religion*. London: Tavistock.

Glob, P. (1969) 'Summary'. In *Rock Carvings in Denmark*, trans. P. Crabb. Jutland Archaeological Society Publications, vol. 7. Copenhagen: Gyldendal.

Goodwyn, E. (2010) 'Approaching archetypes: Reconsidering innateness', *Journal of Analytical Psychology*, *55*: 502–21.

Gottlieb, G. (2001) 'A developmental psychobiological systems view: Early formulation and current status'. In S. Oyama, P. E. Griffiths and R. D. Gray (eds) *Cycles of Contingency: Developmental Systems and Evolution*. Cambridge, MA: MIT Press.

—— (2007) 'Probabilistic epigenesis', *Developmental Science*, *10*: 1–11.

Graves, R. (1960) *The Greek Myths*, vols 1 & 2. Aylesbury: Penguin Books.

Grim, J. (1983) *The Shaman: Patterns of Siberian and Ojibway Healing*. Norman, OK: University of Oklahoma Press.

Grimal, P. (ed.) (1965) *Larousse World Mythology*. London: Hamlyn.

Grinker, R. (1977) 'The borderline syndrome: A phenomenological view'. In P. Hartocollis (ed.) *Borderline Personality Disorders: The Concept, the Syndrome, the Patient*. New York, NY: International Universities Press.

Groesbeck, C. J. (1975) 'The archetypal image of the wounded healer', *Journal of Analytical Psychology*, *20*: 123–45.

—— (1989) 'C. G. Jung and the shaman's vision', *Journal of Analytical Psychology*, *34*: 255–75.

Grof, S. (1976) *Realms of the Human Unconscious*. New York, NY: E. P. Dutton.

Grotstein, J. S. (1981) *Splitting and Projective Identification*. New York, NY: Aronson Press.

Guggenbuhl-Craig, A. (1989) *Power in the Helping Professions*. Dallas, TX: Spring.

—— (1999) 'The necessity of talent'. In M. Mattoon (ed.) *Destruction and Creation: Personal and Cultural Transformations. Proceedings of the Fourteenth International Congress for Analytical Psychology*, Florence, 1998. Einsiedeln: Daimon Verlag.

Gunderson, J. (2001) *Borderline Personality Disorder: A Clinical Guide*. Washington, DC: American Psychiatric Publishing.

Guntrip, H. (1970) *Schizoid Phenomena, Object Relations, and the Self*. New York, NY: International Universities Press.

Gussow, Z. (1960) '*Pibloktoq* (Hysteria) among the Polar Eskimo: An ethno-psychiatric study'. In W. Muensterberger and S. Axelrad (eds) *The Psychoanalytic Study of Society*, *Vol. 1*. New York, NY: International Universities Press.

Halifax, J. (1982) *Shaman: The Wounded Healer*. London: Thames & Hudson.

Harner, M. (1973) *Hallucinogens and Shamanism*. London: Oxford University Press.
—— (1980) *The Way of the Shaman*. San Francisco, CA: Harper & Row.
Harvey, G. (ed.) (2003) *Shamanism: A Reader*. London: Routledge.
Haydu, G. (1970) 'Review of *Shamanism: The Beginnings of Art* by A. Lommel', *Current Anthropology*, *11*: 42–3.
Hayes, J. A. (2002) 'Playing with fire: Countertransference and clinical epistemology', *Journal of Contemporary Psychotherapy*, *32*: 93–100.
Heimann, P. (1967/8) 'The evaluation of applicants for psychoanalytic training'; reprinted in *About Children and Children-No-Longer*; Collected Papers, 1942–80 (1989). London & New York: Tavistock/Routledge.
Hobson, R. F. (1971) 'The archetypes of the collective unconscious'. In M. Fordham, R. Gordon, J. Hubback, K. Lambert and M. Williams (eds) (1973) *Analytical Psychology: A Modern Science*. Library of Analytical Psychology, vol. 1. London: Heinemann Medical Books.
Hogenson, G. B. (1998) 'Response to Pietikainen and Stevens', *Journal of Analytical Psychology*, *43*: 357–72.
—— (2001) 'The Baldwin effect: A neglected influence on C. G. Jung's evolutionary thinking', *Journal of Analytical Psychology*, *46*: 591–611.
—— (2003a) 'Reply to Maloney', *Journal of Analytical Psychology*, *48*: 265–6.
—— (2003b) 'Reply to Raya Jones', *Journal of Analytical Psychology*, *48*: 714–18.
—— (2004a) 'What are symbols symbols of? Situated action, mythological bootstrapping and the emergence of the self', *Journal of Analytical Psychology*, *49*: 67–81.
—— (2004b) 'The Self, the symbolic and synchronicity: Virtual realities and the emergence of the psyche'. Paper presented at the XVI Congress of the International Association for Analytical Psychology, Barcelona, Spain, September.
—— (2005) 'The Self, the symbolic and synchronicity: Virtual realities and the emergence of the psyche', *Journal of Analytical Psychology*, *50*: 271–84.
—— (2010) 'Response to Erik Goodwyn's "Approaching archetypes: Reconsidering innateness"', *Journal of Analytical Psychology*, *55*: 543–9.
Holmes, C. (1991) 'The wounded healer', *Society for Psychoanalytic Psychotherapy Bulletin*, *6*: 33–6.
—— (1998) *There is No Such Thing as a Therapist: An Introduction to the Therapeutic Process*. London: Karnac.
Hultkrantz, Å. (1967) 'Spirit lodge, a North American shamanistic séance'. In C. Edsman (ed.) *Studies in Shamanism*. Stockholm: Almquist & Wiskell.
—— (1973) 'A definition of shamanism', *Temenos*, *9*: 25–37.
—— (1988) 'Shamanism: A religious phenomenon?'. In G. Doore (ed.) *Shaman's Path: Healing, Personal Growth, and Empowerment*. Boston, MA: Shambhala.
Hutton, R. (2001) *Shamans: Siberian Spirituality and the Western Imagination*. London: Hambledon.
Jackson, C. (2004) 'Healing ourselves, healing others: First in a series', *Holistic Nursing Practice*, *18*: 67–81.
Jackson, S. W. (2000) 'The wounded healer'. Presidential Address to the Seventy-Third Annual Meeting of the American Association for the History of Medicine, Bethesda, MD. Retrieved from http://muse.jhu.edu/journals/bulletin_of_the_history_of_medicine/v075/75.1jackson.html
Jochelson, W. (1908) 'The Koryak', The Jesup North Pacific Expedition, vol. 6. In

F. Boas (ed.) *Memoirs of the American Museum of Natural History, 1904–1909*, vol. 10. Leiden: E. J. Brill.

—— (1926) 'The Yukaghir and the Yukaghirized Tungus', The Jesup North Pacific Expedition, vol. 13. In F. Boas (ed.) *Memoirs of the American Museum of Natural History, 1904–1909*, vol. 9. Leiden: E. J. Brill.

—— (1933) 'The Yakut', *American Museum of Natural History Anthropological Papers*, *33*: 35–225.

Johnson, M. H. and Morton, J. (1991) *Biology and Cognitive Development: Case of Face Recognition*. Oxford: Blackwell.

Jones, R. A. (2003) 'On innatism: A response to Hogenson', *Journal of Analytical Psychology*, *48*: 705–14.

Jung, C. G. (1902/1993) 'On the psychology and pathology of so-called occult phenomena'. In *Psychiatric Studies, CW 1*. London: Routledge & Kegan Paul.

—— (1912/1986) *Symbols of Transformation, CW 5*. London: Routledge & Kegan Paul.

—— (1916/1990) 'The structure of the unconscious'. In *Two Essays on Analytical Psychology, CW 7*. London: Routledge & Kegan Paul.

—— (1917/1990) 'On the psychology of the unconscious'. In *Two Essays in Analytical Psychology, CW 7*. London: Routledge & Kegan Paul.

—— (1918/1991) 'The role of the unconscious'. In *Civilisation in Transition, CW 10*. London: Routledge & Kegan Paul.

—— (1919/1991) 'Instinct and the unconscious'. In *The Structure and Dynamics of the Psyche, CW 8*. London: Routledge & Kegan Paul.

—— (1926/1991) 'Spirit and life'. In *The Structure and Dynamics of the Psyche, CW 8*. London: Routledge & Kegan Paul.

—— (1928/1990) 'The relations between the ego and the unconscious'. In *Two Essays on Analytical Psychology, CW 7*. London: Routledge & Kegan Paul.

—— (1929/1993) 'Freud and Jung: Contrasts'. In *Freud and Psychoanalysis, CW 4*. London: Routledge & Kegan Paul.

—— (1930/1991) 'The complications of American psychology'. In *Civilisation in Transition, CW 10*. London: Routledge & Kegan Paul.

—— (1931/1991a) 'The structure of the psyche'. In *The Structure and Dynamics of the Psyche, CW 8*. London: Routledge & Kegan Paul.

—— (1931/1991b) 'Mind and Earth'. In *Civilisation in Transition, CW 10*. London: Routledge & Kegan Paul.

—— (1936/1990) 'The concept of the collective unconscious'. In *The Archetypes and the Collective Unconscious, CW 9i*. London: Routledge & Kegan Paul.

—— (1937/1993) 'The realities of practical psychotherapy'. In *The Practice of Psychotherapy, CW 16*. London: Routledge & Kegan Paul.

—— (1939/1990) 'Conscious, unconscious, and individuation'. In *The Archetypes and the Collective Unconscious, CW 9i*. London: Routledge & Kegan Paul.

—— (1939/1993) 'The symbolic life'. In *The Symbolic Life, CW 18*. London: Routledge & Kegan Paul.

—— (1940/1990) 'The psychology of the child archetype'. In *The Archetypes and the Collective Unconscious, CW 9i*. London: Routledge & Kegan Paul.

—— (1940/1991) 'Psychology and religion'. In *Psychology and Religion: West and East, CW 11*. London: Routledge & Kegan Paul.

—— (1946/1993) 'The psychology of the transference'. In *The Practice of Psychotherapy, CW 16*. London: Routledge & Kegan Paul.

—— (1948/1991a) 'The psychological foundations of belief in spirits'. In *The Structure and Dynamics of the Psyche, CW 8*. London: Routledge & Kegan Paul.

—— (1948/1991b) 'A psychological approach to the dogma of the Trinity'. In *Psychology and Religion: West and East, CW 11*. London: Routledge & Kegan Paul.

—— (1950/1990) 'A study in the process of individuation'. In *The Archetypes and the Collective Unconscious, CW 9i*. London: Routledge & Kegan Paul.

—— (1951/1991) 'On synchronicity'. In *The Structure and Dynamics of the Psyche, CW 8*. London: Routledge & Kegan Paul.

—— (1951/1993) 'Fundamental questions of psychotherapy'. In *The Practice of Psychotherapy, CW 16*. London: Routledge & Kegan Paul.

—— (1952/1991a) 'Synchronicity: An acausal connecting principle'. In *The Structure and Dynamics of the Psyche, CW 8*. London: Routledge & Kegan Paul.

—— (1952/1991b) 'Foreword to White's *God and the Unconscious*'. In *Psychology and Religion: West and East, CW 11*. London: Routledge & Kegan Paul.

—— (1952/1992) 'Individual dream symbolism in relation to alchemy'. In *Psychology and Alchemy, CW 12*. London: Routledge & Kegan Paul.

—— (1953/1993) 'Letter to Père Bruno'. In *The Symbolic Life, CW 18*. London: Routledge & Kegan Paul.

—— (1954) 'Letter to G. A. van den Bergh von Eysinga, 13.2.54'. In G. Adler and A. Jaffé (eds) (1976) *C. G. Jung: Letters, 1951–1961*, vol. 2. London: Routledge & Kegan Paul.

—— (1954/1981) 'The philosophical tree'. In *Alchemical Studies, CW 13*. London: Routledge & Kegan Paul.

—— (1954/1990a) 'Concerning the archetypes, with special reference to the anima concept'. In *The Archetypes and the Collective Unconscious, CW 9i*. London: Routledge & Kegan Paul.

—— (1954/1990b) 'Psychological aspects of the mother archetype'. In *The Archetypes and the Collective Unconscious, CW 9i*. London: Routledge & Kegan Paul.

—— (1954/1990c) 'On the psychology of the trickster figure'. In *The Archetypes and the Collective Unconscious, CW 9i*. London: Routledge & Kegan Paul.

—— (1954/1991a) 'On the nature of the psyche'. In *The Structure and Dynamics of the Psyche, CW 8*. London: Routledge & Kegan Paul.

—— (1954/1991b) 'Transformation symbolism in the Mass'. In *Psychology and Religion: West and East, CW 11*. London: Routledge & Kegan Paul.

—— (1959/1990) *The Archetypes and the Collective Unconscious, CW 9i*. London: Routledge & Kegan Paul.

—— (1963/1990) *Memories, Dreams, Reflections*. London: Flamingo.

Jung, C. G. and Pauli, W. (1955) *The Interpretation of Nature and the Psyche*. London: Routledge & Kegan Paul.

Karmiloff-Smith, A. (2009) 'Nativism versus neuroconstructivism: Rethinking the study of developmental disorders', *Developmental Psychology*, 45: 56–63.

Kaufmann, W. A. (1992) *Discovering the Mind, vol. 3: Freud, Adler, and Jung*. New Brunswick, NJ: Transaction Publishers.

Keble, J. (trans.) (1872) *Five Books of Irenaeus Against Heresies*. Oxford: Library of Fathers of the Holy Catholic Church.

Kent Reilly, F. (1996) 'Art, ritual and rulership in the Olmec world'. In M. Coe (ed.) *The Olmec World: Ritual and Rulership.* Princeton, NJ: The Art Museum, Princeton University.

Kerényi, C. (1959) *Asklepios: Archetypal Image of the Physician's Existence.* New York, NY: Pantheon.

Kirmayer, L. J. (2003) 'Asklepian dreams: The ethos of the wounded-healer in the clinical encounter', *Transcultural Psychiatry, 40:* 248–77.

Kirsch, T. (1982) 'Analysis in training'. In M. Stein (ed.) *Jungian Analysis.* Chicago, IL: Open Court.

Klein, M. (1946) 'Notes on some schizoid mechanisms'. In J. Riviere (ed.) (1952) *Developments in Psycho-analysis.* London: Hogarth Press.

Klementz, D. (1910) 'The Buriats'. In J. Hastings (ed.) *Encyclopaedia of Religion and Ethnography,* vol. 3. Edinburgh: T & T Clark.

Knox, J. M. (2001) 'Memories, fantasies, archetypes: An exploration of some connections between cognitive science and analytical psychology', *Journal of Analytical Psychology, 46:* 613–35.

—— (2003) *Archetype, Attachment, Analysis: Jungian Psychology and the Emergent Mind.* London: Brunner-Routledge.

—— (2004) 'From archetypes to reflective function', *Journal of Analytical Psychology, 49:* 1–19.

—— (2010) 'Response to Erik Goodwyn's "Approaching archetypes: reconsidering innateness"', *Journal of Analytical Psychology, 55:* 522–33.

Kottler, J. A. (1986) *On Being a Therapist.* San Francisco, CA: Jossey-Bass.

Krader, L. (1954) 'Buryat religion and society', *Southwestern Journal of Anthropology, 10:* 322–51.

Kramer, M. (1969) 'Manifest dream content in psychopathological states'. In M. Kramer (ed.) *Dream Psychology and the New Biology of Dreaming.* Springfield, IL: Charles Thomas.

Kraus, R. F. (1972) 'A psychoanalytic interpretation of shamanism', *Psychoanalytic Review, 59:* 19–32.

Krippner, S. C. (2002) 'Conflicting perspectives on shamans and shamanism: Points and counterpoints', *American Psychologist, 57:* 962–77.

Kroeber, A. (1940) 'Psychosis or social sanction?', *Character and Personality: A Quarterly for Psychodiagnostic and Allied Studies, 8:* 204–15.

La Barre, W. (1970) *The Ghost Dance. The Origins of Religion.* New York, NY: Dell Publishing.

—— (1972) 'Hallucinogens and the shamanic origins of religion'. In P. Hurst (ed.) *Flesh of the Gods: The Ritual Use of Hallucinogens.* London: Allen & Unwin.

Lajoux, J. (1977) *Tassili n'Ajjer (Art rupestre du Sahara Préhistorique).* Paris: Edition du Chéne.

Laskowski, C. and Pellicore, K. (2002) 'The wounded healer archetype: Applications to palliative care practice', *American Journal of Hospice & Palliative Care, 19:* 403–7.

Laufer, B. (1917) 'Origin of the word shaman', *American Anthropologist, 19:* 361–71.

Le Guillou, Y. (2003) 'Depictions of humans'. In J. Clottes (ed.) *Return to Chauvet Cave. Excavating the Birthplace of Art: The First Full Report,* trans. P. Bahn. London: Thames & Hudson.

Leroi-Gourhan, A. (1967) *Treasures of Prehistoric Art*, trans. N. Guterman. New York, NY: Harry N. Abrams.

—— (1977) 'Le préhistorien et la chamane', *L'Ethnographie, 118*: 19–25.

Lewis-Williams, J. (1991) 'Wrestling with analogy: A problem in Upper Palaeolithic art research', *Proceedings of the Prehistoric Society, 57*: 149–62.

Lewis-Williams, J. and Dowson, T. (1988) 'The signs of all times. Entoptic phenomena in Upper Palaeolithic art', *Current Anthropology, 29*: 201–45.

—— (1989) *Images of Power: Understanding Bushman Rock Art*. Johannesburg: Southern Book Publishers.

Lewontin, R. C. (2001). 'Gene, organism and environment: A new introduction'. In S. Oyama, P. E. Griffiths and R. D. Gray (eds) *Cycles of Contingency: Developmental Systems and Evolution*. Cambridge, MA: MIT Press.

Loeb, E. (1929) 'Shaman and seer', *American Anthropologist, 31*: 60–84.

Lommel, A. (1967) *The World of the Early Hunters*, trans. M. Bullock. London: Everlyn, Adams & Mackay.

Lopatin, I. (1940–1) 'A shamanistic performance to regain the favor of the spirit', *Anthropos, 35–6*: 352–5.

—— (1946–9) 'A shamanistic performance for a sick boy', *Anthropos, 41–4*: 365–8.

Lorenz, K. (1952) *King Solomon's Ring: A New Light on Animal Ways*. New York, NY: Crowell.

Lot-Falck, E. (1953) *Les Rites de Chasse Chez les Peuples Sibériens*. Paris: Gallimand.

—— (1970) 'Psychopathes et chamans yakoutes'. In J. Pouillon and P. Maranda, *Échanges et Communications. Mélanges Offerts à Claude Lévi-Strauss pour son 60ᵉ Anniversaire*. The Hague: Mouton.

Lowie, R. (1948) *Primitive Religion*. New York, NY: Liveright.

McDowell, M. J. (2001) 'Principle of organization: A dynamic-systems view of the archetype-as-such', *Journal of Analytical Psychology, 46*: 569–71.

McNeely, D. A. (2010) *Becoming: An Introduction to Jung's Concept of Individuation*. Carmel, CA: Fisher King.

Makkay, J. (1953) 'An important proof to the prehistory of shamanism – the interpretation on the masked human portrait of the cave Les Trois Frères', *Alba Regia, 2–3*: 5–10.

Mander, G. (2004) 'The selection of candidates for training in psychotherapy and counselling', *Psychodynamic Practice: Individuals, Groups and Organisations, 10*: 161–72.

Merchant, J. (2006) 'The developmental/emergent model of archetype, its implications and its application to shamanism', *Journal of Analytical Psychology, 51*: 125–44.

—— (2009) 'A reappraisal of classical archetype theory and its implications for theory and practice', *Journal of Analytical Psychology, 54*: 339–58.

—— (2010) 'Response to Erik Goodwyn's "Approaching archetypes: reconsidering innateness"', *Journal of Analytical Psychology, 55*: 534–42.

Mikhailowski, V. M. (1894) 'Shamanism in Siberia and European Russia, being the second part of *Shamanstvo*', trans. O. Wardrop, *Journal of the Royal Anthropological Institute, 24*: 62–100, 126–58.

Miller, G. D. and Baldwin, D. C. (1987) 'Implications of the wounded-healer paradigm for the use of the self in therapy'. In M. Baldwin and V. Satir (eds) *The Use of Self in Therapy*. New York, NY: Haworth Press.

Mimica, J. (2007) *Explorations in Psychoanalytic Ethnography*. New York, NY: Berghahn Books.

Mithen, S. (1996) *The Prehistory of the Mind: A Search for the Origins of Art, Religion and Science*. London: Thames & Hudson.

Mogenson, G. (1999) 'Psyche's archetypes: A response to Pietikainen, Stevens, Hogenson and Solomon', *Journal of Analytical Psychology*, *44*: 125–33.

Montefiore, A. (1894–5) 'Notes on the Samoyeds of the Great Tundra. Collected from the journals of F. G. Jackson, Esq., FRGS', *Journal of the Anthropological Institute*, *24*: 388–407.

Moore, R. and Gillette, D. (1993) *The Magician Within: Accessing the Shaman in the Male Psyche*. New York, NY: William Morrow.

Moss, L. (2001) 'Deconstructing the gene and reconstructing molecular developmental systems'. In S. Oyama, P. E. Griffiths and R. D. Gray (eds) *Cycles of Contingency: Developmental Systems and Evolution*. Cambridge, MA: MIT Press.

Murphy, H. B., Wittkower, E. D., Fried, J. and Ellenberger, H. (1963) 'A cross-cultural survey of schizophrenic symptomatology', *International Journal of Social Psychiatry*, *10*: 237–49.

Murphy, H. B., Wittkower, E. D. and Chance, N. A. (1967) 'Cross-cultural inquiry into the symptomatology of depression: A preliminary report', *International Journal of Psychiatry*, *3*: 6–22.

Murphy, J. M. (1964) 'Psychotherapeutic aspects of shamanism on St. Lawrence Island, Alaska'. In A. Kiev (ed.) *Magic, Faith and Healing: Studies in Primitive Psychiatry Today*. New York, NY: Collier-Macmillan.

—— (1976) 'Psychiatric labeling in cross-cultural perspective', *Science*, *19*: 1019–28.

Natterson, J. (1980) (ed.) *The Dream in Clinical Practice*. New York, NY: International Universities Press.

Nelson, C. A., de Haan, M. and Thomas, K. M. (2006) *Neuroscience of Cognitive Development: The Role of Experience and the Developing Brain*. Hoboken, NJ: John Wiley & Sons.

Neumann, E. (1955) *The Great Mother: An Analysis of an Archetype*. London: Routledge & Kegan Paul.

Noll, R. (1983) 'Shamanism and schizophrenia: A state-specific approach to the "schizophrenia metaphor" of shamanic states', *American Ethnologist*, *10*: 443–59.

—— (1985) 'Mental imagery cultivation as a cultural phenomenon: The role of visions in shamanism', *Current Anthropology*, *27*: 443–61.

—— (1989) 'What really has been learned about shamanism?', *Journal of Psychoactive Drugs*, *21*: 47–50.

—— (1990) 'Comment on "Individuation and Shamanism"', *Journal of Analytical Psychology*, *35*: 213–17.

Novik, E. (1984) 'The archaic epic and its relationship to ritual', trans. R. Radzai. In M. Balzer (1997) *Shamanic Worlds: Rituals and Lore of Siberia and Central Asia*. New York, NY: North Castle Books.

O'Connor, P. A. (1993) *The Inner Man*. Sydney: Sun Books.

Okladnikov, A. (1966) 'Sur la tradition paleolithique dans l'art des tribus néolithiques de la Sibérie'. Paper presented at the VIth Congress of the

International Union for Prehistoric and Protohistoric Sciences, Section 5–8, Rome.

Opler, M. (1936) 'Some points of comparison and contrast between the treatment of functional disorders by Apache shamans and modern psychiatric practice', *American Journal of Psychiatry*, 92: 1371–87.

Oremland, J. D. (1987) 'Dreams in the borderline and schizophrenic personality'. In A. Rothstein (ed.) *The Interpretations of Dreams in Clinical Work*. Workshop series of the American Psychoanalytic Association, Monograph 3: 105–23.

Oyama, S. (2000) *The Ontogeny of Information: Developmental Systems and Evolution*. Cambridge: Cambridge University Press.

Oyama, S., Griffiths, P. E. and Gray, R. D. (2001) *Cycles of Contingency: Developmental Systems and Evolution*. Cambridge, MA: MIT Press.

Pallas, S. (1788a) 'Travels through Siberia and Tartary'. In J. Trusler, *The Habitable World Described*, vol 3. London: Literary Press.

—— (1788b) 'Travels through Siberia and Tartary'. In J. Trusler, *The Habitable World Described*, vol 4. London: Literary Press.

Paterson, S. J., Brown, J. H., Gsodl, M. K., Johnson, M. H. and Karmiloff-Smith, A. (1999) 'Cognitive modularity and genetic disorders', *Science*, 286: 2355–8.

Peters, L. (1978) 'Psychotherapy in Tamang shamanism', *Ethos*, 6: 63–91.

—— (1981a) 'An experiential study of Nepalese shamanism', *Journal of Transpersonal Psychology*, 13: 1–26.

—— (1981b) *Ecstasy and Healing in Nepal*. Malibu, CA: Undena Publications.

—— (1982) 'Trance, initiation, and psychotherapy in Tamang shamanism', *American Ethnologist*, 9: 21–46.

—— (1987) 'The Tamang shamanism of Nepal'. In S. Nicholson (ed.) *Shamanism*. Wheaton, IL: Quest Books.

—— (1988) 'Borderline personality disorder and the possession syndrome: An ethnopsychoanalytic perspective', *Transcultural Psychiatric Research Review*, 25: 5–46.

—— (1989) 'Shamanism: Phenomenology of a spiritual discipline', *The Journal of Transpersonal Psychology*, 21: 115–37.

—— (1994) 'Rites of passage and the borderline syndrome: Perspectives in transpersonal anthropology', *Anthropology of Consciousness*, 5: 1–15.

—— (1996) 'The contribution of anthropology to transpersonal psychiatry'. In B. W. Scotton, A. B. Chinen and J. R. Battista (eds) *Textbook of Transpersonal Psychiatry and Psychology*. New York, NY: Basic Books.

—— (1997) 'The "calling", the *yeti*, and the *ban jhakri* ("forest shaman") in Nepalese shamanism', *The Journal of Transpersonal Psychology*, 29: 47–62.

Peters, L. and Price-Williams, D. (1980) 'Towards an experiential analysis of shamanism', *American Ethnologist*, 7: 398–418.

—— (1983) 'A phenomenological overview of trance', *Transcultural Psychiatric Research Review*, 20: 5–39.

Pietikainen, P. (1998a) 'Archetypes as symbolic forms', *Journal of Analytical Psychology*, 43: 325–43.

—— (1998b) '"Archetypes as symbolic forms": Response to Hester McFarland Solomon, George B. Hogenson and Anthony Stevens', *Journal of Analytical Psychology*, 43: 379–88.

Popov, A. A. (1968) 'How Sereptie Djaruoskin of the Nganasans (Tavgi Samoyeds) became a shaman'. In V. Diószegi (ed.) (1997) *Popular Beliefs and Folklore Tradition in Siberia*. Richmond, Surrey: Curzon Press.

Radin, P. (1914) 'Religion of the North American Indians', *Journal of American Folklore, 27*: 335–73.

—— (1937) *Primitive Religion: Its Nature and Origin*. New York, NY: Viking Press.

Ränk, G. (1967) 'Shamanism as a research subject'. In C. Edsman (ed.) *Studies in Shamanism*. Stockholm: Almquist & Wiskell.

Remen, N., May, R., Young, D. and Berland, W. (1985) 'The wounded healer', *Saybrook Review, 5*: 84–93.

Richardson, G. and Moore, R. (1963) 'On the manifest dream in schizophrenia', *Journal of the American Psychoanalytic Association, 2*: 281–302.

Ring, K. (1988) 'Near-death and UFO encounters on shamanic initiations', *Revision, 14–22*.

Rivers, W. H. R. (1923) *Conflict and Dream*. London: Kegan Paul.

Robert-Lamblin, J. (2003) 'An anthropological view'. In J. Clottes (ed.) *Return to Chauvet Cave. Excavating the Birthplace of Art: The First Full Report*, trans. P. Bahn. London: Thames & Hudson.

Roesler, C. (2010) 'A revision of Jung's theory of archetypes in the light of contemporary research: Neurosciences, genetics and cultural theory – a reformulation'. Paper presented at the XVIII Congress of the International Association for Analytical Psychology, Montreal, Canada, May.

Rogers, C. (1961) *On Becoming a Person: A Therapist's View of Psychotherapy*. Boston, MA: Houghton Mifflin.

Rolt, C. E. (trans.) (1920) *Dionysius the Areopagite. 'On the Divine Names and the Mystical Theology'*. London & New York: Translations of Christian Literature.

Ryan, R. (2002) *Shamanism and the Psychology of C. G. Jung: The Great Circle*. London: Vega.

Saliba, J. A. (1998) 'Shaman'. In *Microsoft Encarta Encyclopedia 99*. Redmond, WA: Microsoft Corp.

Samuels, A. (1985a) 'Countertransference, the mundus imaginalis and a research project', *Journal of Analytical Psychology, 30*: 47–71.

—— (1985b) 'Symbolic dimensions of eros in transference-countertransference: Some clinical uses of Jung's alchemical metaphor', *International Review of Psycho-Analysis, 12*: 199–214.

—— (1993) *The Political Psyche*. London: Routledge.

—— (1994) *Jung and the Post-Jungians*. London: Routledge.

—— (2006) 'Transference/countertransference'. In R. K. Papadopoulos (ed.) *The Handbook of Jungian Psychology: Theory, Practice and Applications*. New York, NY: Routledge.

Samuels, A., Shorter, B. and Plaut, F. (1993) *A Critical Dictionary of Jungian Analysis*. London: Routledge.

Sandler, J. and Fonagy, P. (eds) (1997) *Recovered Memories of Abuse: True or False?* London: Karnac.

Sandner, D. F. and Wong, S. H. (eds) (1997) *The Sacred Heritage: The Influence of Shamanism on Analytical Psychology*. New York, NY: Routledge.

Santayana, G. (1926) 'Normal madness'. In *Dialogues in Limbo*. New York, NY: Scribner.

Satinover, J. (1985) 'At the mercy of another: Abandonment and restitution in psychosis and psychotic character', *Chiron: A Review of Jungian Analysis*, *47–86*.

Saunders, P. and Skar, P. (2001) 'Archetypes, complexes and self organization', *Journal of Analytical Psychology*, *46*: 305–23.

Schmideberg, M. (1947) 'The treatment of psychopaths and borderline patients', *American Journal of Psychotherapy*, *1*: 45–55.

Schore, A. N. (1994) *Affect Regulation and the Origin of the Self: The Neurobiology of Emotional Development*. Hillsdale, NJ: Lawrence Erlbaum.

—— (2000) 'The self-organization of the right brain and the neurobiology of emotional development'. In M. Lewis and I. Granic (eds) *Emotion, Development, and Self-organization: Dynamic Systems Approaches to Emotional Development. Cambridge Studies in Social and Emotional Development*. New York, NY: Cambridge University Press.

—— (2001) 'The right brain as the neurobiological substratum of Freud's dynamic unconscious'. In D. E. Scharff (ed.) *The Psychoanalytic Century: Freud's Legacy for the Future*. New York, NY: Other Press.

—— (2005) 'Attachment, affect regulation, and the developing right brain: Linking developmental neuroscience to pediatrics', *Pediatrics in Review*, *26*: 1–14.

Scott, W. (ed.) (1985) *Hermetica: The Ancient Greek and Latin Writings which contain Religious or Philosophic Teachings Ascribed to Hermes Trismegistus*. Boston, MA: Shambhala.

Searles, H. (1975) 'The patient as therapist to his analyst'. In H. Searles (1979) *Collected Papers on Countertransference and Related Subjects*. New York, NY: International Universities Press.

Sedgwick, D. (1994) *The Wounded Healer: Countertransference from a Jungian Perspective*. London: Routledge.

Shaw, R. (2003) *The Embodied Psychotherapist*. London: Brunner-Routledge.

Shimkin, B. D. (1939) 'A sketch of the Ket, or Yenisei "Ostyak"', *Ethnos*, *4*: 147–76.

Shirokogoroff, S. (1923) 'General theory of shamanism among the Tungus', *Journal of the Royal Asiatic Society*, *54*: 246–9.

—— (1929) *Social Organization of the Northern Tungus*. Shanghai: The Commercial Press.

—— (1935) *Psychomental Complex of the Tungus*. London: Routledge & Kegan Paul.

Sieroszewski, W. (1902) 'Du chamanisme d'après les croyances des Yakoutes', *Revue de l'Histoire des Religions*, *46*: 204–33, 299–338.

Siikala, A.-L. (1978) *The Right Technique of the Siberian Shaman*. Helsinki: Academy of Science.

—— (1980) 'Two types of shamanizing and categories of shamanic songs. A Chukchi case'. In L. Honko and V. Voigt (eds) *Genre, Structure and Reproduction in Oral Literature*. Budapest: Akadémiai Kiadó.

—— (1984) 'Finnish rock art, animal ceremonialism and shamanic worldview'. In M. Hoppál (ed.) *Shamanism in Eurasia*. Göttingen: Herodot.

—— (1987a) 'Siberian and Inner Asian Shamanism'. In M. Eliade (ed.) *The Encyclopedia of Religion*, vol. 13. New York, NY: Macmillan.

—— (1987b) 'Siberian and Inner Asian Shamanism', In A.-L. Siikala and M. Hoppál (eds) (1998) *Studies on Shamanism*. Budapest: Akadémiai Kiadó.

194    References

—— (1989) 'The interpretation of Siberian and Central Asian Shamanism'. In A.-L. Siikala and M. Hoppál (eds) (1998) *Studies on Shamanism*. Budapest: Akadémiai Kiadó.

Siikala, A.-L. and Hoppál, M. (eds) (1998) *Studies in Shamanism*. Budapest: Akadémiai Kiadó.

Silverman, J. (1967) 'Shamans and acute schizophrenia', *American Anthropologist*, *69*: 21–31.

Skar, P. (2004) 'Chaos and self organization: Emergent patterns at critical life transitions', *Journal of Analytical Psychology*, *49*: 245–64.

Smith, C. M. (1997) *Jung and Shamanism in Dialogue: Retrieving the Soul/Retrieving the Sacred*. Mahwah, NJ: Paulist Press.

Smith, N. (1992) *An Analysis of Ice Age Art: Its Psychology and Belief System*. New York, NY: Peter Lang.

Smith, R. C. (1997) *The Wounded Jung: Effects of Jung's Relationships on his Life and Work*. Evanston, IL: Northwestern University Press.

Solomon, H. M. (1998) 'Response to Petteri Pietikainen's "Archetypes as symbolic forms"', *Journal of Analytical Psychology*, *43*: 373–7.

Spencer, R. F. (1968) 'Review of C.-M. Edsman (ed.) *Studies in shamanism*', *American Anthropologist*, *70*: 396–7.

Sperber, D. (1996) *Explaining Culture: A Naturalist Approach*. Oxford: Blackwell.

Stein, M. (1984) 'Power, shamanism and maieutics in the countertransference', *Chiron: A Review of Jungian Analysis*, *67–87*.

—— (1987) 'Looking backward: Archetypes in reconstruction'. In N. Schwartz-Salant and M. Stein (eds) *Archetypal Processes in Psychotherapy*. Wilmette. IL: Chiron Publications.

—— (2006) 'Individuation'. In R. K. Papadopoulos (ed.) *The Handbook of Jungian Psychology: Theory, Practice and Applications*. New York, NY: Routledge.

Steinberg, W. (1989) 'The therapeutic utilization of countertransference', *Quadrant*, *22*: 11–26.

Stern, A. (1938) 'Psychoanalytic investigation of and therapy in the borderline group of neuroses', *Psychoanalytic Quarterly*, *7*: 467–89.

Stevens, A. (1982) *Archetype: A Natural History of the Self*. London: Routledge & Kegan Paul.

—— (1998) 'Response to P. Pietikainen', *Journal of Analytical Psychology*, *43*: 345–55.

—— (2002) *Archetype Revisited: An Updated Natural History of the Self*. London: Brunner-Routledge.

—— (2006) 'The archetypes'. In R. K. Papadopoulos (ed.) *The Handbook of Jungian Psychology: Theory, Practice and Applications*. New York, NY: Routledge.

Stevens, A. and Price, J. (1996) *Evolutionary Psychiatry: A New Beginning*. London: Routledge.

Stevens, A., Hogenson, G. and Ramos, D. G. (2003) 'Debate: Psychology and biology'. In R. Hinshaw (ed.) *Analytical Psychology and Psychoanalysis. Proceedings of the Fifteenth International Congress for Analytical Psychology*. Cambridge, 2001. Einsiedeln: Daimon Verlag.

Stone, D. (2008) 'Wounded healing: Exploring the circle of compassion in the helping relationship', *The Humanistic Psychologist*, *36*: 45–51.

Stone, M. (1979) 'Dreams of fragmentation and of the death of the dreamer: A manifestation of vulnerability to psychosis', *Psychopharmacology Bulletin, 15*: 12–13.

—— (2006) 'The analyst's body as a tuning fork: Embodied resonance in counter-transference', *Journal of Analytical Psychology, 51*: 109–24.

Stutley, M. (2003) *Shamanism: An introduction*. London: Routledge.

Sumner, W. G. (1901) 'The Yakuts. Abridged from the Russian of Sieroszewski', *Journal of the Royal Anthropological Institute, 31*: 65–110.

Taussig, M. (1989) 'The nervous system: Homesickness and Dada', *Stanford Humanities Review, 1*: 44–81.

Tresan, D. I. (1996) 'Jungian metapsychology and neurobiological theory', *Journal of Analytical Psychology, 41*: 399–436.

Turkheimer, E., Haley, A., Waldron, M., D'Onofrio, B. and Gottesman, I. I. (2003) 'Socioeconomic status modifies heritability of IQ in young children', *Current Directions in Psychological Science, 14*: 623–8.

van Gennep, A. (1908/1960) *The Rites of Passage*, trans. M. B. Vizedon and G. L. Caffee. London: Routledge & Kegan Paul.

Vitebsky, P. (1995) *The Shaman*. Boston, MA: Little, Brown & Co.

Wach, J. (1958) *The Comparative Study of Religion*. New York, NY: Columbia University Press.

Waddington, C. H. (1957) *The Strategy of the Genes*. London: Allen & Unwin.

Walsh, R. (1990) *The Spirit of Shamanism*. Los Angeles, CA: Tarcher.

Whan, M. (1987) 'Chiron's wound: Some reflections on the wounded-healer'. In N. Schwartz-Salant and M. Stein (eds) *Archetypal Processes in Psychotherapy*. Wilmette, IL: Chiron Publications.

Wheelwright, J. (1989) Interview in S. Segalier (Producer) *The Wisdom of the Dream*, Part 1 [Video]. Wilmette, IL: Public Media Incorporated.

Whitmont, E. C. (1991) *The Symbolic Quest: Basic Concepts of Analytical Psychology*. Princeton, NJ: Princeton University Press.

Whitney, H. (1910) *Hunting with the Eskimo: The Unique Record of a Sportsman's Year among the Northernmost Tribe*. New York, NY: The Century Co.

Williams, M. (1963) 'The indivisibility of the personal and collective unconscious'. In M. Fordham, R. Gordon, J. Hubback, K. Lambert and M. Williams (eds) (1973) *Analytical Psychology: A Modern Science*. Library of Analytical Psychology, vol. 1. London: Heinemann Medical Books.

Winnicott, D. W. (1941) 'The observation of infants in a set situation', *International Journal of Psycho-Analysis, 22*: 229–49.

—— (1945) 'Primitive emotional development'. Reprinted in D. W. Winnicott (ed.) (1958) *Collected Papers: Through Paediatrics to Psycho-analysis*. London: Tavistock.

—— (1948) 'Paediatrics and psychiatry'. Reprinted in D. W. Winnicott (ed.) (1958) *Collected Papers: Through Paediatrics to Psycho-analysis*. London: Tavistock.

—— (1952a) 'Anxiety associated with insecurity'. Reprinted in D. W. Winnicott (ed.) (1958) *Collected Papers: Through Paediatrics to Psycho-analysis*. London: Tavistock.

—— (1952b) 'Psychoses and child care'. Reprinted in D. W. Winnicott (ed.) (1958) *Collected Papers: Through Paediatrics to Psycho-analysis*. London: Tavistock.

—— (1955) 'Metapsychological and clinical aspects of regression within the psychoanalytical set-up', *International Journal of Psycho-Analysis, 36*: 16–26.

—— (1956) 'Primary maternal preoccupation'. Reprinted in D. W. Winnicott (ed.) (1958) *Collected Papers: Through Paediatrics to Psycho-analysis*. London: Tavistock.

——. (1964) 'Review of *Memories, Dreams, Reflections*'. Reprinted in C. Winnicott, R. Shepard and M. Davis (eds) (1989) *D. W. Winnicott: Psycho-Analytic Explorations*. Cambridge, MA: Harvard University Press.

—— (1968) 'The use of an object and relating through identifications'. Reprinted in D. W. Winnicott (ed.) (1992) *Playing and Reality*. London: Routledge.

Wisdom, J. O. (1961) 'A methodological approach to the problem of hysteria', *International Journal of Psychoanalysis*, *42*: 224–37.

—— (1964) 'A methodological approach to the problem of obsessional neurosis', *British Journal of Medical Psychology*, *37*: 111–22.

Wolgien, C. S. and Coady, N. F. (1997) 'Good therapists' beliefs about the development of their healing ability: The wounded healer paradigm revisited', *Clinical Supervisor*, *15*: 19–36.

Znamenski, A. A. (2003) *Shamanism in Siberia: Russian Records of Indigenous Spirituality*. Dordrecht: Kluwer Academic Publishers.

# Index

abandonment, infant 18
Ackerknecht, E. H. 37
active imagination 45–6, 47
affectivity: as activator of archetypal
    imagery 72, 73, 75, 78; and
    compensation 71–2; and
    constellation of the archetype 72;
    image schema formation driven by
    67–9; and the pre-initiatory illness
    of shamans 72, 73; and
    synchronicity 72–3
Agapitoff, N. N. and Khangaloff, M. N.
    95–6
Aiñanwa't 148
Ainsworth, M. et al. 128
Ainu 114
Aki'mlakê 133–4
alchemist archetype 1
Alekseev, N. A. 94–5
Altaians 96, 115, 140
Altaics 54–5
Altered States of Consciousness (ASCs)
    30–1, 36, 37, 39
amnesia 91, 134
analysts: countertransference see
    countertransference; the 'good
    analyst' 1–4, 40, 71, 151, 152, 153,
    155, 156–7, 162; neurosis of the
    analyst 8, 10; and the proto-
    borderline model 162–4; psychic
    infection see psychic infection;
    selection 1, 3, 13–14, 163; self-cure
    162, 164; susceptibility to influence
    10–13; 'taking over' the sufferings of
    patients 11–12, 15–16, 20;
    therapeutic relationship see
    therapeutic relationship; training
    163–4; 'true Jungians', functioning

as shamans 3–4, 151, 152, 153, 155,
    156, 157, 159, 163, 164; wounded
    healer/shaman archetype and the
    selection of 1, 3, 13–14, 163; as
    wounded healers 13, 15–16
analytical psychology schools 168
Anfilov, V. 139
anger: amongst Siberian shamans
    137–8; as a Borderline Personality
    Disorder (BPD) criterion 173;
    Chukchi (Chukchee) propensity for
    145, 147–9
animism 29
Anokhin, A. V. 140
Anuchin, V. I. 36
apathy 91, 92
archetypal imagery 16, 42, 60, 67, 70, 72,
    79; activation by affectivity 72, 73,
    75, 78; autochthonous revival 41–2,
    47–9, 75, 80–1, 155–6; divorced
    from personal experience 79;
    influence of Jung's personal
    experience on 80–1; primordial
    images 42, 83, 85
archetypal predispositions 43–4, 48, 62
Archetypal school of analytical
    psychology 168
archetype theory: a priori view 44, 47–8,
    58, 59, 60, 61, 62, 74–5, 85, 88, 154,
    156 see also autochthonous revival;
    biological base 42, 60, 61–2; classic
    2, 14–16, 71–2 see also subheadings:
    a priori view (above) and Jung
    (below); contemporary 59–70,
    154–6; developmental models see
    emergent/developmental models of
    archetypes; emergent models see
    emergent/developmental models of

archetypes; gene–environment coaction 62–4; image schema model (Knox) 67–70, 73–4, 82–3, 84–8, 154–5; innatism *see* innatism; and instinct 165–6 *see also* instinct; Jung 21–2, 41–8, 53–4, 61, 69, 71–84, 154, 155–6, 165–6, 168, 174–5n9, 176nn1–3; neuroscience and *see* neuroscience; place of the environment in 74–5, 166–7; re-evaluation of Jung's classic theory in light of emergent/development model 71–88, 155–6; 'sacred heritage' view 2, 59, 156, 168
archetypes *see also* archetypal imagery: activation by resonance 69, 73, 74, 76, 77, 86–7, 88; affectivity and the constellation of 72; alchemist archetype 1; archetype-as-such 68–9, 75, 86, 87; autochthonous revival of 41–2, 47–9, 75, 80–1, 155–6; autonomy of 43, 46, 47–8, 59, 75–83; biological approach to 42, 60, 61–2; and the collective unconscious 2, 41–2; compensatory 71–2; Eliade and 54–6; and environmental conditions 74–5, 166–7; essential features of Jung's theory of 41–5, 71–5; healer archetype 1 *see also* wounded healer; and imagery 53–4; innateness of *see* innatism; instinct *see* instinct; opposite poles of 15; projection of archetypal figures 13, 15; proving existence of (Jung) 45–8; shaman *see* shaman archetype; sociocultural conditions and archetypal expressions 43–4, 45; and synchronicity 72–4; theories of *see* archetype theory; wounded healer *see* wounded healer
'Arctic hysteria' 37, 90–1, 107–8, 112–13, 116
Arctic shamanism 34 *see also* Siberian shamanism
'army officer' case of Jung 75–8
Athanasy (Yukaghir shaman) 139
Atkinson, J. 37
autochthonous revival 41–2, 47–9, 75, 80–1, 155–6
avoidance customs 103

Banzaroff, D. 27
Barnett, M. 14
Baron-Cohen, S. 66
Barry, H. *et al.* 108, 110
Basilov, V. 20, 29, 37, 38, 129, 133, 179n4
bear mythology 52
biological base of archetypes 42, 60, 61–2
blood vengeance 101, 114
Boas, Franz 175n2
Bogoras, W. 37, 38, 94, 111–12, 114, 115, 130, 133–4, 135, 137, 138, 142–9, 175n2
borderline disorders/'type of case' 126–8; BPD *see* Borderline Personality Disorder; and infant development 118–26; and the Siberian shaman *see* proto-borderline psychology of the Siberian shaman
Borderline Personality Disorder (BPD) 38–9, 97, 127–8, 130–1, 134, 143; DSM-IV criteria 133, 137–8, 144, 145, 147, 173
Boss, M. 179n1
Bourguignon, E. 131
BPD *see* Borderline Personality Disorder
brain *see also* neuroscience: emergence of mind/brain structures 65–6; interaction between early life experience and brain development 67–8; and language acquisition 65–6; neural plasticity 66, 67
'breakthroughs' of collective unconscious 3, 151, 158
bride-price systems 102, 114, 116
Buddhism 27
Buryats 95–6, 99, 115

Campbell, J. 49, 51, 56, 94
cannibalistic imagery 93, 94
Casia, V. M. *et al.* 66
Castagné, J. 94, 96
cave art 28, 50–2
centaurs 17, 18, 157
chaos 121, 122; 'no other chaos' and development of a shaman 125–6; place of 'no other chaos' in infant development 117, 122–4, 125–6
Chauvet cave 51, 52

Chichlo, B. 51–2
childbirth: Chukchi (Chukchee) 111–12;
    Gilyak 112; Sakha (Yakut) 103–5;
    Samoyed 113–14; Yukaghir 111
children: infants see infants;
    mother–infant relationship; Sakha
    (Yakut) 100, 105–7, 108–11
Chiron myth 17; psychology of 17–19
Chomsky, N. 65
Chukchi (Chukchee) 94, 111–12, 114,
    115, 133–4, 135, 138, 142–3; case
    study 144–9; propensity for anger
    147–9; propensity to suicide
    144–7
Clark, G. 157, 162–3
Classical school of analytical
    psychology 168
Clottes, J. 28, 50, 51, 52; and Courtin, J.
    50–1; and Lewis-Williams, J. 50, 51,
    52
collective unconscious: archetypes and
    2, 41–2; 'breakthroughs' of 3, 151,
    158; collapsing of difference between
    personal unconscious and 69, 82,
    156, 169; operation with
    autochthonous revival 41–2, 47–9,
    75, 80–1; projection of archetypal
    figures from 13; and the wounded
    healer archetype 15
compensation 71–2
complexes 60
complexity theory 60
compliance 121
containment, of 'no other chaos' 117,
    122–4, 125–6
Conti-O'Hare, M. 6
conversion disorder/states 75, 91, 92,
    177n3
cosmology 54–5
Cosquer cave 50
countertransference 3, 174n1; embodied
    4, 10, 14, 161, 162 see also psychic
    infection; Freud 8; Jung 9, 10, 20;
    and the proto-borderline model
    162–3; psychic infection as
    countertransferential reaction 8–10,
    19 see also psychic infection
cryptomnesia 47, 78
Czaplicka, M. 26, 37, 95–6, 112

De Prokofyeva, Y. 142
deMause, L. 39

depressive position 92–3, 177–8n4
developmental models of archetypes see
    emergent/developmental models of
    archetypes
Developmental school of analytical
    psychology 168
Developmental Systems Theory 62,
    169–72
Devereux, G. 37, 38, 143
Dieterich, A. 78
Diószegi, V. 29, 38, 140–2
dismemberment 2, 25, 39, 49, 92, 131–3,
    150, 158, 160; example 132–3; and
    reintegration cycle 153, 158
dissociation 91, 93, 120, 134–5
divorce 114
Dolgikh, B. 135–6
Dordogne Gabillou cave 50–1
dreams: army officer's dream image
    (case of Jung) 75–8; borderline
    dynamics 132; clinical categories
    132; dream work and the shaman
    archetype 1; Jung 45–6, 75–8, 79;
    and the shamanic call 95
Drosophilia 170
drugs, psychoactive 39
drums/drumming 26, 95, 139, 140, 141,
    144, 179n1
Ducey, C. 56, 89–94, 97, 98, 99–100,
    108, 110, 117, 127, 136, 160
Dynamic Systems Theory 60

ecstasy 30, 31, 32, 36
Eigen, M. 118, 178n2
Eliade, M. 2, 19, 24–6, 27–8, 29, 30, 36,
    37, 49, 52–3, 54–6, 94, 96, 131–2,
    152, 164, 174n6, 175n5, 179n1
embodiment 31; embodied
    countertransference 4, 10, 14, 161,
    162 see also psychic infection;
    shamanic 31
emergent/developmental models of
    archetypes 4, 154–6; and the
    archetype–environment nexus
    166–7; and the Classical/
    Developmental school division 168;
    and the collective/personal
    unconscious division 169; and
    Developmental Systems Theory
    169–72; explanatory power of
    165–6; image schema model 67–70,
    73–4, 82–3, 84–8, 154–5; and

innatism 67, 69, 86, 87, 166; and the nature/nurture debate 167–8; and re-evaluation of Jung's classic theory 71–88, 155–6; and the 'sacred heritage' view 168; and the self-organization of complexes 60; and the shaman archetype 111, 116–17, 125, 129, 157
emergentism 60, 154, 165, 176n2
emotional containment, of 'no other chaos' 117, 122–4, 125–6
empathy 6–7, 14; empathic wounding 20
environment: archetype–environment nexus with emergent/developmental model 166–7; and archetypes 74–5, 166–7; and 'Arctic hysteria' 107–8; and Developmental Systems Theory 169–72; environmental impact and the infant 119–20; gene–environment coaction 62–4; Sakha (Yakut) 100–1
epigenetics 63, 171
epilepsy 37, 91
Evenks (Tungus) 26, 27; Yukaghirized 138–9
evolution 42, 61–2, 172
extrasensory perception 73

face recognition 66
Fairbairn, W. R. D. 92
false self (Winnicott) 117, 121, 122, 123–4
family shamanism 143–4, 150, 179n1
fantasies 41; hallucinatory 91 see also hallucination; of stolen soul removed to upper world 93–4
fasting 39
Federn, P. 92
female imagery 93–4, 161
Findeisen, H. 30
flight 31, 36 see also soul journeys
Fonagy, P. 63, 66, 167
French cave art: Chauvet cave 51, 52; Cosquer cave 50; Dordogne Gabillou cave 50–1; Lascaux caves 50; Les Trois Frères cave, Ariège 28, 51
Freud, S. 8, 86, 118; Jung's split with 80, 81
Friedman, R. 132
Frobenius, L. 50

Garrett, Eileen 73
Gebler, Mr 104–5
Geertz, C. 26
genetics: Developmental Systems Theory 62, 169–72; epigenetics 63, 171; gene–environment coaction 62–4; genetic/biological determinism 62, 67; preformationism 62, 67, 169, 171
Ghindia (Orochi shaman) 95
Gilyak 112, 114
Gottlieb, G. 62–3, 167, 171
Graves, R. 17
Grim, J. 23
Grinker, R. 126
Groesbeck, C. J. 2, 3, 13, 15–16, 40, 151, 163, 164
Grotstein, J. S. 134
Guggenbuhl-Craig, A. 1, 2, 3, 13, 15, 16, 24, 71, 151, 152, 162
Gunderson, J. 97, 127–8
Guntrip, H. 92

hallucination 91, 92; the infant's readiness to hallucinate 120–1; 'solar phallus' case 46–7, 75, 78–80
Harvey, G. 26
Hayes, J. A. 6, 8
healer archetype 1
Heracles 17, 18
Hobson, R. F. 46, 48, 49
Hogenson, G. B. 60, 62, 83, 172, 176n2, 177n1
Holmes, C. 15
Hoppál, M. 23, 33
Hultkrantz, Å 28–9, 32, 34, 35, 36
Hutton, R. 38, 132, 157, 160
hysteria: 'Arctic hysteria' 37, 90–1, 107–8, 112–13, 116; conversion disorder/states 75, 91, 92, 177n3

iiekyyl (beast-mother) 94–5
image schema model of archetypes 67–70, 73–4, 82–3, 84–8, 154–5 see also emergent/developmental models of archetypes
imagery: archetype and 53–4; cannibalistic 93, 94; dismemberment 131–3, 150, 158, 160 see also dismemberment; female 93–4, 161; mythic 76–8, 156; primordial images

42, 83, 85; shamanism and 53–4, 93, 95, 131–3, 161; transpersonal 57, 125, 161
imaging 31, 64, 165 *see also* visualization
impulsivity 18, 137–8, 145, 150, 173
individuation 2, 20–2
infanticide 106, 112, 115, 116
infants: abandonment 18; achievement of non-madness 118, 121, 126; development of false self (Winnicott) 117, 121, 122, 123–4; environmental impact and the infant 119–20; infant development and mental health (Winnicott) 97, 98, 118–25; 'kernel' and 'shell' personality development 124–6, 178n2; mortality 100; mother–infant relationship *see* mother–infant relationship; place of 'no other chaos' in infant development 117, 122–4, 125–6; and primary madness *see* primary madness; readiness to hallucinate 120–1; trauma 18, 93–8; use of intellectual processes in development 122
inheritance, extended 171
initiation of shamans 2, 3, 24–5, 33, 49; pre-initiatory illness *see* pre-initiatory illness of shamans; sex change in 93
innatism 43, 59, 60, 62 *see also* archetype theory: *a priori* view; apparent innateness 65–7; arguments and findings against 3, 58, 69; and the biological base of archetypes 61–2; and emergent/developmental models of archetypes 67, 69, 86, 87, 166; and left-hemisphere dominance for language processing 65
instinct 18, 43, 165–6; neurological underpinning processes of 68; primordial image as instinct's self-perception 85
Inuit 112–13

Jesup North Pacific Expedition 29, 99, 130, 175n2
Jochelson, W. 37, 99, 101, 103–5, 106, 107–8, 111, 114, 138–9, 175n2, 179n1
Johnson, M. H. and Morton, J. 66

Jung, C. G.: archetypal predispositions 43–4, 48; archetypes 21–2, 41–8, 53–4, 61, 69, 71–84, 154, 155–6, 165–6, 168, 174–5n9, 176nn1–3; 'army officer' case 75–8; cannibalistic imagery 94; collective unconscious 156; compensation and affectivity 71–2; countertransference 9, 10, 20; dreams 45–6, 75–8, 79; environmental conditions 74; individuation 20–2; and Lamarckism 83–4; life 151; life experiences as influence on archetypal imagery 80–1; and Pauli, W. 79–80; Philemon experience 57, 80–1, 84; primordial images 42, 83, 85; psychic infection 4, 7–8, 9, 10–13, 164; re-evaluation of his theory of archetype in light of emergent/development model 71–88, 155–6; separation of personal and collective psychic content 82–3; shamanism 1–2, 19–22, 153–4, 174n8; 'solar phallus' case 46–7, 75, 78–80; split with Freud 80, 81; synchronicity 72–4; transference 10–13; wounded physician 2–3, 5–6, 13, 19, 21–2, 39
Jungians: analytical psychology schools 168; functioning as shamans, 'true Jungians' 3–4, 151, 152, 153, 155, 156, 157, 159, 163, 164

Kalmuk 115
Kamchadal 114, 115; shaman 135
Karmiloff-Smith, A. 64
Kaufmann, W. A. 81
Kazak Kirgiz 94, 96
Kele'wgi (Chukchi shaman) 137
Kent Reilly, F. 52
Kerényi, C. 17, 160
'kernel' personality development 124–6, 178n2
Ket 35–6, 113, 116
Kirsch, T. 3
Klein, M.: depressive position 92–3, 177–8n4; paranoid-schizoid position 89, 93, 177n1, 177–8n4
Knox, J. M. 67–8, 69–70, 71, 72, 73, 74, 75, 82, 84, 85–6, 87, 88, 154–5, 157, 165–8, 169, 171–2
Koryak 114, 139

Krasheninnikoff, O. K. 115
Kraus, R. F. 32–3, 34, 36, 37, 53, 56, 151
Krippner, S. C. 38
Kroeber, A. 37, 38
Ksenofontov, G. V. 94
Kusnetsky, Boris 148

La Barre, W. 29
La Venta 52
Lamarckism 83–4
language acquisition 65–6
Lascaux caves 50
Laufer, B. 26–7
Le Guillou, Y. 51
Leroi-Gourhan, A. 50
Lewis-Williams, J. 28, 50, 51
Lewontin, R. C. 170
liminality 89, 119, 121, 130, 136–7, 150, 160
Loeb, E. 37
Lopatin, I. 95
Lorenz, K. 68
Lot-Falck, E. 90
Lowie, R. 175n2

Makkay, J. 28
Mander, G. 14, 174n3
marriage 101, 102–3, 114; bride-price systems 102, 114, 116
Mikhailowski, V. M. 96, 175n2
Miller, G. D. and Baldwin, D. C. 6, 20
Mimica, J. 89
Montefiore, A. 113
Moore, R. and Gillette, D. 40
Moss, L. 172
mother–infant relationship: and the development of a false self 117, 121, 122, 123–4; environmental impact and the infant 119–20; infant development, mental health and (Winnicott) 97, 98, 118–25; Jung's 'army officer' case 76–8; primary maternal preoccupation and the place of 'no other chaos' in infant development 122–4; and psychopathology 97–8, 103; sado-masochistic 93; Sakha (Yakut) 101, 106, 107, 116–17; and separation 106, 114; shamans and difficulties in 90, 93–5, 97, 111, 116–17, 125

Murphy, J. M. 37
mutilation 39, 105; self-mutilation in Siberian shamanism 133–6, 150
myth 16–17; bear mythology 52; Chiron 17–19; mythic imagery 76–8, 156

Narzale (Enet shaman) 135–6
native Americans 35, 37, 175n5
nature/nurture debate 167–8
Nelson, C. A. et al. 62, 65–6
Neumann, E. 82, 177n6
neural plasticity 66, 67
neuroscience 62, 64–5 see also brain; emergence of mind/brain structures 65–6; gene–environment coaction 62–4; and the image schema model of archetypes (Knox) 67–70, 154–5; and language acquisition 65–6; neurological underpinning processes of instinct 68
neurosis 179 (Table N.1); of the analyst 8, 10; 'Arctic hysteria' 37, 90–1, 107–8, 112–13, 116
Nigalai (Samoyed shaman) 139–40
Noll, R. 23, 30–1
North Eurasian shamanism 34–5, 55
Novik, E. 94, 135
Nuwa't (Chukchi herdsman) 149

Ohlmarks, A. 37
Olmec art 52
Opler, M. 37
orphanhood 93–6, 178n5
Ostyak see Ket
Oxtotitlan cave 52
Oyama, S. et al. 169, 170, 171

palaeolithic origins of shamanism 28–9; cave art 28, 50–2
Pallas, S. 113–14
paranoid-schizoid position 89, 93, 177n1, 177–8n4
Paterson, S. J. et al. 64
Pauli, W. 79–80
personal unconscious 41, 69, 82, 156, 169
personality development, infants see under infants
Peters, L. 27, 31–2, 36, 38–9, 57, 89, 127, 130–1, 178–9n3; and Price-Williams, D. 28, 36, 52, 53, 56

Philemon experience of Jung 57, 80–1, 84
Pietikainen, P. 61, 70, 165, 167
polygamy 100, 114
Popov, A. A. 132–3, 142
pre-initiatory illness of shamans 2, 25, 33, 36, 153; affectivity and 72, 73; and the proto-borderline model 157–8, 159; and self-cure 19, 39, 53, 98, 100, 153, 159; and Siberian shamanism as psychopathology 37–9, 90–4; stage one 90–1; stage two 91–2; stage three 92; and their later healing function 39
preformationism 62, 67, 169, 171
primary madness 118, 121, 125, 126; zone of 119, 121, 122, 123, 126, 128, 129
primary maternal preoccupation 123–4
primordial images 42, 83, 85 see also archetypes
projection 161 see also countertransference; transference; of archetypal figures 13, 15; and bifurcation of roles in analysis 15; and susceptibility to influence 11–13; of unconscious complexes 161
proto-borderline psychology of the Siberian shaman 126, 128–9, 130–50; anger and 137, 147–9; application to analysts 162–4; and the 'borderline type of case' 118–29; Chukchi (Chukchee) case study 144–9; connection between Siberian shamanism and psychological derangement 138–43; and the debate over shaman's psychopathology 159–61; dismemberment example 132–3; dismemberment imagery and 131–2, 150; evidence of being proto-borderline 130–50; impulsivity and 137–8, 145, 150; liminality and 136–7; literature hints 130–1; and the pre-initiatory illness 157–8, 159; self-mutilation and 133–6, 150; and the shamanic call 158–9; and the shaman's deviance from cultural norms 162; and the shaman's female imagery 161; and the shaman's transpersonal imagery 161; suicide propensity and 144–7

psychic infection 7–13, 19, 162, 164; case example 8–10; concept of 7–8; Jung 4, 7–8, 9, 10–13, 164; and shamanism 4; susceptibility to influence 10–13
psychic resonance see resonance, psychic
psychoactive drugs 39
psychoanalysis: bifurcation of roles in 15; countertransference see countertransference; psychic infection see psychic infection; schools, and the emergent/developmental models of archetypes 168; 'taking over' the sufferings of patient by analyst 11–12, 15–16, 20; training 163–4; transference see transference
psychoanalysts see analysts
psychokinesis 73
psychopathology: 'Arctic hysteria' 37, 90–1, 107–8, 112–13, 116; 'borderline types of case' 118–29 see also proto-borderline psychology of the Siberian shaman; BPD see Borderline Personality Disorder; connection between Siberian shamanism and psychological derangement 138–43; debate over shaman's 121, 159–61; and the mother–infant relationship 97–8, 103; primary madness see primary madness; proto-borderline shamanic psychology see proto-borderline psychology of the Siberian shaman; re-emergence 91, 96, 97; and the Siberian shaman's pre-initiatory illness 37–9, 90–4
psychosis 122, 123, 132, 179 (Table N.l); 'hysterical psychosis' 93, 117

Radin, P. 38, 175n2
Ränk, G. 23, 26, 30, 34–5, 39, 55, 160
rejection trauma 18
religion: shamanic spirituality 57; and shamanism 29–30
Remen, N. et al. 6–7
repetition compulsions 86–7, 167
resonance, psychic 76, 77, 86; and the countertransference 163; of early infant material 19, 69, 86–7, 162, 163; empathic 14; with image schema template 73, 74, 88, 167

Rhine, J. B. 73
Ring, K. 57
Rivers, W. H. R. 79
Robert-Lamblin, J. 51, 52
Rogers, C. 6

Sakha (Yakut) 52, 94; 'Arctic hysteria'
    107–8; case study 99–117; child
    behaviour 106–7; childbirth 103–5;
    childrearing 105–6, 108–11;
    comparisons and corroborations
    from other Siberian groups 111–16;
    environment and life 100–1; infant
    mortality 100; marriage 101, 102–3;
    neolithic rock art 52; suicide 101,
    103; women's status and position
    101–3
Samoyed 113–14, 139–40; shaman 142
Samuels, A. 4, 8, 9–10, 14, 59, 161, 168,
    174n1
San people 51
Sandner, D. F. and Wong, S. H. 40,
    59
Sandschejew, G. 96
Santayana, G. 121
Satinover, J. 82
Saunders, P. and Skar, P. 60
Savone (Enet shaman) 142
schizoidal symptoms/tendencies 91, 92,
    121, 123
schizophrenia 91, 121, 124, 128, 132;
    'solar phallus' patient 47, 78–9
Schmideberg, M. 90, 126
Schore, A. N. 67, 167
Scratching Woman (Chukchi shaman)
    135, 137
séances 25–6, 39 see also trance
Searles, H. 14
Sedgwick, D. 3, 14, 174n1
self-cure: of analysts 162, 164; of
    shamans 19, 39, 53, 98, 100, 135,
    153, 159, 160
Sereptie Djaruoskin 132–3, 142
shaman archetype 1, 2, 48–57, 154 see
    also wounded healer; and the
    emergent/developmental model of
    archetypes 111, 116–17, 125, 129,
    157
Shamanic State of Consciousness 30–1,
    36, 37
shamanism 23–39 see also shamans;
    Altaic 54–5; as an archaic religious
experience 29; as an archetype 40,
    154 see also shaman archetype;
    wounded healer; Arctic 34 see also
    Siberian shamanism; and Borderline
    Personality Disorder 39; 'classical'
    shamanism 35; classical view of 2; as
    a cluster of typical phenomena with
    functional meaning 53; as
    conceptually central to analytic
    work 1; cosmology 54–5; cultural-
    historical origins 27–9; definitional
    debate about 26, 32, 151–2;
    dismemberment see
    dismemberment; drumming see
    drums/drumming; ecstasy 30, 31, 32,
    36; Eliade's work and views on
    24–6, 54–6 see also Eliade, M.;
    ethnographers' views on 54–7 see
    also individual ethnographers;
    etymology 26–7; family shamanism
    143–4, 150, 179n1; and imagery
    53–4, 93, 95, 131–3, 161; as
    'irrepresentable disposition' 53; Jung
    1–2, 19–22, 153–4, 174n8; and
    liminality 89, 119, 121, 130, 136–7,
    150, 160; locus classicus of see
    Siberian shamanism; North
    Eurasian 34–5, 55; palaeolithic
    origins 28–9, 50–2; and psychic
    infection 4; as reflective of an
    individuation archetype 20–1; and
    religion 29–30; shamanic spirituality
    57; Siberian see Siberian
    shamanism; Siikala's work on 23–4
    see also Siikala, A.-L.; as a
    sociocultural phenomenon 35, 48–9;
    soul journeys see soul journeys; and
    spirits see spirits; trance see trance;
    transcultural phenomenological
    approach to 32–3, 54–7; as a
    universal phenomenon 28, 33, 50–3;
    and the wounded healer 2, 19–22,
    39, 40, 48–58, 154 see also wounded
    healer
shamans: Altaic 54–5; communal
    sociocultural healing focus of 33,
    152; definitions 1, 32, 33, 36;
    developmental aspects of the
    shamanic wounded healer 89–98;
    deviance from cultural norms 38,
    162; dismemberment see
    dismemberment; ecstatic states of

30, 31, 32, 36; embodiment by 31;
evidence for developmental
components to the shamanic
wounded healer 94–8; evidence for
shaman's developmental 'wounds'
90–4; female imagery 93–4, 161;
imaging by 31; initiation *see*
initiation of shamans; instruction
by master shamans 25, 33, 92, 152;
liminal characteristics of 89, 119,
121, 130, 136–7, 150, 160; mastery
over derangements 2; meaning of
word 'shaman' 26–7; and the
mother–infant relationship 90,
93–5, 97, 111, 116–17, 125; 'no
other chaos' in infancy, and the
development of 125–6;
orphanhood and 93–6, 178n5; pre-
initiatory illness *see* pre-initiatory
illness of shamans; proto-
borderline psychology of *see*
proto-borderline psychology of the
Siberian shaman; recruitment/call
of 24, 39, 40, 49, 95–6, 151, 158–9;
self-cure of 19, 39, 53, 98, 100, 135,
153, 159, 160; Siberian shaman's
proto-borderline psychology *see*
proto-borderline psychology of the
Siberian shaman; soul journeys of
*see* soul journeys; and spirits *see*
spirits; trance states of *see* trance;
transpersonal imagery 57, 125,
161; visualization by 31; as
wounded healers *see* wounded
healer
'shell' personality development 124–6,
178n2
Shirokogoroff, S. 20, 27, 37, 38
Siberian Sakha *see* Sakha (Yakut)
Siberian shamanism 144–9; anger
amongst shamans 137; and a
Chukchi (Chukchee) tribe case study
144–9; connection with
psychological derangement 138–43
*see also* proto-borderline psychology
of the Siberian shaman;
dismemberment imagery 131–3, 150;
essential features 35–6; evidence for
developmental components to the
shamanic wounded healer 94–8;
evidence for shaman's
developmental 'wounds' 90–4;

impulsivity in 137–8, 145, 150;
initiation of shamans 25; liminality
in 136–7; and the mother–infant
relationship 90; pre-initiatory illness
37–9, 90–2; proto-borderline
shamanic psychology *see* proto-
borderline psychology of the
Siberian shaman; as
psychopathology 37–9, 90–4; and a
Sakha tribe case study 99–117 *see
also* Sakha (Yakut); self-mutilation
133–6, 150; Siberia as *locus classicus*
of shamanism 33–5, 152–3
Sieroszewski, W. 38, 99, 100, 102–3
Siikala, A.-L. 23–4, 26, 27, 28, 29–30,
32, 35–6, 37, 39, 52, 55, 94
Silverman, J. 37
Skar, P. 60, 70, 87–8
Smith, C. M. 20, 40
Smith, N. 50
Smith, R. C. 81
'solar phallus' case 46–7, 75, 78–80
soul journeys 26, 31, 36; fantasy of
stolen soul removed to upper world
93–4
Spencer, R. F. 26, 35
spirits: crises caused by 36; evil spirits
and childbirth 104, 105; helping
spirits 29, 33, 36, 94, 151–2; and the
pre-initiatory illness of shamans
90–1, 92; spirit possession 26, 31,
90–1
splitting: in Borderline Personality
Disorder 134; and the Chiron myth
17, 18; in conversion disorder 92;
dissociation 91, 93, 120, 134–5;
Ducey 93, 94; infant trauma and 18,
93–4; and psychotic illnesses 121;
and voluntary death 147
Stein, M. 52, 82
Steinberg, W. 14, 161, 174n4
Stevens, A. 61–2, 83, 155, 165, 176–7n3,
177n4
Stone, M. 132, 179n2
Stutley, M. 26
suicide 101, 103, 144–7; voluntary death
146–7, 149, 150, 162
Sumner, W. G. 100, 101–2, 103, 105,
106–7
supervenience 60
Suzukpen (Soyot shaman) 140–1
synchronicity 72–4

Taussig, M. 26
Te'lpiñä [Chukchi (Chukchee) shaman]
    137, 138
therapeutic relationship 6, 15;
    susceptibility to influence 10–13
thinking, use of intellectual processes in
    infant development 122
trance 25–6, 31–2; control over 31, 36,
    37; and dissociation 135; and
    embodiment 31; uncontrolled 91
transcendence 37; symbols of 131;
    wounds as avenue to 6
transcultural phenomenological
    approach to shamanism 32–3, 54–7
transference: love 86, 167; and
    susceptibility to influence 10–13
transpersonal imagery 57, 125, 161
trauma: abandonment 18; in childbirth
    104–5; infant 18, 93–8; re-
    emergence of symptoms 91, 96, 97;
    rejection 18
Les Trois Frères cave, Ariège 28, 51
Tungus see Evenks

the unconscious: collective see collective
    unconscious; infant trauma residing
    in deep unconscious 18; personal 41,
    69, 82, 156, 169; and susceptibility
    to influence 11–13; unconscious
    projection 11–13, 161

van Gennep, A. 90
visualization 31, 42 see also imaging
Vitebsky, P. 26, 161
voluntary death 146–7, 149, 150, 162 see
    also suicide
von Franz, M.-L. 3, 151, 157
vulnerability 4, 5, 6, 16, 159, 163, 178n5

Wach, J. 32
Waddington, C. H. 170
Walsh, R. 164
Whan, M. 7

Wheelwright, J. 158
Whitney, H. 112–13
Williams, M. 82
Williams syndrome 64
Winnicott, D. W. 97, 98, 117, 118–25,
    178n2
Wisdom, J. O. 178n2
women: abduction of 114; bride-price
    systems 102, 114, 116; childbirth see
    childbirth; harsh treatment in
    Siberian tribes 104–5, 111–12,
    113–14; mother–infant relationship
    see mother–infant relationship;
    status and position in Sakha
    (Yakut) society 101–3
wounded healer 5–22; analyst as 13,
    15–16; archetypal approach to
    14–16; as archetype in its own right
    2, 14–15, 40; as an archetype in
    relation to shamanism 40, 48–58,
    154; Chiron myth 16–19;
    developmental aspects of the
    shamanic wounded healer 89–98;
    evidence for developmental
    components to the shamanic
    wounded healer 94–8; evidence for
    shaman's developmental 'wounds'
    90–4; Jung 2–3, 5–6, 13, 19, 21–2,
    39; and psychic infection 7–10;
    shaman archetype see shaman
    archetype; and shamanism 2, 19–22,
    39, 40, 48–58, 154; shaman's wound
    as a 'borderline types of case' see
    proto-borderline psychology of the
    Siberian shaman; susceptibility to
    influence 10–13; woundedness and
    the call/vocation of the
    psychotherapist 3, 13–14

Yukaghir 111, 114, 115, 135, 138–9

Zelenin, D. 30
Znamenski, A. A. 38, 139–40